DON'T QUOTE ME!

DON'T

Washington Newswomen

QUOTE

and the Power Society

ME!

by WINZOLA MC LENDON
and SCOTTIE SMITH

New York / E. P. DUTTON & CO., INC. / 1970

Published simultaneously in Canada by
Clarke, Irwin & Company Limited, Toronto and Vancouver

Library of Congress Catalog Card Number: 73-108896

SBN 0-525-09472-5

"Newswomen are a breed all their own—hard-working, elastic, supersensitive to events, compassionate, not afraid to feel the human side of the situation, deeply sentimental, and usually blessed by a sense of humor."

LADY BIRD JOHNSON
December 1968

"I've always enjoyed the Washington press girls. We've gotten along for twenty-two years, and I've learned from them. Most of them have a sense of history because of the important events they have covered. They're the best in the world, otherwise they wouldn't be in Washington."

PAT NIXON
June 1969

ACKNOWLEDGMENTS

This book was written from our experiences as Washington newswomen and from the experiences of our friends and colleagues, so generously shared in countless hours of interviewing. We are grateful to these people, particularly those who searched through their scrapbooks and files for certain stories and dates we needed to round out a chapter. We want to thank the following publications whose files we researched: The Associated Press, *Editor and Publisher*, Feature and News Incorporated, Hearst Headline Service, King Features News Syndicate, Knight Newspapers, *New York Daily News*, *The New York Times*, *Newsday*, North American Newspaper Alliance, *Portland Oregonian*, *The Reporter*, Scripps Howard, United Press International, *The Wall Street Journal*, *Washington Daily News*, *Washington Star*, *Washington Post*, *Washington Times Herald*, *Women's Wear Daily*, *Esquire* magazine, *Ladies' Home Journal*, *Life*, *Newsweek*, *Time*, and the *Washingtonian*. While gathering material, we read, and are grateful to the

7

authors of: *The Autobiography of Eleanor Roosevelt*, by Eleanor Roosevelt; *Cissy*, by Paul Healy; *Dateline Washington, the Story of National Affairs Journalism*, edited by Cabell Phillips; *Entertaining in the White House*, by Marie Smith; *The Honeycomb*, by Adela Rogers St. John; *Jacqueline Bouvier Kennedy*, by Mary Van Rensselaer Thayer; *Ladies of the Press*, by Ishbel Ross; *Leaning on a Column*, by George Dixon; *Perle*, by Perle Mesta; *The Press in Washington*, edited by Ray Eldon Hiebert; *The Right People*, by Stephen Birmingham; *Soul Sister* by Grace Halsell; and *Washington Dateline*, by Delbert Clark.

We especially want to thank Peggy Brooks of E. P. Dutton who approached us with the idea for this book and then, with wit and understanding, so graciously guided it to publication. We quarreled with her about the use of the latest edition of *The Manual of Style*, the guidebook of the publishing business, which dictates that capitals should no longer be used in naming anybody from a president to a pope, and though she won the argument, we have halfway forgiven her.

WINZOLA MC LENDON

SCOTTIE SMITH

Following page 122

President Johnson with Betty Beale

Mrs. Nixon is interviewed by Wauhillau La Hay, Isabelle Shelton, Nan Robertson, and Mary Wiegers

President Kennedy with Marianne Means

President Nixon with Nancy Dickerson

Mrs. Nixon shows the president's office to newswomen

Tricia Nixon with Marie Smith

Betty Beale, Kandy Stroud, Tricia Nixon, and Ymelda Dixon

Attorney General and Mrs. Mitchell with Malvina Stephenson and Vera Glaser

Press briefing

Mrs. Robert Kennedy with Kandy Stroud

10 · *Illustrations*

Clare Crawford interviews First Lady Pat Nixon's staff director, Connie Stuart

Press briefing in White House library

Barbara Coleman interviewing Mrs. Johnson

Shirley Elder interviewing Congressman Anderson

Anne Chamberlin with Senator Brooke in Ghana

There are no people on earth more fearful and anxious when written about than members of the press. Just as doctors are known to be impossible patients, and many pilots are said to panic when they're passengers in planes flown by others, so professional journalists, having spent their lifetimes extracting information from people who often would rather not give it out, are petrified when the tables are turned, and they're the ones being interviewed. They end practically every statement with "Don't quote me!" In an effort to "tell it like it is" without getting our friends either fired or excommunicated, we sometimes have not revealed our sources.

It was impossible for us to write about all the women whose work we admire, or whose courage upon entering what is still essentially a man's world deserves documentation. We have described the scenes and people most familiar to us during our combined 37 years of reporting, without, we hope, casting any reflection on those we have not included. But this book is dedicated to all Washington newswomen, whether their names appear in it or not. It is also dedicated to Captain John Benjamin McLendon (U.S. Navy, Retired) who proved that husbands also serve who only stand and wait to deliver copy, fix tape recorders, check facts, make photo copies, and look things up in the Library of Congress.

WINZOLA MC LENDON
SCOTTIE SMITH

June 1970

DON'T QUOTE ME!

1

"What I like about Washington is that everybody is *somebody*, which puts gossip on such a high plane."—From *First Lady*, a play by George S. Kaufman and Katherine Drayton

"Nixon reminds you of a good head-waiter: he wants to take care of everybody."

"Kennedy was charming but his personal life wasn't above reproach. Because he did it elegantly, did it well, it was all right. But poor old Lyndon, sitting scratching, was chewed up by everyone. It has reached the point where it's all right to be immoral but not to be vulgar."

"He may not be the new Nixon, but she sure is the new Pat. Something happened to that woman in those eight years. The blood is running and with proper handling she can be great."

So it goes, on and on, in press planes following the president or the First Lady, in bars during a Democratic or Republican national convention, over lunch in crowded little restaurants on Capitol Hill, while sipping champagne at an embassy reception, in Georgetown postage stamp–sized gardens on summer evenings, on the telephone, behind typewriters, in taxis and in the corridors where press people must so often wait, wait, wait for the thing to happen which is going to make a great news story tomorrow.

A Washington newswoman, whether in her early twenties or mid-sixties, a fashion plate or a fashion joke, quiet and soft-spoken or an object of mock terror, has one thing in common with other members of her sex: a passion for gossip. In her case, gossip about the quirks of the mighty. If there's a little sex mixed up with it, so much the better of course; but Washington, despite an occasional juicy scandal, is not a sexy city compared to Paris,° New York, or Hollywood. On the whole the men haven't got the time for romantic liaisons, and the women are too tired from a hectic social life for high-level flirtations.

What goes on here is politics. In Washington, politics is breakfast, lunch, and dinner, and in bed at night. Newswomen not only look for the political angle while covering such obvious places as the White House and the Hill, but while they are covering ladies' luncheons, benefit balls, and even food and fashion stories. One of the most widely read stories during the 1960 campaign was about fashion—who spent the most on her clothes, Jacqueline Kennedy or Pat Nixon? Jackie said she couldn't spend as much on clothes as Pat Nixon did "unless I wore sable underwear."

Nan Robertson of *The New York Times* got the story about Jackie's clothes while doing a running interview with her which started in the bedroom of a Waldorf Towers suite (while Nan helped Jackie try on maternity clothes by "buttoning her up") and ended at the Commodore Hotel where Jack Kennedy was making a campaign speech. "The male reporters were simply furious when I followed Jackie into the ladies' room and they had to stand outside," says Nan. "But not as furious as Jack Kennedy was when he read the story. One of his aides said he hit his forehead and cried, 'Good Christ!' That was the last interview they let Jackie do until after the election."

With its bottomless pit of news and its revolving-door popula-

---

° Claudine Lebel, the attractive blonde wife of former French Minister to Washington Claude Lebel, said once that Paris is getting almost as unromantic as Washington. "In our case, it's the traffic jams. My friends say that if they have a *cinq-à-sept* engagement, they arrive at 6:10 and have to leave at 6:30. How much romance can you have in twenty minutes?"

tion, Washington is probably the world's greatest fishing-ground for any woman reporter. In some ways the women's page reporters have a more interesting time of it than the others. They cover the great policy makers, even the president, under relaxed, informal conditions; they chat with First Ladies and ambassadors, they talk to key senators and congressmen over a gin and tonic, a special advantage because it's difficult for a man to refuse to answer a woman's question when the two are chatting over a drink at a party together.

Newswomen learned while covering a White House reception that President Nixon was sending Governor Nelson Rockefeller to Latin America on a fact-finding mission; Dorothy McCardle of the *Washington Post* got the first hint that Robert McNamara was resigning as secretary of defense while talking to Mrs. McNamara at a Pakistani diplomat's party; and Wauhillau La Hay of Scripps Howard was at a Georgetown dinner when she heard that a letter Jackie Kennedy wrote to Lady Bird Johnson was being sold at auction in New York. That story made front pages around the world, as did the follow-up when the Secret Service moved in and the letter was withdrawn from the sale.

Mary Hoyt, the pretty former Peace Corps worker who heads *Ladies' Home Journal's* Washington bureau, summarizes: "Washington is where it all starts." LHJ opened its first office here in early 1970, says Mary, because "this is the pivot point of everything—the issues, society, volunteerism."

McCall's magazine has just recently put the talented young Susanna McBee in charge of its Washington office. Susie, who came to *McCall's* from *Life* after having spent her cub reporter days on the *Washington Post,* has her master's degree in political science and as a reporter is not usually associated with typical women's stories. She was lured to *McCall's* by its new editor, Shana Alexander, whose pages, according to Susie, will reflect women's interest in "everything." She points out that Washington "is the starting point for a lot of things . . . it has the personalities and the people who are responsible for how America lives."

Since Society here is dominated by politics, all Washingtonians read the news of who was invited to the White House for dinner, what the ambassadors of Russia and Iran said to each other at a reception, or who shows up at a national day celebration. Patty Cavin, who had a daily NBC-Radio talk show until she went with Radio Corporation of America, puts it this way: "The social coverage here is like a blueprint to who is doing what and where, and it has political undertones that are quite fascinating to the veteran Washingtonian." So there's probably no other place on earth where reading the newspapers is as essential to survival as eating and breathing. Any aspiring hostess who's not sure who's been appointed to or fired from what might as well cancel her facial appointments on Elizabeth Arden's fifth floor. How would she look asking the Brazilian ambassador about his summer plans, when it had just been announced by society columnist Betty Beale that he has been recalled? Not to mention the real-estate agents, the busiest birds of prey in this constantly changing city. How is he or she to beat out the competition without reading in a Marie Smith story that the President is naming Joe Doe of Arabella, New Mexico, deputy assistant secretary for administration at HUD?

It is mandatory, if one would be "with it" out on the party circuit, to read the three local dailies—the *Washington Post,* the *Washington Star,* and the *Washington Daily News*—and *The New York Times* and *Women's Wear Daily* (which is always upsetting applecarts by getting the first story on what Jackie, Lynda, Luci, Julie, or Tricia will wear at their own or other people's weddings, not to mention whom they will marry). Society has become important business here since Washington became a world power center rather than a sleepy capital, and even the editors now admit that who does what to whom after 6:00 P.M. is as avidly read by men as by women.

For instance, Clare Crawford of the *Washington Daily News* gave her readers something to think about when she wrote that the Republican National Committee was picking up the tab for a large portion of President and Mrs. Nixon's expanded entertainment. According to Clare, the committee was paying for "quite a bit" of the Evenings at the White House, a new type of entertaining inaugurated by the Nixons, to which some 200 guests are invited for buffet supper and to hear a big-name performer. Clare pointed out that the manner in which the "Evenings" are financed would probably be "a surprise to the guests who think of themselves as personal guests of the President of the United States rather than just another voter being courted from the coffers of a political party." She also noted: "The White House is a political asset and the Nixons have used it more adroitly than any President with the help of the Republican National Committee."

Both shocking and amusing are such tid bits served up with one's morning coffee and orange juice as this Spiro Agnew quote, found in Maxine Cheshire's "Very Important People" column in the *Washington Post:* "Agnew [speaking at a dinner given by President Nixon for Prince Philip] began by reassuring anyone who was worried that he might say something out of place. 'All of you with tightened sinews and constricted sphincters can relax,' he promised with man-to-man bonhomie."

But many readers were not amused when they read what at first appeared to be an innocuous little story by Helen Thomas of United Press International on the occasion of Tricia Nixon's 24th birthday. Tricia told Helen how much she admired Vice President Agnew: "I feel I should write him a letter. He's amazing what he has done to the media . . . helping it to reform itself. I'm a close watcher of newspapers and TV. I think they've taken a second look. You can't underestimate the power of fear. They're afraid if they don't shape up . . ."

The women handling the news in Washington as full-time reporters, editors, and columnists number 300 or so and are roughly divided into three categories:

(1) Those who write so-called women's news, about society, Pat Nixon, Tricia, Julie Eisenhower, the Daughters of the American Revolution (who convene here every spring), embassies, what's said at State Department receptions, what Betty Beale defines as "politics after six," what's going on in the charity world, and what the government is planning to do about the issues the charity world cares about, as well as fashions, food, advice to the lovelorn, and all the other departments loosely lumped under the heading, "Women."

(2) Those who do traditionally men's jobs, jobs that have nothing whatever to do with being male or female. One shining example is probably Eileen Shanahan of *The New York Times,* who won the Publisher's Award from *The Times* for her cover-

age of the 1969 tax bill and who is one of the most respected writers on financial matters. Another is Helen Dewar, who blankets Virginia politics for the *Washington Post* and predicted a year in advance that Virginia would, on November 4, 1969, elect its first Republican governor in 93 years.

Then there are Pulitzer Prize winners Miriam Ottenberg and Mary Lou Werner, both of the *Washington Star*. Miriam, the first reporter to reveal publicly that the Mafia was still thriving in America as the Cosa Nostra, is a top-notch investigative reporter whose exposés have won her the Pulitzer for a series of articles on used car dealer frauds, and the National Headliners' Award for her consumer stories. Mary Lou Werner, now the *Star's* state editor—one of the most important jobs in the newsroom—received her Pulitzer for stories on Virginia's moves to desegregate its schools. Judith Randal, the *Star's* medical reporter, is another award-winner in a field usually covered by men. She won the Albert and Mary Lasker Foundation Award for medical reporting in 1969; was one of the first reporters to write about "L-Dopa" in the treatment of Parkinson's disease; and broke the story that John Knowles, general director of Massachussets General Hospital, after having been offered the job of assistant secretary of HEW, had had the offer withdrawn because of opposition by the American Medical Association. The AMA, Judith said, vetoed Dr. Knowles because he was an outspoken advocate of the need for reorganization of medical care.

(3) Those who do both jobs, like Frances Lewine of the Associated Press and Helen Thomas of United Press International, who cover both the President's side and the First Lady's side of the White House, and Barbara Furlow who is *U.S. News & World Report's* "number two" White House correspondent, covering the president yet dashing off for cross-country trips with the first lady.

Another reporter who covers both "hard" and "soft" news is Lillian Wiggins of *Afro-American*. Though she has the title of society editor, she says, "When you are on a Negro paper, it's the same as working on a weekly, you cover everything." Lillian was in Africa for three months in 1969, covering the Nigerian-Biafran war; she also was in Barbados the same year, doing a series on the Blacks there and the island's black tourist trade

("They have little because it costs so much to get there"). The African embassies are on her beat and she was at the Ivory Coast covering a seated black-tie dinner the night of the 1968 riots in Washington. "I got a call from my office in the middle of dinner," recalls Lillian. She dashed home, changed from evening dress to slacks and leather jacket, and went to Fourteenth Street, the center of the rioting. Not daring to show her notebook, Lillian had to depend on her memory except for the few things she was able to jot down when she could hide behind a building. She was in the middle of the looting and burning until seven in the morning.

All together, as they frequently are at Women's National Press Club and American Newspaper Women's Club functions (such as the annual dinner for Congress or the reception for a new press secretary), newswomen seem strident, unmanicured, and faintly hysterical. Individually, however, it is a different story.

Some, like Mary McGrory, syndicated columnist for the *Washington Star*, are so feminine they've been known to burst into tears when emotionally involved with an issue or a candidate; others maintain the detachment and apparent disinterest more traditionally associated with men.

Some, like Marianne Means of the Hearst papers, or Nancy Dickerson of NBC, are flashingly good-looking and well-turned out; others show the wear and tear of much hard work on their faces and in their wardrobes.

Some are extremely nice, others are downright bitchy. Some are true wits, like Liz Carpenter, who was Lady Bird Johnson's press secretary, and Wauhillau La Hay of Scripps Howard; others take themselves so seriously that they lose all sense of humor.

Except for the syndicated columnists, women reporters make relatively little for their labors—the average is somewhere around $250 a week—but their reward is what has been called "a ringside seat at the best show on earth." A reporter can own exactly one evening dress and not know the difference between *boeuf bourguignon* and an Irish Stew, yet lunch with the wife of the French ambassador, cocktail with several senators, and dine with the president all in one day.

"You have to act like a lady, look like a girl, think like a man, and work like a dog."

The elite of the writing press are the political columnists. They write what they think, not just the what, when, where, why, and how. People throughout the nation, or even the world, form their opinions from what the columnists say is going on in Washington. Presidents seek them out for advice, they are the ones who get the nod if they want to ask a question at a press conference, and Cabinet members, even occasionally the president or vice president, accept their invitations for dinner. Nearly every bureau in Washington, in addition to the three local papers, has at least one columnist analyzing the situation, giving advice to the administration, and interpreting for the public the motives of those who are in power.

Probably the only women political columnists in Washington whose names might be considered household words are Mary McGrory and Marianne Means. Mary's home paper is the *Washington Star*. Marianne is with King Features, the Hearst syndicate, so her columns do not appear in Washington, which she considers a great disadvantage. Marianne would like the *Wash-*

ington Post to run her column but says she was told on good authority that the reason the *Post* does not do so is that "I am a woman," a fact she finds ludicrous, since the owner of the *Post* is Katherine Graham.

One of the most intriguing newswomen in town, Marianne looks like the actress a casting agency would pick to play a glamorous girl columnist in Washington. Though she's got determination and stick-to-it-iveness equal to any man's, her sex-kitten quality reminds one of Marilyn Monroe, with her big, baby-blue eyes made more liquid by contact lenses; tousled blonde hair, china-type white skin, and a deceptive I-am-an-innocent-little-milkmaid-and-will-always-remain-one quality. The only blemish on her movie image is the unmistakable trace of Sioux City, Iowa, where she was born, in her voice. It is not the least of her charms that she is as honest about that as she is in her writing. "If it wasn't for my middle-western voice, I would probably have gone on TV long ago," she admits. "God knows it couldn't be any harder than writing a national column three times a week."

Marianne is now syndicated in 129 papers with such hard-hitting columns as one headed "PRESIDENT NIXON: MR. ORDINARY," in which she wrote: "As President Nixon embarks upon his second six months in office it is difficult not to wonder whether the whole point of his administration is that it has no point. . . . It is all very well to create an impression of tranquility by spending the evening at ball games and the weekends sunning with Florida friend 'Bebe' Rebozo. But what does an unhurried non-leader do in a crisis?"

Marianne, who is as unlucky in love as she is lucky in her work (she has had two unfortunate marriages), has exposed such matters as:

· An angry scene behind closed doors when the top Republican governors blasted GOP National Chairman Rogers B. Morton for the party's inattention to Blacks. According to Marianne, when Morton told the 26 GOP governors that the party intended to make a special effort to attract members of minority groups, Delaware's Governor Russell Peterson admonished Morton, "Look around you. Where are the black faces in this room?"

and proceeded to denounce the conference as typical of a "traditional Republican tendency to talk a lot and do very little in the field of equal opportunity." Governor James Rhodes of Ohio observed, "You can talk all you want about attracting Negroes and the underprivileged into the party, but it won't do any good unless you hire them for responsible jobs, help to educate them, and provide decent housing."

· The vice president's new chores as head of the White House 1970 congressional campaign task force.

· Lyndon Johnson's two specific suggestions to Nixon as they rode up Pennsylvania Avenue on their way to the inaugural: First, to get rid of Kennedy administration holdovers still in important government jobs; second, to urge that Cabinet members see each other socially at least once a week, so as not to be divided by the press on major policy issues.

· Nixon's offer to former Florida Senator George Smathers of the post of attorney general before it went to his long-time law partner, John Mitchell.

· A conversation between Hubert H. Humphrey and former President Lyndon Johnson during which they discussed a replacement for Senator Fred Harris as chairman of the Democratic National Committee. Senator Harris saw the column, which ran on January 25, 1970, and telephoned Humphrey who did not deny that such a conversation took place. The senator announced his resignation as chairman soon after his far-from-friendly telephone conversation with Humphrey. Marianne refuses to say how she heard of the HHH-LBJ conversation, but adds, "You will have to presume I had a good primary source."

Marianne came here 12 years ago as green as a sprig of corn on a Nebraska prairie, having majored in journalism and English at the University of Nebraska and simultaneously worked on the copy desk of the *Lincoln Journal*, "a paper that had a tremendous bias against women on the desk but happened to be so desperate at the time that since I had learned the mechanics at college, they took me on." Before she left in '57 she was the assistant wire editor, which meant getting to work every morning at six, making up the front page and deciding what was to be the lead story, a discipline she feels has stood her in good stead ever since.

She was through college, married, and working full-time at the paper when then-Senator John F. Kennedy came to the campus, and Marianne and her husband, then a senior, were assigned the job of showing him around. "One thing I remember is Ted Sorensen riding in the back seat with the Senator," says Marianne, "and the Senator was chewing gum. Sorensen said, 'Presidential candidates do not chew gum in public,' and Kennedy threw it out."

When they took Kennedy to the airport, Marianne told him they wanted to come East, and he suggested her husband apply at George Washington University, which neither of them had ever heard of. "It sounds incredible now," Marianne recalls, "but we came East knowing not one soul but Kennedy . . . I went around to all the traditional places and the *Washington Post* offered me a job at $40 a week. Somehow I landed in Arlington at the *Northern Virginia Sun* for $65 a week, and within a few weeks I became women's editor there, even though I had never set foot on Virginia soil before."

The *Sun* was an exciting paper to work for between 1957 and 1961, when it was owned and run by Clayton Fritchey (now a syndicated columnist), Philip Stern, author of the *Great Treasury Raid* and *The Oppenheimer Case*, George Ball, later famous as LBJ's "dove-ish" undersecretary of state, and Arnold Sagalyn, later director of law enforcement coordination for the Treasury Department under Kennedy and Johnson.

In those days Marianne chewed gum, wore tight sweaters that left little to the imagination, and was thoroughly detested by all the other women in the city room because not one man could keep his eyes off her. After a time, though, even Shirley Elder, now covering the Hill for the *Washington Star*, came to respect her, for she was the first in the office in the morning and the last out at night, and her women's pages were the most readable in the paper. By the time the paper had to be sold because of a titanic struggle with the typesetters' union, Marianne had so thoroughly established herself as a competent professional, not just a Baby Doll, that with Clayton's help she landed a general assignment reporter's job with the Hearst papers' Washington bureau.

"Nearly two years later, I was assigned to Kennedy's campaign, and then when he won, to the White House. Though I wanted to get away from women's news, Jackie was such good copy that every once in a while I did features on her . . . I went on the first Kennedy trip to Europe in May 1961, to Paris and Vienna. It was the first time that three of us from Nebraska, Evelyn Lincoln,° Ted Sorensen, and me, had ever set foot outside the U.S. I was in Dallas when the president was shot, and I stayed at the White House through Johnson's 1964 campaign. But it's such a nomadic life that I got tired of traveling, so I persuaded them to let me write a column. In January of 1966 King Features picked it up, so I've been syndicated a little more than four years."

Hers is a spectacular success story, and there is no doubt but what her good looks have played a part in it. Some of her colleagues, furious about the fact that presidents-elect and presidents from Kennedy to Nixon so often answer her questions first, suggest that she uses techniques you don't learn in journalism school. Entering a dinner party one night, Barbara Howar was heard to say loud and clear, "I'm so glad to meet you at last. Everybody tells me I'm the biggest bitch in town, except for you." This sort of remark does not go down well with Marianne, who is, in fact, not a "bitch," and it is doubtful whether she and Barbara will become firm friends.

John Kennedy always had an eye for the ladies—with that characteristic Kennedy confidence he seldom made an effort to hide it—so it was quite natural that Marianne should catch his eye in the midst of the rather drab, tired faces that is the press *en masse* when they have waited hours in the rain, wind, or hot sun for a presidential candidate to arrive somewhere. Marianne's goose, in one sense, was cooked when Kennedy got off his boat at Hyannisport shortly after he had been nominated and addressed her, her *only*, by name, with a hundred or so other reporters and photographers hovering nearby. However, it

---

° Evelyn Lincoln was President Kennedy's personal secretary.

was a goose a lot of other women would have adored to have cooked, and Marianne went on from that first triumphal moment to a situation millions of women would envy.

"Men, as a rule, have a hard time taking a young woman seriously," says Marianne. "They want to pat you on the knee, but not give you serious information. Kennedy was different. For example, he once gave me a tip that he was going to name Jim Rawley head of the Secret Service, and I wrote it. Jim's brother, who was a friend of our national editor, called and said, 'My God! What has this idiot girl done? If Jim ever had a chance, she has ruined it now.' What had happened was that Kennedy had told me, but had forgotten to tell Rawley."

Marianne travels today on such important assignments as Nixon's first presidential trip abroad and the governors' conferences ("you get a chance to talk to them in a way you don't when you have to call them up"), but the bulk of her writing is done either in her private office at Hearst's Washington bureau office or in the upstairs study of her sunny, book-filled Georgetown house where she lives with two dogs and a cat. There, she wrote *The Woman in the White House*, about 12 First Ladies who had had an impact on the country, which finally established her reputation as a serious reporter.

"There is a great deal of discrimination in this business," she says. "Some of it is subtle, because it *looks* as if the paper has a lot of women reporters, but most editors assign them to the soft things, like health, education, or welfare. There's no reason why there should only be two women, Mary McGrory and myself, writing a political column, except that men editors just don't take women seriously.

"All I want is to have access to the same sources the men do. For example, Godfrey Sperling of the *Christian Science Monitor* has a regular series of breakfasts to which he invites Cabinet members, senators, and anybody else in the news to brief a couple of dozen of my competitors on what's really going on. These sessions are off-the-record, but often those things you see quoted as 'coming from an unimpeachable source' or 'stated by a high government official' originate at those sessions. He's told me to my face he simply doesn't want a woman there, and that's unfair."

Marianne doesn't like to talk about it much, but part of this true Cinderella story is that she and her most recent former husband became close personal friends of the Johnsons, dining with them privately at the White House several times a month and frequently going boating with them down the Potomac on one of the presidential yachts. She visited them at the ranch along with the small group who made up the Johnson circle of intimates: Representative and Mrs. Jake Pickle of Texas, Representative and Mrs. Jack Brooks of Texas, Presidential Assistant Jack "I sleep better at night knowing that Lyndon Johnson is in the White House" Valenti, of Texas, who married a pert blonde former secretary of LBJ's, Representative and Mrs. George Mahon of Texas, and the Dale Millers of Texas. The Johnsons never seemed to feel really comfortable without Texas people around, but Marianne was an exception, even going up to Camp David for several weekends, never saying a word about it, so that during the entire five years of LBJ's presidency, this was one of the best-kept secrets in Washington.

"I never used any information that came out of our discussions, just anecdotes and background . . . we liked him very much and felt he was grossly misunderstood. His faults were terribly exaggerated, in my opinion. He has a fascinating mind, and he was always so generous. I want to do a serious study of him some time.

"One of my favorite memories from down at the ranch dates back to when Nicholas Katzenbach was still attorney general. Some town had given Johnson its old fire engine, why I don't know, and he climbed into it and raced it around the ranch clanging the bell, with Katzenbach in the seat beside him, and as he drove by me standing there watching he shouted, 'This is why Barry Goldwater wanted to be President!' He was always telling great stories, and there was always a moral to them.

"You probably remember that magazine story back in '64 about him speeding around the Texas roads, while I was supposed to be batting my blue eyes and drinking beer on the seat beside him. Well, that was a typical misinterpretation because I hate beer, and I was sitting on the back seat and if I had been batting my blue eyes it would have had to have been at his back. What happened was that he had invited the members of the press corps out to the ranch and they had served beer and being a gracious host, he had said 'Come on, get in the car and we'll go for a ride.' Lady Bird took another group in her car, and the ones who were left out went back to Austin absolutely furious. Even though I've lectured at Rutgers and spoken to two seminars of the American Political Science Association, there are still people who think of me only as batting my blue eyes at Lyndon Johnson."

An unusual thing about Marianne is that this heady wine seems not to have affected her in any deleterious way. When asked to comment on success as it affects her personally, her answer is, "I don't think I'm all that sucessful yet. I want to have 1,000 papers instead of 124, and I want to write a couple of really good books.

"The glamor—it is marvelous, fascinating, rewarding if you're willing to sacrifice enough for it—carries a tremendous responsibility with it, because here you are in the seat of power of the free world. Also, you have to work so hard in a man's world . . . I wish I could remember who first said, 'You have to act like a lady, look like a girl, think like a man, and work like a dog.' "

Despite her Kennedy and Johnson identification, Marianne has survived the change of administrations. She was riding back from the first Nixon trip to Europe with the President on Air Force One when Henry Kissinger, a most important Nixon assistant and an attractive "bachelor," asked her who she was. Later, on a date (both were recently divorced), he told her that Secretary of State Rogers had overheard his question, taken him aside, and said "Next thing you know, you'll be asking Walter Lippmann who *he* is!"

Another White House aide, Steve Hess, told Marianne a story about President Nixon one day when she and Hess were lunching together. The first time Richard Nixon appeared on color TV, Hess recalled, he and John Whitaker, secretary to the Cabinet, were with him. After the show, Nixon asked, "Well, how do I look in color?" Whitaker said, "You were green." Nixon said, "Well, isn't it too bad they don't have it developed yet, it will take a little time." Whitaker answered, "The interviewer wasn't green."

It is typical of Marianne that, with all the possibilities open to

her, when she gave a dinner in honor of Spiro Agnew at the
City Tavern (a Georgetown club remodelled in Federal period
style), she invited as many of her buddies from *Northern Virginia Sun* days as famous-name officials. That is a rare sort of
thing to do in Washington, where generally a dinner party is
less an exercise in friendship than in the collection of celebrities.

Mary McGrory occupies a rarefied summit in Washington:
She is a leading political writer for the *Washington Evening
Star,* and her syndicated columns are carried by papers all over
the country. Most men and women in the trade would give their
typewriters, if not their eyeteeth, for a chance at such a prominent spot. She brings a refreshing, highly personal point of view
to the goings-on in the capital, uncluttered by doctrine, theory,
or catch phrases. Politicians for Mary are men and women
caught in the same predicament as the rest of the human race.
She chronicles their hopes, frailties, triumphs, and disasters with
merciless candor, surgical precision, and compassion. In contrast
to the sharp use of elbows and fancy footwork that are the customary weapons in this competitive trade, Mary scores her
newsbeats by intuitive understanding. She was the first to see,
for example, when she journeyed to New Hampshire, that Senator Eugene McCarthy's "Children's Crusade" was a political
force to be reckoned with.

Mary's writing has won prizes and honors for herself and the
Star, but perhaps her most flattering reward is the fact that her
male colleagues and competitors not only salute her compe-
tence, but battle for the pleasure of carrying her typewriter.

The mistress of indignation via the printed word, Mary ham-
mers away, four times a week, with what can only be described
as genius at the eccentricities of the political world she covers.

Here are a few excerpts from her much-read columns:

· On Mayor John Lindsay of New York, when he had to
second Spiro T. Agnew's nomination for vice president at the
1968 Republican Convention: "The mayor of New York, who may
have been the most miserable delegate of all, stood with a
frozen half-smile. He was being sacrificed on the altar of party
regularity."

· On the postal workers' strike: "The president said in his stern message to the postal workers that what was at stake was 'the survival of government based on law.'

"And part of the trouble seems to be that the government has been distributing the logic, and justice as badly as the mail has been distributed for the last four days, and the postal workers, who are the coal miners of government service, stopped in their tracks to deliver the message."

· On the Senate's turndown of Judge G. Harrold Carswell: "The battle for the impossible dream—the defeat of Judge Carswell—began on an unlucky day, Friday, March 13, at the Statler-Hilton Hotel. Clarence Mitchell, the doughty warrior of the NAACP, stood before a thoroughly demoralized emergency gathering of civil rights leaders considering the shambles of school integration and said, 'Carswell can be beaten.'

". . . The record showed only Carswell's 'white supremacy' speech at age 28—tut-tutted to an indiscretion in knee-pants by Minority Leader Hugh Scott—and the Judge's part in segregating a public golf course. It was not enough.

"But the following Monday, Sen. Hruska (R-Neb.), the resolute middle-American who was managing Carswell's fortunes, gave the country an issue it could understand. He conceded that Carswell might be mediocre, but harrumphed confidently that the mediocre people deserved representation on the Supreme Court.

"His blunder galvanized the law schools, the bar associations and other groups who have not officially abandoned excellence as a goal."

· On Senator Eugene McCarthy, one of her heroes early in his campaign because of his anti-Vietnam war stance, just after his primary victory in Wisconsin: "At his best he conducts a dazzling dialogue with audiences. In Madison, before a university crowd of 18,000, his words were so closely attended that the throng was like a great fish leaping out of the water to catch the bait of his sentence."

· On Governor Nelson Rockefeller of New York: "Nelson Rockefeller's decision to enter the Presidential race after all has visibly heartened the moderates of his party. It has, however, brought the gravest apprehension to those who love the English language.

"The press conference in which he announced that, 'the speed of the changes in American life' had caused him to change his mind was a perfect example of his marshy prose style and the lamentable imprecision of his expression.

"The Governor displays a poverty of vocabulary that is startling in a man so visibly endowed with this world's goods. The adjective eludes him. He has few verbs. His favorite noun is 'prahblems' and he can scarcely speak of anything from paving-blocks to world peace without reference to our Judaeo-Christian heritage.

"He substitutes for the King's English a kind of body English. He is a great arm-squeezer and backslapper. He winks, grins and shrugs. He does not answer questions. He gives the impression of not having heard them."

Mary has been quoted in *Newsweek* as saying, "I want to be read, but I don't want to be a personality." Small, pert in a pug-nosed Irish sort of way, highly emotional and quite controversial, because she not only wears her heart on her sleeve but wraps it around her typewriter, there's not much she can do to *keep* from being a "personality." Theodore H. White has anecdotes about her in every one of his *The Making of the President* books. In the 1960 book, he has her with Hubert Humphrey at the poignant moment when he conceded not just West Virginia, but in effect the presidential nomination to John F. Kennedy; in 1964 with President Johnson the day after the Walter Jenkins case broke; in 1968 with Senator McCarthy, who read poetry to her, along with some of his other press favorites, in her hotel room the night of the Wisconsin primary.

Mary is reluctant to talk about herself, but lets her hair down once in a while. She says, "The best part of being a newspaper-woman is newspaper*men*. I cannot speak too well of them. They are always communicative and sometimes witty; approached noncompetitively they are capable of chivalry. Gruffs and bores and stuffed shirts—the kind who say 'I've broken with the administration, you know'—there are. They are exceptions in a princely company."

Mary feels that there is a good deal of institutionalized prejudice against women in the news business. During her progress from the book review department to the front page, she was occasionally lectured about not being "difficult." She claims that being "difficult," if you're a woman, means in translation asking for a raise or a particular assignment, requests which if you're a man are deemed perfectly reasonable.

She crept into this man's world "like Elsie Dinsmore," she says, "ready to nod, listen, and be grateful." She rarely asked questions at press conferences and saved her opinions for the next day's paper. It worked. "Men naturally like to explain things to women, and I have given them exceptional opportunity in this regard. I would be lost without the experts who surround me in the White House foyer and the Senate press gallery."

Though admitting that the mark of having arrived as a political reporter is covering presidential campaigns, she calls them "pulverizing rituals . . . As Spiro said of slums, when you've seen one campaign, you've seen them all. One airport is like another, and the police are the same everywhere with the possible exception of Chicago."

Mary never went to journalism school or covered police stations or courts. She has always been a good speller ("the Phineas Bates School in Roslindale, Mass., was firm about that") and an enthusiastic memorizer of poetry ("I'm one of the few people I know who can recite the first ten lines of the *Aeneid* in Latin"). Her first job was as secretary to the literary editor of the *Boston Herald*, where she was told by the managing editor that she was too shy ever to make a good reporter.

"When I came to Washington,° I travelled sedately to the capital city in company with a friend breaking in a new car. I liked it on sight, the trees and the sense of being incognito. In Boston, your name or your face froze you into place. In Washington, nobody knew exactly who anybody else was, so there was more mobility.

° Her first job was reviewing books for the *Washington Star*.

"I liked the *Star* right away, too. Like many evening papers, it is loosely structured, and everyone is free 'to do his or her thing.' Eccentricity is indulged, and so is freedom of expression. I have always felt at home there. For seven years, I reviewed three or four books a week."

Occasionally, she was what she called "unleashed" to wander around Capitol Hill and write profiles for the *Star*'s Sunday section. A true Bostonian brought up with the rogueries of James Michael Curley (the mayor who did a good deal of time in jail), she felt at home with politicians. "Interpreting their evasions is fun, like doing crossword puzzles." In the spring of '54, she was summoned by Newbold Noyes, then national editor, to his desk in the cluttered old building at the corner of Pennsylvania Avenue and 11th Street which served for so long as headquarters for the *Star:*

"Say, Mary, aren't you ever going to get married?" he roared at her in his friendly way, "because if you're not, we think you ought to try something different. You should give color, humor, and charm to the news columns."

Her first trial by fire was to be the Army vs. McCarthy hearings the following week, and Newby reassured the terrified Mary that if she couldn't handle it, she could go right back to her books without anybody knowing the difference. She arrived in the Senate Caucus Room gulping with apprehension and "stone-cold about the issues." The kindest words she ever heard were those of the late Edwin A. Lahey, a Chicago reporter known for his intuition. When she took her seat, trembling inside, he stood up at the long press table and said, "Nice to see you on the news side, honey."

The first sight of the dreaded senator was also steadying. "I had seen his like all my life, at wakes, at weddings, at the Junior Prom. He was an Irish bully-boy, with high shoulders and wicked grin; he was at once the judge, the jury, the prosecutor and the defendant. When I struggled back to the *Star*, overburdened with notes and impressions, Newby Noyes was waiting for me.

"He cut through my babblings with the one phrase I have clung to over the years: 'Write it like a letter to your favorite aunt.'

"I did have a favorite aunt, named Sarah. She was my father's sister, old and frail, had been a history teacher in the Brockton High School, and liked to hear how the principles she had put forth were working out down in the capital."

It took Mary six hours to write the first "letter," and for the next 34 days, with Newby exhorting her to "keep it simple," she produced a series which made her famous. She was the first reporter in the U.S. to dare suggest that Joe McCarthy was indeed "putting the country on" with his accusations and allegations. The managing editor was swamped with calls from people wanting to know what had happened to the *Star*. One letter began, "So, you have joined Alger Hiss and Judith Coplon in attacking our noble Senator McCarthy."

When the hearings ended, so did her days as a book reviewer. "Some old hands took a dim view of having a woman on the national staff, particularly one with such wispy credentials and provocative views. But ancient cub as I was, I was launched at last."

Once launched, acceptance came harder. The first time she went to New York to cover Averell Harriman's re-election campaign for governor, one of his aides, seeing her in the back row at a press conference, asked if she was chairman of the Westchester County Volunteers. "As I started to reply, he amended his question to whether I was the governor's secretary. He'd been brought up in an era when women only made the sandwiches for the house rallies, and when I confessed my business, he was stupefied."

Mary greatly admired the late Doris Fleeson, the syndicated columnist who broke the ice for many women. But it wasn't until the Eugene McCarthy campaign of 1968 that she felt the ice had truly melted.

"The Senator's young helpers, who knew a great deal, not only knew who I was but swamped me with speech transcripts, coffee, aspirin, and tolerance of my anti-social early morning moods. They shared their peanut-butter and jelly sandwiches with me, and their unnerving insights about their elders. Whenever they complained about something I had written, they would start out: 'My mother didn't like what you said about . . .' Readers complained about a loss of objectivity. They were probably right. It's a little hard to keep your head with 21-year-old press aides who tell you that you're their substitute mother-figure. Mass solicitude from a generation that hasn't been speaking to anyone over 30 can be pretty undoing."

She feels, nonetheless, that politicians of the old school still regard the woman political reporter as a contradiction in terms. Senator John Stennis of Missouri, chairman of the Armed Services Committee, blushes and bows when he sees her. "Good mawnin', Miss Mary," he says, "it's mighty nice to see you . . . why no, I wouldn't have anything to say about that matter". . . then stomps down the hall to the waiting television cameras to tell the story to the men. Mary wishes she had more courage about fighting back; she claims that she's brave at the typewriter, but never in person.

Politicians, she finds, tend to tell women their troubles rather than their news. "I've heard more than I care to know about unhappy wives and wayward children. Unless accompanied by some heavyweight like Robert Healy of the *Boston Globe,* I rarely get to hear the obscene expletive that signalled the delivery of a delegation or the end of an impasse on a bill."

Senator Eugene McCarthy was a friend of 20 years, but she was one of the last to learn he was going to challenge Lyndon Johnson. Henry Brandon of the *London Sunday Times* told her he thought McCarthy would, but she told him in October of 1967 that it would be "too preposterous."

The myth that female scribblers spend their evenings over candlelight and wine, with high officials whispering state secrets in their ears, is deeply imbedded in the public mind, according to Mary. "*Advise and Consent* may have something to do with it. Allen Drury worked on the *Star* before he went to *The New York Times,* and should have known better. All I can say is that even if I were bidden to such momentous gatherings, I would never get there. As the hired butler glides through with the first tray of martinis, or as the company is digging into the catered chocolate mousse, I am finding out that the last line I have written is really the lead of the dispatch, and am preparing to turn the whole thing upside down and begin again. Such continuing un-facility is a hang-up, and perhaps I ought to consult a psychiatrist. But I'd never get *there,* either."

Except at Hickory Hill, a pocket of strenuous merriment once upon a time, Mary's convinced that the idea of just having fun has never been seriously entertained by Washington hostesses. "The cares of the day and of status are always present at the festive board, and once I heard a reporter say to Robert McNamara, by way of lightsome gambit over a glass of champagne, 'I thought your second paragraph didn't really take into account the San Antonio formula.'"

She went to dinner once at the White House, asked by President Kennedy in a fit of remorse. It had been called to his attention that he had given first-anniversary interviews to the entire press corps with the exception of Mary, who had shadowed him from the start. She was seated next to the pantry, but had a marvelous time; and there were no competing memories, since it was her first visit to those hallowed halls.

"During the Johnson years, there was no cause to venture out unless you had an appetite for shattering scenes, with old friends screaming at each other about the bombing halt and 'negotiating from strength.' After the Chicago Convention of 1968, it got even worse." The single woman journalist, Mary thinks, is in any administration a problem to her hostess. The other guests are not quite sure whether to treat her as a woman or a newspaperwoman, and the men tend to end sentences with "Now, don't print that." Sometimes the wife of a high official or a colleague will say a bit coyly: "I'm just a housewife." The assumption is that the working newswoman is a career girl who summarily rejected the love of a good man for a by-line.

It is better, she discovered, to invite people to your own small apartment. *Chez elle,* it is not forbidden to discuss the indigestible topics of the day, but it is discouraged. They sing instead. Four senators in all have crossed the threshold over the years, gotten the drift right away and pitched into singing and serving. Robert Kennedy won all hearts by his rendition of his camp song. He did one stanza, left, and reappeared 15 minutes later saying he had recalled the second. An editor's wife said it was just like her girlhood evenings back on the farm in South Dakota. So much for the glamorous social life of the Washington reporter.

She enjoys most of the events she attends in line of duty. "I feel a responsibility to the people waiting in line outside the hearing-room—the night club of my working hours, intimate and contained—and hope I can describe it so they will think they got there. 'Why should I?' said Charlotte Bronte when someone asked her why she didn't go out in society. 'My sister Emily will bring it all home to me.' "

Mary has been to a lot of funerals since 1963. She shared a hymnbook with Richard Nixon at Martin Luther King's touching obsequies at his home church in Atlanta. A black woman came up to her in tears in Birmingham to thank her for being at the funeral of a 13-year-old boy who had been shot in the back. She saw blood on the floor of the McCarthy headquarters in the Hilton Hotel in Chicago, and blood on the streets outside.

Mary also has more cheerful memories, most of them predating the Vietnam war, which "blighted everything." She remembers John Kennedy's telling May Craig that he was sure the government was not doing enough for women, and Robert Kennedy entering the Greek Theater at Berkeley with a 100-piece band playing "Yankee Doodle" as if it had just been written, President Eisenhower trying to keep his temper when Sarah McClendon asked him a question, the lovely speeches of Adlai Stevenson, and furious old Arthur Watkins gavelling down Joe McCarthy. "The company is excellent, the diversion endless. The only snag is the typewriter."

She vehemently disagrees with Marianne's comment that the shortage of women columnists "is disgraceful." To her, "that's the sort of meaningless feminism (is there any other kind?) that is really aggravating. What's disgraceful to me is that there's no political columnist of the calibre of Doris Fleeson, Dorothy Thompson, or Anne O'Hare McCormick. When you compare us with those Valkyries, you realize how insipid we are. Those girls made governments quake. There is no one comparable on the scene today."

Mary's fans think she's wrong. Any woman makes things quake who can write, on the day after President Nixon left for the new White House in San Clemente, "Barry Goldwater, in his halcyon days, used to suggest that the Eastern seaboard be sawed off and floated out to sea. Nobody thought it was a practical idea until Richard Nixon came along and did it."

New as Washington columnists, although not as Washington newswomen, are Vera Glaser and Malvina Stephenson, who write an entertaining and informative syndicated column called "Off Beat Washington" for the Knight newspapers. They aren't as political as Mary McGrory and Marianne Means, or as society-oriented as Betty Beale or Ymelda Dixon, but their column covers a wide range of subjects. One day it might be an exposé of how the Navy bought 17 new-style patrol gunboats for $68 million, only to discover they were so poorly made they might have to be junked; another day, an interview with Attorney General John Mitchell's talkative wife Martha.

The two first collaborated on election night of 1968 when they fast-talked their way into the Nixon inner sanctum on the 35th floor of the Waldorf Towers while some 1,000 of their colleagues were stuck on the third-floor press room set up by the Nixon press aides.

Vera, a good-looking blonde, and Malvina, an equally attractive redhead, were walking around looking for any story that wasn't a handout from the Nixon press office when they spotted handsome young Robert Finch—former secretary of Health, Education and Welfare, then one of Nixon's closest friends and campaign adviser.

The girls talked him into doing a taped interview and convinced him a quiet corner of the 35th floor would be the best locale in which to tape it. Finch led them through police corridor-blocks and past the Secret Service right into the area where campaign manager John Mitchell (now attorney general), and top aides Richard Kleindienst, Fred LaRue, and Peter Flanagan were ensconced. Vera and Malvina taped short interviews with all of them; they also interviewed Murray Chotiner, who had been Nixon's adviser for many years and was now back on the team.

By the time Vera and Malvina were spotted by Director of Press Relations Herb Klein's secretary and told to leave, they had not only the interviews but the mimeographed copy of campaign director Robert Ellsworth's confidential guide to election returns which one of them had casually picked up from a table.

To make sure their scoop was holding, the girls stopped by the third-floor press room and innocently asked if there had been any statements from the high command. "They're closeted with Nixon on the 35th floor, and no one can get through," answered Don Irwin, ace political reporter for the *Los Angeles Times*. "No kidding!" exclaimed Malvina.

Vera at that time was with the North American Newspaper Alliance and Malvina had (as she still does), her own bureau servicing several Oklahoma papers and TV—radio stations. They went to their rooms, got on the long-distance line to Malvina's stations, and went on the air with the announcement that "no matter what Nixon strategists say at this moment, here is what the insiders really think. . . ." They then explained Bob Ellsworth's guide to the returns and said, "The winner in Illinois, according to Ellsworth, will be the next president. Illinois is unexpectedly close and still uncertain." All night they fed bulletins to Malvina's stations, giving Ellsworth's predictions as each state went either for Humphrey or Nixon. Vera was also pounding out stories for NANA. Malvina's stations later told her that she beat the networks by two hours all night long, and Vera wound up with five exclusive interviews for NANA.

A few weeks later, they started writing their "Off Beat" column, and one scoop has followed another ever since. Some of them are:

· Shirley Temple Black, Nixon's appointee as a delegate to the United Nations General Assembly, charged a $500 fee for every speech she made at a major GOP function, plus double travel expenses; she even received $500 for appearing at her own birthday party, given by the GOP women at their 1968 Spring Conference.

· Mrs. Robert B. Rheault, wife of the special forces colonel in charge of the Green Berets, blasted the military for its handling of the Berets' "murder" case. Vera and Malvina, after an exclusive interview, quoted Mrs. Rheault as saying that General

Creighton Abrams, U.S. commander in Vietnam, had "egg on his face," and that the government was trying to keep the Green Beret wives from talking but "try and stop me!"

· Director of the Central Intelligence Agency Richard Helms and Russian Boris Strelnikov, a correspondent for *Pravda,* live in the same apartment building. In a column starting, "Who is spying on whom . . ." Vera and Malvina pointed out that the two cloak-and-dagger foes bed down every night under the same roof, sharing the same plumbing and the same switchboard.

· Information that members of the House Foreign Affairs Committee were unhappy about the Nixon Administration using expensively trained astronauts on nonspace jobs. Vera and Malvina wrote that "Astronaut Michael Collins soared to the moon and back in eight days, but seems unable to get into orbit at the State Department after four months as assistant secretary of public affairs." They quoted Representative Wayne Hays, a Democrat from Ohio, as saying that Collins "is about as qualified to hold that job as a pig is to be a figure skater."

· The Nixon Administration's appointment of what the two called "a Republican segregationist" to a $20,000 a year job at the State Department. As soon as the Glaser-Stephenson story appeared the White House moved swiftly to dismiss the woman, Mrs. Peter Cameron, of Bethesda, Maryland, from the job. Vera and Malvina in their story revealed that Mrs. Cameron in 1964, at a Wallace rally in Rockville, Maryland, carried a placard reading, "They *say* intergration [sic]. They *mean* miscegenation." They also produced a picture of Mrs. Cameron carrying the sign. In her State Department job, which Mrs. Cameron held for 48 hours, she would have been traveling extensively to work with local people in India, Pakistan, Nepal, Ceylon, Burma, Poland, Yugoslavia, Israel, Tunisia, Guinea, Morocco, and Egypt.

Vera and Malvina, like the others, never reveal their sources, but it's safe to say the Cameron information came from one or more Bethesda GOP women who had worked for Nixon during the campaign, and were incensed that Mrs. Cameron had been handed such a plum.

The pair also are known to have many congressional friends who leak information to them. Probably it was a member of Congress, anxious to stop the Army's court-martial proceedings against the Green Berets, who set up their interview with Mrs. Rheault. Congressman Carl Albert of Oklahoma has admitted that he gave Malvina the scoop that Robert McNamara had been named head of the World Bank. Malvina, who has her master's degree in journalism and history from the University of Oklahoma, came to Washington in 1940, and has been developing good congressional news sources ever since. Vera for a while left newspapering to become women's news director for the Republican National Committee and from there went to the Hill as press secretary to Kenneth Keating (then a senator, now U.S. ambassador to India). The connections she made then are invaluable to her now as a columnist. Ken Keating was a member of the exclusive Chowder and Marching Society, a group whose members are present or past Republican congressmen including Richard Nixon, Melvin Laird, Thruston Morton, and Gerald Ford. One of the early parties given by President and Mrs. Nixon in the White House was a dinner for the still-active Chowder and Marching Society, and many of its members have been appointed to important jobs in the administration.

Vera had the first story that Arthur Goldberg, then ambassador to the U.N. but waiting for his successor to be appointed, favored the admission of Red China to the U.N. The story, says Vera, "scooped the world."

Recalling how she got it, Vera says, "The extraordinary thing about this was that there were six or eight people sitting there when I asked Goldberg this question and none of them got it. He was talking about who should be admitted to the U.N., and he said he thought everybody should be admitted. I asked if that included countries like Red China and he said 'yes.' This was the story of all time, because he had voted against it three times, because this was the policy of our government, and he felt, I guess, that now that he was leaving he could express his private opinion."

Vera is proud of the exclusive interview she had with Passport Director Frances Knight, at a time when certain people at the State Department were trying to get Miss Knight fired.

Frances Knight had been forbidden to give interviews, but Vera told the secretary that Miss Knight was being persecuted from all sides, that she should let someone tell her story, and that she, Vera, was the one to tell it. Miss Knight called her back within a few hours and Vera went to her office.

Miss Knight started off by saying that if the men in the State Department would spend more time doing the job they were supposed to do they wouldn't be in such a mess; instead, she said, they spent all their time trying to get rid of her.

"I learned something from that interview," says Vera. "I had heard that Miss Knight was mean, an absolutely impossible woman, and she turned out to be delightful; and it proved one thing to me: if a woman knows what she is doing, and Frances Knight does, it makes a lot of men livid. The rumors and barbs about that poor woman are just incredible and she's just as nice as can be. There are 450 people in her department and the morale is just terrific, they all adore her."

Perhaps the best remembered exclusive story Vera and Malvina have had was when they were able to get copies of Jacqueline Onassis' memos to her staff when she was First Lady Jacqueline Kennedy. (Again, this was information leaked by an unnamed source.) This was before Mary Gallagher, the First Lady's tell-all secretary, had her book published. Vera and Malvina told their readers that: Jackie Kennedy worried about drunken behavior by White House guests, possible damage to the Red Room rug, and demeaning the presidential seal by possible use on cigarette packs; that there was a bitter clash between Jackie and her social secretary, Letitia "Tish" Baldrige because "when Tish destroyed all of Jackie's detailed directions for the glittering Kennedy entertainments, the First Lady's sense of history was assaulted."

The memos had a surprise for newswomen who always thought they got along quite well with President Kennedy, if not with his wife. Jackie wrote her press secretary that "JFK was a bit disturbed last night about the press ladies. They hang around with their pads and make everyone nervous—and, though they were very nice about last night, they had the McCones [CIA Director John McCone] rather apprehensive as they had said something in their hearing."

CHAPTER

3

"The tools of the trade include stamina, flexibility, binoculars, track shoes and an affinity for a phone booth."

No matter how many times a reporter walks into the White House she always gets a sense of awe and wonder that so much power could be concentrated in one relatively small dwelling. The White House is "THE" beat. Those regularly assigned to it belong to a sort of aristocracy of the press; only a columnist like Mary McGrory or a network commentator like Nancy Dickerson has more standing.

Like Gaul, the White House is divided into three parts: the West Wing, the East Wing, and the middle. The West Wing contains the president's offices, the offices of his assistants, and a lobby where anyone coming to see the president or one of his aides is whisked through on his way to the appointment. If the visitor is so important that the White House wants to keep his visit secret from the press, he is sneaked in through the other side of the building. Next to this lobby is the office of the press secretary, a gentleman whose role approximates that of Daniel among the lions. If he can toss out the right number of pieces of red meat each day, he may with luck manage to avoid being eaten up himself.

President Nixon's press secretary is handsome, 31-year-old Ron Ziegler who worked for an advertising firm in Los Angeles until he joined the Nixon campaign staff. He is personally popular with the press, though they complain that he's kept on a tight leash. "He's very likable," says Bonnie Angelo of *Time* magazine, "and he does his job competently enough, but he's too mechanical. I feel if he said the president wants Polly to have a cracker, and I asked whether Polly prefers a Saltine or a Triscuit, the answer will come back that Polly wants a cracker. I don't think he knows what Polly really wants."

Until early 1970, the press also was quartered in the West Wing, built during the Theodore Roosevelt era so the president could get the White House business offices out of the mansion. It's now in a $574,000 "West Terrace Press Center," built at the president's suggestion in the colonnade connecting the West Wing with the mansion. The colonnade is part of a pavilion constructed when Thomas Jefferson was president, opening on the south to the rose garden with a swimming pool on the north, built for polio-crippled Franklin Roosevelt with funds donated by American citizens. It was enhanced with a handsome mural —a scene of the harbor at Christiansted in the Virgin Islands by French artist Bernard Lamotte—donated by former Ambassador Joseph Kennedy when his son was president. When President Nixon, a salt-water swimmer, announced that the pool area— dressing rooms, lockers, plus the flower room where White House pets used to be parked—was being made into a press room, *The New York Times'* James M. Naughton wrote: "President Nixon plans to send the White House correspondents to the locker room and the radio-television reporters to the dog house."

President Nixon took President Johnson on a tour of the new press center, only a few days after it opened. LBJ, who had his troubles with the press, said it was a great improvement and asked, "Is there the same improvement in the stories?" "It's only a hope, I assure you," answered RMN.

Everyone except Tass, the official Soviet government news agency, likes the new setup, which is a two-floor arrangement with a small stage for briefings and informal press conferences, a lounge area with tufted suede Chesterfield sofas, Currier and Ives reprints on the walls, Muzak piped in, 12 broadcast booths and 40 individual desks for the writing press. Tass is upset because it wasn't assigned a desk, although Reuters, the British news service, and Agence France Presse, the French Government service, were. Although American newsmen in Moscow seldom can question Soviet officials, and they have to get their only official government news by reading *Pravda, Izvestia* or the Tass news service, Tass is still protesting because it has not been given "equal treatment" with other news services in the White House.

Living quarters for the First Family are in the center section, where on the north is the columned portico, and on the south the Truman balcony which caused such a donnybrook at the time it was built. Thousands of tourists ogle at the first two floors of this section daily, except Sunday and Monday.

Balancing, architecturally, the Jefferson colonnade on the West side is another colonnade from the mansion leading to the East Wing, incorporating the family theater and a glassed-in corridor overlooking the First Ladies' Garden, known until the Nixon Administration as the Jacqueline Kennedy Garden.

The East Wing, built during Franklin Roosevelt's administration, is where the military aides have offices, along with the First Lady's staff director, press director, her social secretary, and the batteries of people who grind out invitations to parties (suitable for framing), citations, appreciations, and exhortations. Here emanates the news about who's invited to parties, what they will eat and do before and after dinner, why and where. The press covering this wing is ambulatory: no desks or telephones are provided for it, except on official party nights when a few phones are installed in the theater. Yet almost as many words of copy spill out of the East Wing as the West, when you consider daughters' weddings, choices of clothes designers, and such culinary earthquakes as changes of chefs. This is because the chief society writers, who are usually syndicated all over the world, keep as close watch on what the First Family is doing as hunters on safari do on the game they are stalking. During presidential inaugurals, or a White House birth or wedding, one can almost feel pity for the poor press secretary who must contend with the not-always-ladylike "Ladies" of the press.

Though the activities of the two wings seldom cross for the majority of the news people assigned to the White House, there are two prominent exceptions to this general rule: Frances Lewine of The Associated Press and Helen Thomas of United Press International. Close friends, so much so that they are often called the "Bobbsey Twins" since one is seldom seen covering a news event without the other nearby, Fran and Helen are something of a Washington institution.

Fran is part of a three "man" AP White House staff, headed by Frank Cormier and including Douglas Cornell; Helen and Eugene Risher, who came to Washington from UPI's Saigon bureau about two years ago, cover the White House for UPI. The AP and UPI teams have worked together so long now that they seem to be able to parcel out the day's or night's work without communicating in words: they will come away from a daily press briefing and decide within 60 seconds who will tackle the revolution in South America, who the appointment of an ambassador, and who the president's message on soy bean tariffs. In one sense, they are like a doctor and his head nurse, with this important difference: Fran and Helen are qualified and competent at all times to take over the whole AP or UPI White House operation themselves, and often do. How they manage to do a man's job all day and still stay on top of every rumor or whisper out of the distaff side of the White House is a cause of constant wonder to their envious colleagues.

Fran and Helen follow the president and his family everywhere, and when you read a news story in your local paper about Mrs. Nixon, the children, or any social or civic event in which the First Lady is participating, if it says UPI or AP on it, the chances are that one of them has written it. They follow the family so closely that it sometimes causes amusing incidents. Gerry Van der Heuvel told of one in *Editor and Publisher*:

"On one trip down to Palm Beach, during the kidnap scare about Caroline, a woman reported to the Secret Service that two suspicious looking women were following Mrs. Kennedy. The unsavory characters were Frances and Helen . . .

"The tables were turned a short time later when Frances observed a swarthy, stocky-built man sitting in church when the Kennedys were there on Sunday. What worried her was the obvious bulge of a gun in his pocket. She nudged Helen Thomas and gave her a 'let's get on him' look. He was a Secret Service man."

Like many other newsgirls, Fran and Helen broke into newspapering during World War II. The men were with the Armed Forces, leaving editors no choice but to hire women. The *Washington Post* even put Ann Christmas (now with the *Star*) on its sports staff. One of us, for instance, was one of the first girl reporters ever hired by the *New Yorker* magazine. As she left his office after landing her job, the late, great *New Yorker* editor, Harold Ross, turned to his assistant and exclaimed loudly, "My God! Have we come to *this?*" War's end found women so entrenched in the city room that they've been around ever since.

Neither Fran nor Helen has ever married, which probably is significant: they haven't had time. One being of Arabic and one of Jewish descent hasn't affected their friendship, and neither has their professional rivalry. Both have "gentlemen friends" with whom they are seen frequently; both are charming companions and infinitely knowledgeable about What's Going On In The World. Being based in the new Press Center (they have their own desks and telephones in glass-enclosed booths), and also covering the East Wing from church to champagne, they occupy what one might call the best seats in the House for all important occasions.

Helen was the first woman in history ever to close a Presidential press conference. It was under President Kennedy and absent that day was the late Merriman Smith who had that honor since he was dean of White House correspondents, having headed the United Press staff there since 1939. Helen saw that the time (thirty minutes) was up and said, "Mr. President, thank you." Later she realized she should have said, "Thank you, Mr. President." It didn't matter: President Kennedy was so relieved to be rescued from a tricky question that he said, "Thank YOU, Helen." Since then she has opened and closed press conferences under both Johnson and Nixon.

Helen has managed to have a rapport with all the presidents she has covered.* There's the time when she had been on the "baby watch" when John F. Kennedy, Jr., was born. "For a spinster," she says, "I've had a good record as a midwife. I've delivered more presidential babies than I care to remember." President-elect Kennedy got used to seeing her in the crowd of women reporters every day when he visited his wife at Georgetown University Hospital. One morning Helen's office sent her to stand in front of the Kennedys' "N" Street House in Georgetown to see him off for a conference with President Eisenhower on how to run the country. Startled to see her there, Jack Kennedy said, "Helen, you've deserted my baby!"

Discussing Helen recently, Bill Moyers, former publisher of the prestigious *Newsday* and erstwhile Johnson press secretary, said: "Helen came up with more scoops on her beat than any one male reporter did . . . She exasperated me, humiliated me, embarrassed me . . . and impressed me for doing what a good reporter ought to do: develop sources, comb them relentlessly, and come up with good stories."

Helen broke the news that Jackie Kennedy, then First Lady, was going to Rome and would have an audience with the pope; she told the nation first that Luci Johnson, younger daughter of then-President Johnson, was taking instruction to become a Catholic. She also was first with the news that Luci and Pat Nugent were on their way to the LBJ Ranch to ask her parents' permission to become engaged, an event that caught even Liz Carpenter by surprise.

How does Helen know such intimate family secrets? She'll never tell. Like other members of the press, she fiercely protects her sources. She knows none of them would ever again leak information to her if exposed as the one who fed her a story.

Every president and First Lady since the Kennedys have called Fran and Helen by their first names, even Jacqueline Kennedy, who was ambivalent about the press—and still is, if

* Helen was one of two newswomen President Nixon telephoned in the early morning hours of May 9, 1970, when he was unable to sleep before the protest demonstrations against his Southeast Asia policies. He telephoned Helen at 3:45 A.M., after having called Nancy Dickerson of NBC at 1:30.

the story about her judo grip on the photographer who tried to catch her coming out of the movie, *I Am Curious—Yellow* is to be believed. Having been an "Inquiring Photographer" herself for the Washington *Times-Herald* (later bought by the *Post*), not long after she left Vassar, she understood what the press was up to from its side of the fence. "Who will be Washington's number one hostess now that the Republicans are back in power?" photographer Jacqueline Bouvier asked Patricia Nixon, whose husband had been sworn in as vice president in 1953, just a month earlier. Mrs. Nixon answered:

"Why Mrs. Eisenhower, of course. I think her friendly manner and sparkling personality immediately captivate all who see or meet her. She is equally gracious in small groups or long receiving lines, where she has the knack of getting acquainted with each person, instead of merely shaking hands with the usual phrase, 'How do you do?' The people of America will always be proud of their First Lady."

The aggressive type of reporting she later viewed with horror was used by Jackie when she stalked Ellen Moore, the 11-year-old niece of Mrs. Eisenhower, home from school, and talked to her about Ellen's baby-sitting jobs. The precocious niece of the new First Family told Jackie that she was thinking of raising her rates: "I've been charging fifty cents an hour, but now that my uncle is president of the United States, don't you think I should get seventy-five?" Like so many people when they find themselves a part of the inner White House circle, Ellen's mother wasn't pleased about unsolicited publicity. She asked a newspaper friend, the late George Dixon, to "do something to make that brash camera girl, whoever she is, know her place."

Yet when the shoe was on the other foot, Jackie took it hard. She never seems to have quite understood that there is a price to pay for being the darling of five continents. "She never could stand us," a veteran reporter says.

Her efforts to avoid the press during a Greek isle odyssey furnished Fran Lewine with enough material for a chapter in her book (Fran, like every Washington newswoman, has been "writing a book" for years). The First Lady and her sister, the Princess Lee Radziwill, vacationed on Greek shipping magnate Marco Nomikos' yacht, the *North Wind,* long before anyone dreamed that Jackie would someday marry another Greek ship-ping man and have a luxury yacht of her own. Fran, assigned to cover the First Lady, went armed with history and travel books aboard an AP chartered 53-foot ocean-going cruiser, and set sail on the Aegean Sea with seven shipmates—the captain and crew, two photographers, a Greek reporter, and a photo mes-senger.

"We knew the *North Wind*'s first destination, that was all," says Fran. "But the sea was so rough and the winds so strong, the captain decided we had to pull into a little port and spend the night. It was a dismal evening, because we figured that if we lost them the first day we'd never catch up."

The next morning the sky was blue and clear, but the most beautiful sight to Fran was the *North Wind* anchored alongside, for Jackie's yacht, too, had had to put into port.

From then on it was tracking by-guess-and-by-gosh, until Fran discovered that Jackie's land-based social secretary, Tish Baldrige, and an embassy aide aboard the yacht were talking daily via ship-to-shore radio in French. When all their plans ap-peared on the AP wire, the aide and Tish switched to Italian, which a crew member translated.

"Between us," says Fran, "eight languages were spoken on our cruiser. They couldn't get away!" However, there were such dis-appointments as rowing ashore to a tiny island at midnight and climbing a steep hill, only to find that there was no way to file the story.

Much as First Families want their privacy, they dread even more being ignored. More than 130 reporters signed up for Pres-ident Nixon's first around-the-world trip, but only one indicated she would be following Mrs. Nixon on her rounds of hospitals and such. When the president discovered this, he made a per-sonal appeal to newswomen, two days before the trip started. "Will it help if I call your bosses?" he asked.

The reluctance of editors to send newswomen was not the expense—over $3,000 dollars for transportation, plus hotels, food, cost of transmitting copy—but not knowing if Pat would do anything newsworthy. Her schedule was released only the night before the president made his last-minute appeal, although his own had been out almost a week.

Fran and Helen were assigned to go along on the 12-day, 8-country trip after their bosses received a White House call and thus had one day to get immunization shots, pack, and gather up background material pertinent to the places they'd visit.

On the trip, they averaged two hours sleep a night ("We fell asleep at the palace dinner in Thailand") . . . didn't get their hair done once during the whole trip ("I had a fall along but didn't have time to put it on") . . . had 15 minutes to change into evening dresses ("I wore one dress six times, at the last it looked like something was happening to it") . . . drank five cokes an hour to combat the 115-degree heat, missed baths because there were rust and bugs in some of the water, and ran, ran, ran to catch a plane, a bus, a car, a helicopter.

When Fran's bosses once asked her to send a memo telling them what it was like to cover the White House, she wrote:

"The tools of the trade include stamina, flexibility, binoculars, track shoes and an affinity for a phone booth. It always sounds terribly glamorous to those on the outside—and it really is. But there are times when you've written one more story at 4 A.M. or rushed into long evening gown and long white gloves in 15 minutes flat when you think maybe another profession might be easier on the nerves."

Fran adds that "the opportunities for news coverage and variety probably are unmatched on any beat." Presidents and reporters get on a first-name basis—that is, they call *you* by your first name. It's sometimes hard to realize that this is the seat of power and you're alongside. It gets to be commonplace riding in Air Force One and presidential helicopters and motorcades, chit-chatting with the president.

"Through all this, the press has to maintain its critical, questioning, probing attitude toward the president, his actions and his operations, remembering that you play a watchdog role in the democratic process. When the White House press office begins to take down names of reporters alongside the questions they ask and criticising the way leads are written, you have to be ready to withstand the pressure as well . . ."

Most of the trips that touch other continents are jet-propelled agonies, but they include some fabulous adventures. For Fran, there was the spectacle of a visit to the fabled Khyber Pass to write about Jacqueline Kennedy wearing new wrap-around sun-glasses . . . getting a lift in a French police paddy wagon after being stranded 12 miles outside of Paris on Kennedy's visit . . . holding a phone line open from Moscow to London for one hour of constant talking (lest she be cut off) awaiting a Nixon-Khrushchev communiqué . . . losing a shoe running through the black soil of Garst's farm in Iowa on Khrushchev's return visit to the U.S.A. . . . being rescued by helicopter from amid a million milling Koreans in Seoul on President Johnson's Asian trip.

Fran summarizes: "The biggest requirement of this job, I think, is ingenuity. I've learned such tricks as keeping a dime in my shoe on a running story, to jump carefully from a moving bus to avoid falling flat in the street as I did covering Queen Elizabeth's royal tour in Canada and to remember to get in-structions in Chinese and Thai on how to call the AP office in Malaysia.

"I've learned the hard way not to come home and try to tell colleagues the vicissitudes of your travels. They always greet you with: 'How was the vacation?' "

Though Fran and Helen are the only women covering both wings of the White House day by day, Muriel Dobbin, a pert, red-headed Scottish girl who represents the *Baltimore Sun* is the only woman covering strictly the West Wing side for a daily paper. This is both by choice and by luck, for she doesn't enjoy covering family and social activities and the *Sun*, though physi-cally so close to Washington and with a sizeable readership in the Maryland commuter towns around Washington, doesn't want any more detail about them than the wire services can provide.

"When I first came here," she says, "I covered one or two of the White House dinners, but I wasn't fond of all that standing around. When Mrs. Johnson first came in, I followed her on about three of those beautification trips, and she made those sugar-coated speeches until the *Sun* said they weren't going to spend any more money having me watch her plant azaleas."

Muriel was on the White House beat just helping out, writing about Jackie Kennedy, which she didn't like because clothes and parties don't interest her, when President Kennedy was shot. "Incredible!" An ex-police reporter, it was the kind of thing she knew how to do: cover a murder. So she met President Johnson when he arrived that night, and wrote mood pieces about Mrs. Kennedy as well. When it was over, the *Sun* started using her regularly at the White House and eventually she graduated to White House correspondent. She's never had anything but help from the men, especially on presidential trips where the ratio of men to women is about 98 to 2. Obviously, says Muriel, "any man would rather have lunch, a drink, or dinner with a woman, as long as she washes and doesn't go stamping around about women's rights."

When asked to compare Nixon and Johnson, Muriel says:

"President Johnson generated his own uproar, and it extended beyond his staff to the press, consequently permeating the entire White House. He took an interest as intense and personal in the White House press corps as the reporters took in him."

When Johnson was worried, troubled, agonizing, euphoric or about to go into surgery, Muriel feels he wanted everybody to suffer or celebrate with him, including the press. Johnson's idea of being solitary was to have an audience of at least four. She says: "His alternate wooing and abuse of the press were responsible for the steady decline of his relations with the fourth estate, which spent much of its time talking and complaining about him, yet which has found since his departure that it is possible actually to miss him, much as one would miss a crotchety grandfather.

"President Nixon's press philosophy is to stay as far away from reporters as possible and when he does see them, to do so on terms of careful formality. His manner when dealing with reporters at the few off-record gatherings he has had with them has been manicured in its politeness but careful. He gives the impression of being determined to learn from his predecessor's mistakes, and he obviously feels the latter's handling of the press was one of the largest of those."

To Muriel, the most striking difference between the two men in relation to the press is that the press not only knew Johnson was there, but Johnson also knew the press was there. "He may have frequently detested it, but at least it was familiar. Nixon is unobtrusive in manner and physical appearance, and the presidential aura seems to sit uneasily on those neatly tailored shoulders. Johnson wore it like a halo, twirling it around his head." On the days of crisis, the Nixon White House remains composed. Briefings may be delayed, but the atmosphere of gathering storm clouds is gone, possibly because the chief storm cloud is gone. Every member of the Nixon staff stresses the president's civility and self-control under all circumstances. The most the Johnson staff would say was that his temper wasn't really as bad as it was reputed to be.

Traveling with Nixon is much more organized, in keeping with the rest of the picture, and is even announced days or weeks in advance. There is little secrecy about the president's travel plans, or even about his legislative plans. And there is no uproar behind the scenes when such plans are revealed, as was the case with Johnson.

"In a nutshell," Muriel summarizes, "I suppose you might say this is a sedate and tidy administration run by a sedate and tidy president. But it isn't nearly as interesting."

Every administration is interesting to Marie Smith of the *Washington Post,* who has covered the White House since the Eisenhowers and still finds "something great and wonderful and exciting" about her beat. A brunette with Dresden-china skin, deep dimples, and a way about her that makes you want to tell her everything you know immediately, Marie is not only one of the top White House reporters, but the only one who has really made the White House a specialty, having written three books about it: *White House Entertaining, White House Brides,* and *The President's Lady,* a biography of Lady Bird.

Although Marie is mostly an East Wing reporter, she comes up with West Wing scoops regularly. She probably has as many political contacts as anybody in town, and her loyal sources see to it that she is first with such stories as that the president would appoint Maryland State Senator Louise Gore, who introduced Spiro Agnew to Richard Nixon, as U.S. ambassador to UNESCO, and that Chicago multi-millionaire Clement Stone gave Nixon at least part of the secret for his big political comeback by introducing him to his own book, *Success Through a Positive Mental Attitude.*

Through one of her informants, Marie learned in 1963 that a maternity suite at the Otis Air Force Base in Massachusetts, near the Kennedy compound at Hyannisport, had been redecorated in anticipation of the First Lady's using it. A picture of an Air Force officer attached to the military hospital ran along with Marie's story. President Kennedy was extremely displeased. He called in his Air Force aide, Brigadier General Godfrey McHugh, waved the newspaper in front of his nose, and bellowed, "Doesn't that fellow have anything else to do besides have his picture taken?"

"The biggest scoop I've ever had," Marie says, "was when President Kennedy decided that he would change the order of precedence and put the Speaker of the House ahead of the Chief Justice at all official occasions." Order of precedence is a monumentally important matter in Washington. Speaker Sam Rayburn had wanted the change for a long time, as Marie found out at the capitol while covering the 1961 inaugural ceremonies. She wrote it as a front-page story even though she couldn't get official confirmation. "This is always a dangerous thing to do, but I knew my sources well enough to be sure it was true."

The profile she did of Pat Nixon during the 1960 campaign still remains one of the most perceptive ever written about the First Lady. In it, she disclosed Pat's Catholic ties right at the time when the religious issue was one of the key factors in the campaign:

"Pat Nixon was never a Catholic but her father and all his family were," she wrote. Then she told how Pat came East in the early thirties to work for two years as an X-ray assistant in the old Seton Hospital, owned by New York City but operated by the Catholic Sisters of Charity. Pat's aunt, Sister Thomasina, worked in the hospital pharmacy and helped her get the job. Will Ryan, Pat's father, had been baptized a Catholic, but during his years of prospecting and travel in the West had lost contact with the Church. When he married a Lutheran widow he permitted his children to be reared in her faith, but returned to the Catholic Church during a long illness before his death.

Another scoop was Marie's interview with Zephyr Wright, the Johnson family cook. This was one of the few occasions when Liz Carpenter was outsmarted, for when she gave permission for Marie to talk with Zephyr, she had no idea that Zephyr was going to "tell it like it was." Under a headline proclaiming, "Zephyr Wants Out of the Kitchen," Marie wrote that Mrs. Wright was looking forward to retirement, that she considered the White House a prison, and that the tension of working there for five years had caused her to become a compulsive eater whose weight had increased from 130 to 210 pounds.

Zephyr never knew when she would serve meals, she told Marie. "Sometimes the president buzzes that he will come to lunch in 10 or 15 minutes and is bringing 25 people with him." That wasn't the worst of it; sometimes he would have dinner guests and she would be told to serve dinner at 8:30, but "Mr. Johnson didn't bring his guests to the dining room until 10, 11, or 12 at night." It's difficult to hold popovers, one of LBJ's favorite foods, she said, so this caused the boss to bellow at her one night when the three-hour-old popovers were almost burned.

Among other secrets Mrs. Wright revealed were: that President Johnson had gone from 184 to 212 pounds, that he loved everything fattening, and that when she, on orders of the White House physician, cooked him low-calorie meals and something else for the guests, "he ends up eating both."

Liz and her staff were pretty upset when this story appeared, and Simone Poulain, assistant press secretary to Mrs. Johnson, lamented: "We had dozens of requests for an interview with Zephyr, but we thought we could trust Marie!"

4

"The only time press relations between a First Lady and Washington newswomen have been perfect was during the Franklin Roosevelt era—Eleanor Roosevelt was her own press secretary."

When the Nixons are in residence at the White House at 1600 Pennsylvania Avenue, newswomen covering the East Wing go each Monday and Thursday to the White House theater for the bi-weekly press briefings held by Connie Stuart, Mrs. Nixon's staff director. Ten to 40 (the number depends on whether there have been any hints dropped about "big news" that day) attend these sessions at 10 A.M. on Mondays and 3 P.M. on Thursdays.

The briefings were started by the 31-year-old, redheaded Connie the day she took over press operations for Mrs. Nixon from the First Lady's first Press Secretary, Gerry Van der Heuvel. *Newsweek*, writing about Gerry's "Closed Door Policy," had accused her of choking off information, giving out releases late, being chronically unavailable, and favoring certain reporters over others. Various newspapers had voiced the same complaints and had added a few of their own. Clare Crawford wrote in the *Washington Daily News:* "The attractive Mrs. Van der Heuvel may be the first press secretary in history who is una-

vailable to the press." And the Society of American Social
Scribes had given Gerry its "Lassie Award . . . for being such a
dog of a press secretary." Gerry, with her soft voice and quiet
ways, was not one to survive the rough-and-tumble press secretary vs. press fracas.

There's always a battle between writers and those they write
about. The job of the president, his family, and his staff is to
continue to build up the image smart Madison Avenue types
have sold to the public during the campaign; the job of the
press is to reveal exactly what's behind that man-created façade.

George Reedy, one of LBJ's many press secretaries and a
newspaperman himself, said at a Woman's National Democratic
Club meeting while he was still in the White House:

"During the years that I have spent in Washington, there has
been no topic of conversation quite so persistent as the presidency and the press . . . The watch on the White House as-
sumes a greater intensity and a greater persistence than the
watch on the Rhine . . . The watch focuses not only on the
president but on the members of his family . . . it is a mistake
to believe that this is a situation arising out of bad manners . . .
The facts are that the constant watch on the White House and
the First Family is merely a reflection of the attitude of the
American people themselves . . . They are not satisfied with a
mere chronicle of his official activities. They want to know all of
the little, but revealing, acts which uncover his personality; the
activities of his family which they believe give them insight into
the man himself . . ."

Helen Thomas takes this view of people who live in the
White House: "I feel that they really tried hard to get there, so
their sudden protestations about privacy are just a bit much for
my taste. I think people who submit themselves to campaigning
and go out of their way to be publicized to the hilt, to be photographed beyond the pale, to be interviewed and so forth during the campaign, and suddenly get into the White House and
say they are *private people,* are people consumed with their
own power. Once you've whetted the appetite of the public
about you, once you've told them every time you sneeze, you
can't suddenly tell them you are a private person."

Marie Smith of the *Washington Post* has strong feelings on

the subject, too: "I think a First Lady belongs to the public. She knows before she goes into it what the job is, she knows people are interested in what she is doing and that she no longer has a private life. She must accept it. She was elected to her job just as much as her husband was, and is in the White House at the taxpayers' expense. They are entitled to know what she is doing."

Fran Lewine adds: "First Ladies are not really making public policy, but they certainly help us to evaluate a president and what he is like in his lighter moments. The more you can know about what the First Family is like, what they read, what they want to do, their feelings on various subjects, the more you can assess what kind of people are in the White House."

Probably the White House has the advantage in its constant battle with the press since there are so many things a reporter can't write about without cooperation. If she is not put on a "pool," not recognized when trying to ask a question at a press conference, not called back when she telephones, the reporter is the one who's hurt. It's the same when the press secretary calls the reporter's boss to complain about a story. Occasionally, the White House brings out its big guns and gets really rough. A newswoman can have her income tax returns rechecked in detail for the last five years. One woman running her own bureau claims she was dropped by two papers after a president personally called her publisher and applied pressure.

Traditionally, reporters from the three Washington papers are allowed at all functions open to the press. But after Clare Crawford, society columnist for the *Washington Daily News,* a regular on WRC-NBC's early evening TV news, said in her column that White House Social Secretary Lucy Winchester had placed a member of the Mafia on a Nixon guest list and that the mistake had been caught only at the last minute, the White House punished Clare by not letting her cover the next state dinner. Another time the White House discriminated against the *Washington Post.* Dorothy McCardle arrived one Sunday morning to cover church services and wasn't allowed in. That time they were miffed because *Post* reporter Nancy Ross had recently revealed that when for the first time in history a rabbi, Dr. Louis Finkelstein, chancellor of the Jewish Theological Seminary of America, had conducted a worship service in the White House, "Several of the 350 guests, who included prominent members of Washington's Jewish community, expressed surprise that the doxology was included in the order of worship. The chant's last line, 'Praise Father, Son and Holy Ghost,' which affirms Christian belief in the Trinity, runs counter to Judaism's monotheistic concept."

It may be that the White House also was irked about a column Clare wrote, under the head, "Nixon Family Fly Military," in which she told how the Nixons, "in addition to turning on the White House lights, serving French champagne and wearing white tie," were flying in military planes even when the president wasn't along.

Lady Bird flew commercial planes, even tourist class, when traveling without the president. Many of her trips with the press were on commercial planes and both Luci and Lynda went by commercial plane on their honeymoons. Mrs. Nixon uses military planes for all her traveling,° even when dashing up to New York to shop. Julie and David Eisenhower had military planes bring them back and forth from college every week or so. "I hate to think what would have happened to poor LBJ if Luci and Pat had flown on military aircraft," more than one reporter has said.

Jacqueline Kennedy also avoided military planes if her husband wasn't along. But usually she used the Kennedy family's private plane, the *Caroline,* bought for Jack while he was campaigning in 1960.

Harassment can occasionally take some odd forms. One reporter with a common, but strictly female, physical problem was being treated in the out-patient department of the Bethesda Naval Hospital. When she learned that President Johnson was entering the hospital for major surgery, she took a tour of the

---

° She flew on a chartered commercial airline plane on the trip with the press to California and Oregon, but on her second solo venture to publicize volunteerism, in March 1970, she and the press traveled on an Air Force plane. Members of the press paid $375 each for this transportation. It is not known whether Mrs. Nixon and members of her party paid their pro-rata share.

building, discovered a newly created "Presidential Suite," and wrote a story about its elegant curtains, furniture, and paintings on loan from the White House. The day the story appeared, the Navy removed the sign reading "Presidential Suite" and substituted another reading "Senior Officers' Suite." ° Both the president and the Navy were furious at the reporter for describing the décor. The late Merriman Smith of UPI wrote that there were "snippy remarks and jesting suggestions that things could be worse, such as having her White House press card lifted."

What "Smitty" didn't write, at her request, was that the White House physician, who had been the liaison between Mrs. Johnson and the hospital during the decorating period, talked to the reporter's doctor in an effort to find out how she was able to get the story. It might have been a coincidence but within a day or two, much to her embarrassment, the nature of her ailment was common knowledge around the White House press room.

It's easy to see why, with relations difficult at best, the most important appointment the White House makes, as far as the East Wing is concerned, is that of press secretary to the First Lady. She is the press's only official link with the First Family, and newswomen think the job can't be done effectively for either side unless she has both the confidence of her employer and appreciation of the problems of a deadline reporter. She must be available at all times to answer questions, imaginative enough to anticipate most of them, and have a rapport with the newswomen. A sense of humor helps, too.

Mrs. Nixon personally announced the changes in her office staff in October 1969, at a hastily called press briefing in the Family Theater. Gerry said she would go to Rome as a special assistant to the ambassador (for public and community relations), with an undisclosed increase in salary from the $25,000 she received at the White House. "We wish her well," Mrs.

° The "Senior Officers' Suite" stood vacant for months at a time since it could be used only by permission of the president. Both Vice President Hubert Humphrey and Mrs. Humphrey were patients at the Navy Hospital, at different times, during the Johnson Administration, and were not put in the luxurious suite since neither President Johnson nor any of his aides gave the O.K.

Nixon said, but one reporter commented, "That's the Boot of Italy." When asked: "Are you a career diplomat, Gerry?" the toppled press secretary snapped, "I ought to be, by this time."

It would be a whopping understatement to say that Constance Cornell Stuart was a surprise to veteran White House newswomen. That afternoon she took over the briefing with Madison Avenue efficiency, then:

· Handed out white-covered press kits (Patricia Nixon's signature and "The White House" delicately lettered in gold were in the lower right-hand corner) containing seven press releases.

· Announced she would hold bi-weekly press briefings and that they would last 30 minutes. She noted they "sometimes may be even a little shorter, depending on the information we have for you."

· Answered questions about herself in crisp sentences, saying she was a 1960 honor graduate of the University of Maryland and had worked as a public-relations supervisor for the Bell System—first in New York, then transferring to Washington when her husband, Charles ("many people call him Chuck, I call him Charles"), came to town with the Nixon administration. (Charles is the staff assistant to John Ehrlichman, a top assistant to President Nixon and thought to be one of the few men really close to the president.)

· Predicted that she would be reviewing the East Wing staff and making changes.

· Said her starting salary was $30,000,° she was born Republican, and that a White House limousine went with her job, but not with her husband's.

· Answered, "Would you believe it, no," when asked if she had a temper to go with her red hair.

Two days after she took over, Connie said she planned to pro-

° Her salary with the telephone company is reported to have been $12,500.

ject the "humanness" of the Nixons with photographs of the
president, the First Lady, and their daughters to show "how
close the family is and what a tremendous relationship they
have." One she later released of President and Mrs. Nixon
standing just outside his office she called "a lovely and warm
picture of a man and wife." Connie's selling of the First Lady
also includes such things as a five page, single-spaced biography
of Pat Nixon ending, "With her warmth, quiet strength and love
of humanity, there is no doubt that Patricia Nixon will write a
long-remembered chapter in White House history."

Efficient, aggressive, dramatic Connie has made an electric
impression on the newswomen. One says she has the potential to
be a successful press secretary if she doesn't try to program reporters through her computer. Others, while taken by her brisk,
athletic, multi-vitamin charm, aren't sure they will survive it
through the Nixon years. Others feel the Nixons have again
hired someone so full of the Madison Avenue "snow-job" technique that, just as during the campaign, "we won't be able to
hear the message for the words."

At Connie's biweekly briefings, she gives out such information
as the entertainment for a state visitor, which group of women
will visit Mrs. Nixon this week, what Julie and David are doing
over the holidays, but most pointedly not where Tricia will be
going over the weekend. At one briefing, when asked what Tricia would be doing with her friends, Connie answered, "I guess
she'll be doing whatever friends do together on weekends." That
was before one of those friends revealed that the Tricia group
played "sardines" and that on one occasion everyone tried to
hide under the bed in the Queen's Room, which must have
caused many an eyebrow to raise in certain Republican Circles.

Connie, whom Marie Smith of the *Post* describes as one "who
grits her teeth behind a forced smile as she tackles each new
problem," calls attention to newswomen's errors as vigorously as
she said she would. Several newswomen "wondered" if Pat Nixon's planned trip to college compuses in late 1969 was cancelled
because someone at the White House discovered it was in conflict with the November fifteenth moratorium, and that it might
be dangerous for the First Lady to be mingling with students

that day. Connie felt that was nasty reporting since the First Lady, she said, was recovering from the flu.

She has made the predicted changes in her staff, creating what Marie Smith says is "the largest, most expensive press or public relations staff ever assembled to promote the public image of a President's wife." Marie set its cost as something approximating $150,000 a year.° Most veteran White House watchers, while deploring the "Madison Avenue" aspect of Connie's operations, agree that her office is well organized and her personnel cooperative and efficient. Maybe this is because she apparently has had a free hand in hiring her staff. One can't spot any friends of the family or daughters of big contributors among her assistants. For instance, Julie Marr Robinson, who has the title "press coordinator," and among other things is in charge of all pictures taken of the First Lady, Tricia and Julie, and the Mansion itself, got her job simply by writing a letter and applying for it.

White House staff jobs are among the most coveted there are, because they catapult the holder instantly not only into local fame and prestige, but onto the backstage of history. Though little known outside Washington, they wield tremendous power in that they are able to arrange appointments, schedule picture-taking, and generally grease or rust the wheels of any member of the press wanting a story, an interview, pictures, or just hard-to-get information.

While on the subject of staffs: it is an old White House custom, in order to hold down its budget, to "borrow" employees from other government agencies. No one dares mention what it does to the budgets of the agencies carrying these people on their payrolls for years without ever seeing the person drawing the checks. Connie's staff includes one assistant on the Department of Interior payroll, another on loan from Health, Education and Welfare, and two from HUD. One from HUD is Helen Smith, now director of press relations and the only Gerry Van der Heuvel holdover. Helen, a sixth generation "cave-dwelling"

° The cost of keeping President Nixon "staffed, housed, protected, transported, rested and in touch wherever he is" is put at roughly $70 million a year by the *Wall Street Journal.*

Washingtonian, came to the White House from the Washington Bureau of the *New York Daily News*, where she was office manager, and as far as anyone knows, she has never set foot in the HUD building.

Like all those before her handling the press for First Ladies, Connie tries to ban notebooks at parties. "Please, ladies, you are here as guests, and guests do not wander around taking notes, even behind potted palms." She has nixed tape recorders, too. "If I think some of you have gotten exceedingly busty because you are carrying tape recorders around, I might question how you gained so much weight." But the instruction which had the newswomen up tight was: "Let's be fair to guests. Please introduce yourselves just like any nice, well-brought-up lady would do."

(At the next state dinner, Wauhillau La Hay walked up to a Cabinet member and his wife she had known since Eisenhower days and said: "I'm Wauhillau La Hay of Scripps Howard." The astonished Cabinet officer cried, "For God's Sake! What's the matter with you, Wauhillau?")

Actually, the only time press relations between a First Lady and Washington newswomen have been perfect was during the Franklin Roosevelt era, when Eleanor Roosevelt was her own press secretary. She held regular press conferences and, by categorically refusing to let male reporters attend, forced editors to assign women reporters to the White House. A newsgirl with a query simply picked up the telephone, called the White House and asked to speak to Mrs. Roosevelt, who took the call and answered the question, hard as that might be for a present-day reporter to believe. It's doubtful that any newswoman has talked to Pat Nixon on the telephone, although Lady Bird did call frequently to thank a reporter personally for a story she liked.

Mrs. Roosevelt even kept an eye open for stories when she was out of town, and more than once telephoned long distance to tell about some newsy event. Male newsmen not used to her super-open press methods were so confused by her that an AP man turned down a unique opportunity for his wire service to make newspaper history. Mrs. Roosevelt had given the late Bess Furman (then with AP, later with *The New York Times*) a ride from an event starring the First Lady when a Roosevelt dog riding in the limousine bit Bess's lip. Mrs. R. rushed her to the hospital, stood by while the lip was stitched, and called Associated Press to inform them of their reporter's injury. She then suggested that she write the story herself; the AP desk man was so shocked he declined her offer.

One reporter who covered her wondered in print whether Mrs. Roosevelt's successor would realize what a "splendid thing" the First Lady was doing, and would follow suit. She did not.

For her liaison with the press, Mrs. Harry Truman retained as social secretary Edith Helm, who had held the same position with the second Mrs. Woodrow Wilson and with Mrs. Roosevelt. Isabelle Shelton of the *Star* (also a syndicated North American Newspaper Alliance columnist) who began covering the White House then and still does, says, "Mrs. Helm belonged to the old school and as she really believed a lady's name is in the paper only when she is born, married, or dies, her horrified reaction to the simplest question was such that you almost stopped asking. With her it was ladylike and proper and you accepted it."

Things weren't so ladylike for the press during the Eisenhower administration. Mary Jane McCaffree, who was Mamie Eisenhower's social secretary, in the opinion of reporters, viewed her job as "protecting the First Lady from the press."

Isabelle recalls that "she didn't even give out weekly releases. With her it was sort of a catch-as-catch-can thing in which you had to ask the right questions or lose the game. She was much too protective of Mrs. Eisenhower, and wouldn't let people near her, not only in the White House, but when she went out to luncheons and teas. If we could break through the barrier of Mary Jane we found Mrs. Eisenhower delightful and willing to chitchat with us."

Mary Jane also ran the social side of the White House with an iron hand. Once before a state dinner when a group of newswomen came by to look at the table decorations, she wouldn't let them walk on the red carpet in the foyer, requiring them to take mincing steps along the narrow strip of marble at the side. Later when the same reporters, wearing floor-length evening gowns and opera-length white kid gloves, returned to watch and report on the entertainment, Mary Jane insisted that they stand behind potted palms, peeking through the fronds, to observe the guests marching from the dining room to the East Room where the entertainment was staged.

Liz Carpenter, covering the party for her Texas papers, thought the restrictions so ludicrous she gave all the details to newspaperman George Dixon, who wrote a column which amused the reporters, but infuriated Mary Jane.

After much detective work, Mary Jane thought she had nailed down the name of the culprit. Saying nothing, but biding her time, she removed the innocent reporter's name from the White House Christmas list. Just before the holiday, when the usual print of one of President Eisenhower's original oil paintings was passed out to White House correspondents, there was none for Mary Jane's suspect. But Liz Carpenter received one. No one, as far as is known, told Mary Jane about her error.

Liz Carpenter's approach to covering the women's beat changed after she went to work at the White House. Once there, she viewed with horror what she calls "the kid who wets his pants" type of story. She still maintains there is enough going on of interest without reporters singling out such stories as the woman who lost her petticoat while dancing in the East Room; the man who while eating at a State Dinner tilted his gilt chair so far backward he broke one of its legs and crashed to the floor; or the Arabian princess who missed the last step of the stairway from the family quarters to the entrance foyer, stumbled and fell to her knees right in front of a group of White House photographers.

And Liz must have sighed with relief, since it didn't happen when she was responsible for news out of the East Wing, when Nan Robertson, describing a Nixon reception for the diplomatic corps, wrote in *The New York Times:*

". . . Dr. Guillermo Sevilla-Sacasa of Nicaragua, who has been around Washington for a quarter century and thus is first in any diplomatic line-up, set the tone. With forty-three medals hung across his chest, he clanked like a tank as he shook the President's hand . . .

"There were a few setbacks . . . but they were minor. The Israeli Ambassador was detected grinding out his cigarette on the East Room's parquet floor. The Swiss Ambassador stepped on the red net train of the wife of the Ambassador from Cameroon, bringing her to a dead halt in front of the Agnews. The *chargé d'affaires* ad interim of Colombia, dazzled by the bright photographers' lights trained on the Nixons in the Green Room, sailed right by the Agnews in the dimly lit Blue Room until a protocol officer stopped him in his tracks.

"The wife of the Ambassador from Swaziland looked as unhappy as she must have felt—she was the only woman wearing a short skirt . . ."

When Jackie Kennedy appointed Pamela Turnure as her fulltime press secretary, veteran reporters thought it ironic that a young, jet-setting socialite with no newspaper experience should hold the first such post in history.

Pam, with her polite little-girl voice, her sleeveless, A-line dresses and modified Rajah-style coats, low-heeled shoes and slightly bouffant hairdo, fit right into the mold of the Kennedy women. But her lack of knowledge of the press and its needs is still a subject of conversation whenever the East Wing press discusses its favorite subject, "The First Lady's press secretary."

"Pam was a nice girl and a kind person, but she had about as much business being press secretary as I would have directing the Space Agency," says Helen Thomas.

To show just how little Pam knew about the press, Isabelle Shelton tells the following story:

"One day I called the White House about something else, and lucked into the fact that Mrs. Kennedy was down at Mount Vernon—one of the few times I have ever seen someone in the White House carelessly give a piece of news away."

Isabelle grabbed a photographer and dashed down to Mount Vernon, where they found Mrs. Kennedy with Tish Baldrige, her social secretary, Pam, and some other White House staff members wandering around the grounds. There were about 400 tourists following them and Isabelle and the photographer joined the crowd. The tourists were looking at Mrs. Kennedy and taking pictures, so Isabelle and the photographer did the same, without trying to hide their presence. Isabelle couldn't hear all the conversation but she got enough, and this was the first time anyone knew that the White House planned to entertain the

President of Pakistan, General Ayub Khan, with a state dinner at Mount Vernon.

Isabelle recalls: "All of a sudden Tish and Pam, who recognized me, got in a great state of excitement and with indignation said that I was eavesdropping, that this was private. I asked, 'What do you mean, private? There are 400 people here!' I raced for the telephone and got a story in the paper that afternoon."

In the story she mentioned that "Mrs. Kennedy's staff was irritated," but due to a misunderstanding by the girl who took Isabelle's dictation, the story appeared saying, "Mrs. Kennedy was irritated." The next day, Isabelle received a handwritten note from Mrs. Kennedy saying something to the effect, "Isabelle, I wasn't irritated at you. I didn't even see you; I would have been happy to have seen you."

Jackie's attitude toward the press seemed to run hot and cold. She would write reporters gay little notes, praising them for something they had written, then another time try to get them barred from covering official functions.

She once wrote Ellen Key Blunt, then a reporter with the Washington Post, a two-page letter in which she praised Ellen for an "incredibly decent gesture." Ellen had asked Jackie if the Post photographer could take a picture of Caroline, taking part in the "costume class" at a Virginia horse show, and Jackie had answered that she hoped he wouldn't. When the picture wasn't taken, Jackie wrote the letter which ended: "I know that newspapers need to print different—or rather unusual—pictures and there is always the conflict of trying to raise one's children fairly normally—So when you—who are torn both ways—respect a little girl's chance to have a happy day with other children who fortunately treat her as just another four year old (that is almost the only public place where she isn't singled out and fawned over)—it is amazing and consoling. I think you made the right decision—the humane one—but what you did is rare—and I do want you to know how impressed and deeply grateful her father and I are—" The letter brought $750 at a New York auction in early 1970.

Although none of the newswomen knew it then, Jackie, while in the White House, thought of the female press as "harpies."

This didn't come out until July of 1969, when Vera Glaser and Malvina Stephenson published in their syndicated Knight Newspapers column several secret memos the First Lady had written to her staff. In one memo, she suggested that social aides, equipped with bayonets, be stationed near the "harpies" at the next dinner, complained about reporters hanging around with their notebooks, making everyone nervous and apprehensive about saying something in their hearing, and expressed the wish that the White House didn't have to have reporters covering the after-dinner entertainment, because "that is when they ask everyone questions."

Whether a reporter should or should not carry a notebook is still being argued at the White House and behind the scenes of other official functions. The best argument for not carrying them heard so far is given with tongue in cheek by Mary Wiegers of the *Washington Post:* "One night I dropped mine in the punch bowl and a waiter had to help me fish it out."

Pam Turnure and Tish Baldridge once called a few women reporters into Tish's office to "talk things over." Among other things, they asked them please not to take up so much of President Kennedy's time,° and suggested that they stop talking to the guests. It was O.K., they said, for reporters to question the entertainers ("they want all the publicity they can get"), and there were no objections to interviewing the regulars, such as Vice President Johnson, Secretary of Defense McNamara, or Robert Kennedy, since "they are used to you," but other guests, especially one like Charles Lindbergh, who "is painfully shy," were to be left alone.

Liz Carpenter, who was a reporter for several Texas papers before she was Lady Bird Johnson's press secretary, was the next best thing to having the First Lady act as her own press secretary, most newswomen felt. She knew the pressures of deadline reporting. She didn't think it was her job to "protect"

° This situation still goes on. The press was forbidden to talk to President Nixon at the state dinner for Canadian Prime Minister Trudeau, and didn't go anywhere near the president or his guest of honor; so President Nixon sent an aide to round up the newswomen to come talk to him and the dashing Trudeau.

the First Lady from the press, and was always available to answer questions.

Like Mrs. Roosevelt, Liz saw that reporters had colorful stories—if they didn't develop naturally, Liz created them. In Big Bend National Park she sent out copy by live Pony Express (a sleepy-looking rider on a burro) and played coyote howls on a record player planted behind a cottonwood tree when the coyotes she promised didn't show up.

Occasionally a colorful story out of the White House was not intentional. In a release giving information about Luci's wedding, the press was informed that the bridesmaids would be taught how to *sin* on the back seats of White House limousines without wrinkling their dresses.*

Liz had excellent rapport with women of the press. She showed up for their parties at home, and when one of them was hospitalized Liz sent flowers from the White House flower room, her get-well card neatly tucked in an envelope with "The White House" lettered in the upper left hand corner (the little commercial on the envelope was a sure guarantee of extra-special service from the nurses.) The camaraderie between Liz and the press was so strong that when *Women's Wear Daily*, miffed at being barred from covering Lynda's wedding, printed a two-page spread with the glaring headline "Loud Liz, The Nation's Voice," the newswomen were indignant; at least one cancelled her subscription and has never renewed it.

Discussing her White House job recently, Liz said: "Half the battle is to provide facts, provide access and to have the transmittal facilities handy. The most essential ingredient that I found improved the disposition of newswomen was to have some men on the trips. This isn't as sexy as it sounds; it's be-

---

* Not all slips came from the East Wing; Judith Martin reported in the *Post* that President Nixon, while talking to reporters following a White House church service, explained his policy of consulting people both in and out of the administration when gathering information on such subjects as Vietnamization. "This is consistent with our policy of cross-ruffing everything," said the president. "Rather than just getting the opinions of in-house people, we're checking with out-house people, too."

cause the women are less likely to be tyrants in front of their male counterparts. The second essential is to have a watering hole available at the end of the day. The reporters are exhausted and if the press secretary can ease the pain with a little Scotch, that is fine."

These out-of-town trips are considered the icing on the cake by almost all reporters. They are not only a chance to get out of Washington and "see the world," first-class, but they are also a chance to get to know the president and the First Lady far better than is usually possible in Washington. Trips never fail to etch themselves indelibly on the memories of the reporters, especially the "pool people."

A "pool person" is a reporter chosen by one of the press secretaries to accompany the president or First Lady, or both, on Air Force One, or in a helicopter, chartered plane, etc., while the rest travel in the accompanying press plane.

The reason for the pool is not only to allow the principals to breathe without the full rapacious pack of 100 or more newsmen and women bearing down upon them, but to permit the press to function with efficiency. Pool people travel in a car behind the Secret Service when they land at an airport, while the rest of the press generally arrives at its destination by bus. To keep it fair, representation on the pools alternates each time among the different major news media, except that the AP and the UPI are always included.

Some of the women's pool reports, in contrast to the male reporters' staid reports, are pretty hilarious. ABC's redheaded glamour girl, Marlene Sanders, an out-of-towner who travels often with First Ladies, says that the most memorable things about White House coverage for her are the "hysterical" pool reports; and Lenore Hershey, managing editor of the *Ladies' Home Journal,* the writer who ghosted Perle Mesta's column in *McCalls* for years, says the pool reports on Mrs. Nixon's trip to the West Coast were the funniest things she has read in her long journalistic career.

One she undoubtedly had in mind was given on a bus, speeding along a California freeway in Los Angeles, after Mrs. Nixon had made a night-time visit to the Wesley Social Service Center in Watts, where volunteers teach such skills as sewing, music, and weight lifting to the area's underprivileged youngsters. Kandy Shuman Stroud of *Women's Wear Daily* stood at the front of the swaying bus to give the first pool briefing.

"Mrs. Nixon went into the weight lifting room and 14-year-old Junior Olympic Champion Raymond Morgan raised a 215-pound weight into the air. Mrs. Nixon gasped, 'How he got it up I'll never know!'"

Photographers in the back of the bus were the first to laugh. Within seconds the female reporters and the bus driver were howling, too.

Kandy, a puzzled look on her face, stood waiting for the laughter to die down. A photographer called, "What else did Mrs. Nixon say, Kandy?"

"She said, 'I don't think I could get it down.'"

(Pause for uproarious laughter.)

"Mrs. Nixon told him, 'You're just great, you certainly get up perspiration.' Then she said, 'I haven't seen a weight lifter in a long time.'"

"You're making that up!" cried Wauhillau La Hay.

Ending her part of the briefing, Kandy said, "Mrs. Nixon then went into the music room next door."

"Thank God!" exclaimed Wauhillau.

When reporters and photographers piled off the bus in front of the hotel, the driver told them, "I certainly hope I get to drive you folks tomorrow."

The trip by raft down the Rio Grande was one of the most exciting of the many trips Lady Bird Johnson made to promote beautification, education (Head Start was a pet project) and Discover America. Isabelle Shelton told what it was like when 139 people paddle down a river on 27 rafts carrying all the paraphernalia of civilization "including TV cameras, walkie-talkie radios, and shielded 'his' and 'her' portable toilets (fetchingly named 'John Towers')."

"It must be confessed that eccentricities of certain of the press participants added further to the color of the First Lady's trip. Imperishable memories include the fetching young female who decided a bikini ° was the proper garb for the raft ride with the First Lady, and the scribe who carried a red umbrella at full sail as she climbed a mountain and rode a raft . . . There was also the reporter who disregarded her guide's advice that all personal belongings be stowed in tightly tied plastic bags, as protection from the ever-present water. She . . . stuffed [her notebook and pen] down the front of her blouse. The notes got soaked, making them illegible; the pen, after leaking ink all over her unmentionables, stopped working. And finally there was the Washington society reporter, at home in the capital's best drawing rooms, who decided to reorganize the after-raft-ride square dancing according to the routine followed at Marjorie Merriweather Post's chic soirees. "No, no, no! That's not the way to Allemand Left!' she insisted to her Western-clad Texas partner, who'd been square dancing all his life." °

On all the trips the press women are allowed one suitcase each; on Lady Bird's last junket, which included Cape Kennedy, New Orleans, Denver, and the California Redwoods country, the suitcases held a long dress, short dresses, winter coats, spring coats, raincoats, bathing suit, and boots.

First Lady Jacqueline Kennedy's trip to India and Pakistan, with a stop in Rome, was another where the reporters' one suitcase was far from adequate, since the voyage included a variety of climates and schedules that ran the gamut between a papal interview to digging for ancient stones in the ruins of a town built by Alexander the Great.

Newswoman Marie Ridder took along a pair of blue jeans and some disreputable sneakers for digging, never dreaming she would have to wear them for a more formal occasion as well. Jackie's reputation as a horsewoman encouraged all sorts of equestrian invitations, Marie recalls. She accepted some, delighting her hosts but ruining the careful schedule. Her staff decided to prevent any more of these tempting invitations from reaching Jackie. Then came one from the Khyber Rifles, and "the very name evoked Kipling and heroism." They were determined to exhibit their skills, if not to the First Lady then at least to a

---

° Judith Axler of the *New York Daily News* was the shapely young lady in the bikini; Betty Beale of the *Washington Star* instructed the square dancer; one of us had the pen problem.

member of her entourage, so it was suggested that Marie, an expert horsewoman, substitute for Jackie. She was eager, although ill equipped fashion-wise in her blue jeans and sneakers, for an outing under official gaze.

"I knew Jackie's boots would fit me so I decided to ask her for them," Marie says. "But as I caught her eye she was talking with the president of Pakistan, Ayub Khan. She looked so remote and queenly that I couldn't bring myself to ask for size nine riding boots and reduce the scene to the humdrum. The camaraderie of the hunting fields of Virginia's Piedmont seemed very far away. So off I went in the pink light of early dawn with the sparkling Khyber Rifles in my incredible outfit. Months later when I told Jackie about the ride and how I had decided against asking her for the boots she couldn't believe I had been so 'silly.'"

Nan Robertson of *The New York Times* thinks Lady Bird's whistle-stop tour through the South during the 1964 campaign was the classic trip of all time. It lasted 4 days, with 47 stops in 8 states and a speech at each stop. The train was 19 cars long with the press car in the middle, which meant that at each of the stops reporters had to jump off the train, run down the cinder track, get down Lady Bird's remarks, interview people in the crowd, note down a few signs, and sprint back to the central part of the train and the press car to start typing.

Nan remembers that "Stan Wayman of *Life* magazine got a tooth knocked out by another photographer who shoved him in the photographers' pool car and smacked him in the face with his camera. Dr. Janet Travell was the physician on board and she was in seventh heaven; she is a Florence Nightingale in disguise. She walked happily up and down the aisle, binding up the wounded, for there were a great many scraped and bruised knees and elbows on people who, in their eagerness to get to the back platform for Lady Bird's latest speech, threw themselves off the train while it was still moving.

"It was physically the most grueling of all campaign trips, and if you could survive it and turn out good copy, you could survive anything. Each one of us had a roomette—mine was six cars away from the press car, where tables were set up and where we typed—so I seldom went to it except to sleep. There was a dining car where I had one meal in four days, because there was too much happening, and it was too crowded and far away. There was a snack bar immediately ahead of the press car that most of us used.

"Within a few days the train was a traveling slum. Bathing was a problem which Mary Packenham of the *Chicago Tribune* solved by taking a garment bag, tieing one end, stepping into it and sloshing water on herself."

Early one morning, without benefit of garment bag, Nan was stark naked, taking a sponge bath, as the train rolled slowly through the Southern countryside. The window was open and suddenly there was a frieze of fascinated faces watching Nan scrubbing and soaping. The train had slowed down for a little station and a crowd had gathered to see Lady Bird roll by.

The whistle-stop tour ended when the train pulled into New Orleans and Senator Allen J. Ellender spoke his unforgettable lines, "All the way with LJB!"

Nan Robertson is a general-assignment reporter in *The Times'* Washington Bureau, covering what she calls "poverty to parties." She is one of the few reporters who started as a foreign correspondent and worked her way back to the women's pages. One week after she graduated from Medill School of Journalism at Northwestern University, she sailed for Europe where, after two or three other jobs, including one in Germany with *Stars and Stripes,* Nan worked part time in London for the *Times'* women's pages, covering mostly fashion, before coming back to the *Times* in New York. She was transferred to Washington when her husband, newspaper man Stan Levy, now with Scripps Howard, was assigned here.

Her beat keeps Nan hopping all around the nation, even when not traveling with the First Lady. She did three in-depth nation-wide student surveys within a year, specifically inquiring into political-action groups such as the SDS and the black militants, and covered both 1968 political conventions and campaigns, as well as Mrs. Nixon's only solo trip the first year her husband was in office, when she launched her project "Vest Pockets of Volunteerism," in Oregon and California in June 1969.

For weeks, the women regularly covering the East Wing had

been speculating about what Pat's "own thing" was going to be. How would she follow Jacqueline Kennedy's interior-decorating and Lady Bird's exterior-decorating projects? Gone are the days when a First Lady can spend her afternoons playing bridge or canasta with the girls. Her role as leader of U.S. women, now a majority of the population, is too important.

Thirty-nine reporters and photographers, Pat Nixon, and 22 others (members of her White House staff, the Secret Service, and Eastern Airlines representatives) traveled in a giant Eastern DC-8 "stretch plane" which could hold 203 passengers. As usual the men—photographers and TV and radio crews—spread out on seats nearest the little flight kitchen, whence all liquor flows. There's no limit to the number of drinks served on these flights since they're chartered, but it's hard to recall a time when a member of the White House press was obviously intoxicated on a plane.

Reporters representing the top papers, magazines, and the radio-TV networks had barely settled down to read their press releases and background material when, to their surprise, Mrs. Nixon and Julie appeared. They came back from the first-class section, which is always taken over on these flights for the First Lady and her official party. Notebooks and tape recorders appeared in a hurry, and the photographers were up front with their cameras so fast one wondered how they had had time to park their drinks. The center aisle of a plane, even a DC-8, isn't the ideal place in which to have an informal chat with the First Lady, even standing on a seat and leaning across the back of another. It was hard to hear her answers, but fortunately everybody "pooled."

It was the first time the women had had a chance to question Mrs. Nixon at any length since the campaign, so the conversation ranged from the purpose of her trip ("to encourage volunteerism" because "if more millions would get involved it could change the pace of things and enrich life for all"), to who took a bite out of Pascha, Tricia Nixon's Yorkshire terrier. "It was a beagle, a Johnson left-over," said Julie, and it had happened at Camp David the day before. The aggressive dog was one President Johnson gave to the Navy man in charge at the presidential retreat.

Julie said her father was the only one in the family who had to diet: "He does it with cottage cheese and catsup." Mrs. Nixon, asked what she was giving her husband for a wedding anniversary present, said, "I usually get the present."

She also explained why the plane was so large: "They let us have this plane for the same amount as a smaller one because this one was not in service." The White House refused to disclose the "same amount," but an Eastern official estimated about $20,000.°

A sumptuous lunch, washed down with Paul Masson Emerald Dry or Paul Masson Rubion and a French champagne, didn't mean a thing to anyone on deadline, as all the dailies were. As soon as Mrs. Nixon and Julie retreated to first class, typewriters were whipped out and all thought of food forgotten, since reporters had to have all the details, quotes, and impressions about the First Lady and her daughter ready to throw at Western Union the moment the plane landed.

The noon arrival at Portland airport seemed eerie to the press veterans. The only people there to meet the First Lady were members of the Oregon press. At Mrs. Nixon's request, there were no local politicians and their wives, no cheering supporters lining a fence and waving "We Love Pat" posters, no highschool band playing off-key, no shy little girl shoved forward with a small bouquet of wilted flowers, nor any of those long-stemmed roses always presented by the ranking official's wife. That's how Pat had wanted it, low-keyed, and the press disappointment was almost tangible.†

The Oregon press, desperate for material for a story, interviewed their Washington counterparts on the press bus. As the

° Each of the 39 members of the media was billed $525 for airfare. If the Eastern official's estimate was correct, Mrs. Nixon and her party paid nothing and the newspapers and networks Vice President Spiro Agnew has criticized so severely subsidized the First Lady's launching of her volunteer project.

† Advance men whipped up airport crowds for Mrs. Nixon's solo trip, some 10 months later, and at each stop she was greeted by several hundred sign-carrying people, including what one reporter termed, "Every God-damn Brownie in the country." The Brownie troops were always placed in the front row, leading one Secret Service man to shout to one pushing mob, "Careful, don't squash the Brownies!"

bus made its lumbering way to the hotel, along highways and through sad-looking districts which seemed familiar even to those who had never been to Portland, Isabelle Shelton of the *Star* brought home to everyone the dreary similarity of all airport-to-hotel routes when she told a startled reporter, Milly Wohler of *The* [Portland] *Oregonian,* she wasn't certain if she had been to Portland before, because "I was with Mrs. Johnson in so many places. I remember the redwoods, so I think I would have remembered going to Mt. Hood."

The rest of the trip followed the same low-keyed pattern as Mrs. Nixon visited 10 projects—from adult literacy class to a foundation for the junior blind—on her 5,000 mile, two-state tour. The trip lacked the fun-and-games atmosphere of a Lady Bird tour, but gradually the newswomen learned many things about Mrs. Nixon:

· She is unflappable: Anti-Vietnam hecklers showered her with small pieces of paper, printed with the words, "If this was napalm, you would be dead," as Mrs. Nixon entered a Methodist volunteer emergency help center, but she walked in calmly. She ignored a group of young girls, dressed as witches, who chanted "Mrs. Nixon, trouble's mixin', millions die, but you don't cry. Money to kill against our will: people at home are denied their own. This nix on you will all come true. We'll say no: your kind must go." Discussing the incident later, Mrs. Nixon said, "I was out there doing the very best I could, and if that was the best that they (the demonstrators) could do, that's sad." She showed the same kind of aplomb in South America in 1958. As the vice-presidential caravan made its way through the streets of Caracas, Venezuela, a screaming mob blocked the way and battered the car with clubs and pipes. Local police fled and the Secret Service agents drew their guns. Pat Nixon, riding in a car behind her husband, calmly reassured the frightened wife of the Venezuelan foreign minister. Later a witness said that she showed "cold animal courage."

· She relates to the needy, whether babies, small children, or adults: Visiting a ghetto garden she admired an amateur farmer's vegetables and said, "Gardening is my favorite hobby." In the Los Angeles Watts area she patted children and called them "hon," and outside the Foundation for the Junior Blind in Los Angeles, when a young black boy called, "Mrs. Nixon, let's give the soul shake," she clasped his hand in hers and laughingly went through the twisting and turning ceremony.

· She is compassionate: Along with her daughter Julie and women reporters, Mrs. Nixon was moved to tears at the foundation for the blind boys and girls when they staged, beautifully, two scenes from *The Sound of Music.* Mrs. Nixon, obviously sincerely, rushed up on stage as soon as the last note was sung, kissed the performers, and told them they were "wonderful."

· She can let her hair down: People have often referred to her as a 'Barbie Doll," or even one so "stiff . . . she looks as though a laser beam couldn't melt her expression or her rigid posture"; yet on the jet bringing her and her party back to Washington, she chatted informally with reporters for 45 minutes, an unusual thing for a First Lady to do. She said she was going to visit several colleges to encourage students to do volunteering ("we're going to make it the IN thing to do"), and when asked if she thought the black militants might try to disrupt her visits, she said, "I'm not afraid of anything." *

She also revealed such family secrets as her formula for a successful 29-year-old marriage: "I'm not a nagger;" said her daughters thought the president was a "real swinger," and that when young she belonged to the 4-H club and had raised a prize-winning hog named "Piggy."

The very reporters who had complained about her being stiff and unsophisticated wrote such things as, "The United States has a new First Lady with the potential for becoming a great one." "Mrs. Nixon's venture revealed an effective personal style." "Mrs. Nixon was a model of warmth and graciousness." "Pat Nixon has suddenly emerged from an icy cocoon of literal anonymity and proven herself a living, breathing, thinking, loving woman." And even "the First Lady's handling of her extensive

---

* Mrs. Nixon's first college tour consisted of visiting volunteer projects off campus in four states and an on-campus stop at a small, self-help college in the Ozark Mountains.

projects compare favorably with that of her predecessor, Mrs. Lyndon B. Johnson."

The newswomen's estimate of the First Lady may have been higher than her press secretary's opinion of them. A man on the trip, chatting with Gerry Van der Heuvel on the plane coming home, asked, "Now that you have traveled with the news gals, what do you think of them?" "There isn't a gentleman in the crowd," Gerry answered.

"Mrs. Nixon and I read you. We want your ideas. We want your advice. Whenever we can get it, we want your seal of approval."

A White House party at night can be pretty dazzling, and there's always a sense of anticipation that's felt even by correspondents who have covered First Families for the past three, four, even five administrations. This is especially true of state dinners, the *crème de la crème* of each administration's entertaining. Presidents naturally want to show off a bit when entertaining the head of another country, and traditionally nobody ever refuses an invitation to a state dinner.*

A reporter covering a social event of the magnitude of a state dinner always feels extra special when she walks into the White House. It's one of the few times when a woman has a real advantage over her male colleagues. Newsmen have never been known to dance with a president or a vice-president, but practically all the women covering the social side of the White House have. It was while dancing with Vice President Hubert Hum-

---

* Or any invitation to the White House, for that matter. Poet Robert Lowell refused a Johnson invitation to take part in a White House Festival of the Arts as a protest against the war in Vietnam, but such a rebellion is rare.

phrey that Judith Axler, then with the *New York Daily News*, got the scoop that Bill Moyers was going to resign as President Johnson's press secretary to head up the Long Island publishing company, *Newsday*.

"I found Bill Moyers and said I heard he was going with my old paper," says Judy, who once worked for five weeks at *Newsday*. "He said, 'No, I'm not.' But I knew he was lying, just by the way he said the 'no.'" Moyers told her later that he hadn't even notified his mother and that when she saw the story in the paper she called him and asked, "Billy, did you have a fight with the president?" He also told Judy that she had beaten him by seven hours, because he had planned to announce it himself the next morning. His switch from the White House to *Newsday* surprised Judy even more than it did other reporters; he had told her a few weeks before that he wanted to be ambassador to Vietnam.

During the Johnson administration one reporter made news herself while on the dance floor. Trude B. Feldman, correspondent for a California paper, the *Jewish Press*, took a few turns around the floor with a state visitor, the Arab leader King Hussein I of Jordan. Some of Trude's colleagues gleefully reported that the king had danced with a partner who was the sister of three rabbis and the daughter of another. "The king was quite sophisticated about it when he heard," Trude says, "although I hear he was kidded about it when he got home."

Most male White House correspondents never get near the living quarters, except to be herded in along with hundreds of other reporters for a presidential press conference in the East Room. But female reporters run in and out so much they begin to think of it as home. A favorite story among newswomen is the one about the well-known society columnist who, spotting a cocktail napkin on the floor during a reception, beckoned to a Negro gentleman, resplendent in white tie and tails, to ask him to remove it. It turned out he was not a waiter, but the ambassador from a new African nation.

From the kitchen to the Queen's bedroom,° newswomen

° So named because five Queens have slept in its four-poster bed: Elizabeth, queen mother of Great Britain; Wilhelmina and Juliana of the Netherlands; Frederika of Greece; and Elizabeth II.

have been in practically every cranny of the White House. They've had tea with Pat Nixon in the oval yellow room in the family living quarters, peeked at a secret stairway when Julie Nixon Eisenhower took them on a tour (along with a startled group of tourists, plucked at random from a waiting line outside the East gate), and inspected the presidential bedroom—once, during the Johnson administration, even the bathroom. Nan Robertson wrote in *The New York Times* that the Presidential toothbrush was worn, so the bathroom has been off limits to newswomen ever since. Pat Nixon did show them the men's room next to the library ("I want you to see the new curtains I picked") where Bonnie Angelo of *Time* pointed out to her that a Currier and Ives lithograph, showing Chief Wee Jun Jon's visit to Washington, had an appropriate hanging place.

Mrs. Nixon's first party after she became First Lady was a luncheon for 130 local and out-of-town newspaper women. Then, a few weeks into her husband's second year in office, Mrs. Nixon gave an evening party for ladies of the press and their escorts. There was a screening of the Alfred Hitchcock movie *Topaz* in the State Dining Room, followed by a buffet and dancing in the East Room which had been set up cabaret-style with small tables. Entertainment in the East Room was furnished by Connie Stuart and her girls who did amusing sketches of newswomen as they look to White House staffers.* President and Mrs. Nixon stayed until after midnight, and dancing continued for more than an hour.

The president dropped in at Pat's earlier press luncheon too, just as the main course (chicken and mushroom crêpes) was being served, and noted that Pat's party was the first seated affair given in the State Dining Room during his administration.

"Mrs. Nixon and I read you. We want your ideas. We want your advice. Whenever we can get it, we want your seal of approval," he told the group. This was a joking reference to the ill-starred Willie May Rogers appointment to take Betty Fur-

---

* Not all newswomen were pleased to see themselves portrayed in the show which ended with a song beginning: "There's no business like Press Business, like no business we know. Everything about it is a crisis. Every question needs an answer now. Every writer wants her own exclusive, and when they're granted, the others howl . . ."

ness' place as the presidential consultant on consumer affairs. Her ties with the Good Housekeeping Institute had raised such a howl about conflict of interest that she had resigned within four days of her appointment.

He then read an imaginary telegram from Miss Rogers: "Faces are red. Consumers are blue. Four days of me, four years of you!" Then added wistfully, with the sort of humor the public seldom sees, "I was kind of thinking about eight years." Even the most hostile guests—and a lot of the Washington press has always been somewhat hostile to Nixon because of his old Joe McCarthy witch-hunting days when he had scarcely a kind word for the role of the papers—were softened by his charm that day. *The New York Times'* waspish, razor-sharp women's news editor, Charlotte Curtis, gave the luncheon the ultimate accolade, calling the flower arrangements of pink azaleas and red geraniums "far more Kennedy than Eisenhower."

The reporters were each given a small color print of the White House as it looked in 1848, whereupon Gerry Van der Heuvel, then Mrs. Nixon's press secretary, went to the microphone to point out that the lithographs had been personally autographed by "Mrs. Johnson." After the laughter died down, she explained that "I wish I had not brought it up, but I knew Mrs. Johnson better than I do Mrs. Nixon." Poor Gerry! Some reporters wonder whether this boo-boo (which she later told newswoman Angele Gingras had been her worst on the job) so un-endeared her to her new employer that relations between them remained strained until she was replaced late last year.

It's awfully easy to pull a boo-boo, if you're the impressionable and nervous type, when you're in the presence of the great without adequate preparation. Once a reporter who had known Jackie Kennedy for years was at a farewell party Mrs. Hugh Auchincloss was giving for Letitia Baldrige, Jackie's social secretary. Jackie made a surprise appearance at the party and the reporter, who is something of a horticultural expert, racked her brains for a suitable topic. She decided to mention the new planting Jackie was doing around the Kennedy's weekend retreat in Middleburg, Virginia, which was mostly globe-shaped topiary boxwood.

When Jackie, hand extended and wearing that sub-zero smile

that so terrified people anyway, approached her, the poor woman blurted out, "Jackie, how do you like your new balls?" Jackie simply stared at her, wordlessly. The reporter made a hurried exit from the party and is said to have remained in bed for three days.

Then there was the time when Wauhillau La Hay of Scripps Howard arrived late at the annual dinner Secretary of State Dean Rusk was giving for the heads of foreign missions. She was flustered to find that the host had been taken ill in Florida at the last minute. Nobody knew exactly who was in charge of what for the evening, and she was trying to find out what was going on when she heard someone say, "What are you doing here?" It was President Johnson, who had dropped in with Vice President Humphrey to help out Mrs. Rusk.

"I was so surprised to see him that I blurted out, 'Why, hello, honey, how are you?' right in front of all those ambassadors in their white ties and decorations. Then I went into shock and, trying to pull myself together, said, in a very dignified manner, 'Good evening, Mr. Vice President.' Hubert responded, 'What's the matter? Don't you love *me* anymore?' I promise you that at that moment I had the strongest death wish of my life. It took me about an hour to realize that, thank God, they thought it was funny."

The Kennedys, what with dinner on the lawn at Mount Vernon and other brilliantly imaginative departures from tradition, made state dinners something of an art form. A silver spoon in the mouth from birth helps a great deal when it comes to placing 100 silver or vermeil spoons around perfectly set tables. President and Mrs. Johnson carried on that tradition, though perhaps with a trifle less flair, and the Nixons are trying hard. They entertained over 50,000 people his first 14 months in office (more than any previous administration) and came up with several new types of entertaining, such as a lively cultural series called "Evening at the White House," and Sunday church services in the East Room followed by a social hour. Yet the White House state dinners under the Nixons are proper, sedate, staid and imbued with the unexpressed feeling that, "Let's knock it off early tonight so everyone can be back at his desk before eight o'clock tomorrow morning." One catches this nuance probably because President and Mrs. Nixon escort their guests of honor to the front door immediately following the entertainment, then head straight for their quarters, which is the cue to Vice President and Mrs. Agnew and other bigwigs that they can cut out, too, leaving the lesser lights to accept the President's invitation to stay and dance in the marble foyer. Even Ike and Mamie mingled after what they called the "musicale." President Kennedy also stayed to chat with his guests, and President Johnson, before he became so bogged down with Vietnam, stayed as late as one or two in the morning, dancing.

As far as reporters know, President Nixon hasn't danced at one White House party; neither has Mrs. Nixon except for a short whirl around the floor with Senator Barry Goldwater when a press aide set it up for photographers who had requested a picture of the First Lady dancing. No one knows just when the Nixons gave up dancing (if they actually have); when he was in the Senate, and even when he was vice president, they were regular diners and dancers at the Shoreham Hotel's Blue Room or Terrace.

The press is permitted to cover only the entertainment following a Nixon state dinner, although during the Kennedy and Johnson administrations at least one newswoman (and husband, if any) was invited as a seated guest for every official dinner. They were technically invited as "nonworking" guests, but their colleagues knew they would pool anything unexpected that happened. The Nixons haven't continued this custom. When Ron Ziegler, the presidential press secretary, was asked why, he said, "We didn't stop inviting them. We never started."

Actually, Nixon state dinners haven't scored high for their entertainment value ° (Mrs. Bus Mosbacher, wife of the chief of

---

° One notable exception was the state dinner for German Chancellor Willy Brandt in spring 1970, when Pearl Bailey entertained. The enthusiasm for Miss Bailey's act was so great that President Nixon jumped up and carried his chair onstage for use as a stepping stool when Pearl wanted to sit on top of the piano. He was so carried away with her performance he gave her the chair. He didn't know until later that since all White House property is protected by an act of Congress, he had to pay for it out of his own pocket. She now makes it part of her act, and invites members of her audience to sit in it, and even buys two plane tickets to accommodate it.

protocol, went to sleep during one after-dinner concert), so reporters wouldn't mind missing them too, if they weren't part of the job. *Wall Street Journal* reporter Helene Melzer, in a front-page story titled "The Nixon Touch" said that the Nixon state affairs are "proper, even properly dull," with neither the Kennedy spark nor the Johnson flamboyance. "The state entertainment at the White House," Helene went on, "has been not very different, one can imagine, from what results when the earnest ladies of Peoria or Whittier set out to get themselves some culture . . . as society watchers here note the passing scene, they see the lights are on at the White House these nights, and wonder what there is to stay up for."

When the Kennedys were in the White House, Basil Rathbone and the Consort Players presented a program of Elizabethan poetry and music following a dinner for the Grand Duchess Charlotte of Luxembourg, including a surprise for the president when it turned out Jackie had arranged for Basil Rathbone to do a special reading of Henry's V's St. Crispin's Day speech, a Shakespearean monologue often quoted by President Kennedy. Jerome Robbins' "Ballets: U.S.A." was the entertainment for the shah and empress of Iran, and the American Shakespeare Festival Theater of Stratford, Connecticut, did excerpts from *Henry V, Macbeth,* and *As You Like It* following the dinner for President Abboud of Sudan.

The selection of entertainment at Johnson administration state dinners was equally imaginative. Prima Ballerina Maria Tallchief and Jacques D'Amboise, principal dancer with the New York City Ballet, performed on a shell-backed stage on the South lawn, following a dinner in the Rose Garden honoring Dr. Ludwig Erhard, chancellor of the Federal Republic of Germany. Others, like Carol Channing, did their bit for the country (nobody ever gets paid for entertaining at the White House) in the East Room from the jewel of a portable stage given to the White House by patroness of the arts Rebekah Harkness.

In contrast to their staid state dinners with musicale-type entertainment and big business guest lists, some Nixon parties have produced memorable evenings. Reporters agree that the birthday party President and Mrs. Nixon gave for pianist-composer Duke Ellington was a history-making affair. One hundred and twenty guests were invited for dinner and more joined them for the concert, a program of all Ellington music played and sung by the greats of American jazz. President Nixon, more relaxed than one usually sees him at parties, sat down at the piano ° and played "Happy Birthday" while everyone serenaded the first Black man ever honored at a White House dinner. One California musician told a friend that he had always voted against Mr. Nixon but that "if he ran for Grand Dragon of the Ku Klux Klan I'd vote for him tonight."

The Nixons also gave a dinner for Andrew Wyeth before the opening of an exhibit of the artist's work which the White House said was the "first occasion on which an American painter has been formally honored with an exhibition in the White House." Prominent American artists, gallery and museum directors, and others from the art world were among the guests. Wyeth's brother-in-law, artist Peter Hurd, was there, confirming that LBJ had actually called his Hurd portrait "the ugliest thing I ever saw." Hurd said, "He's denied it since, but I have witnesses—and I'm not deaf."

On George Washington's Birthday, 1970, the Broadway cast of *1776* (Sherman Edwards' musical play about the drafting of the Declaration of Independence) presented the complete show in the East Room. It was the second of the series of evenings at the White House that the Nixons are giving every six weeks or so. The White House went to a lot of trouble to stage that evening since some members of the cast were not pro-Nixon and had to be persuaded to perform. According to Clare Crawford of the *Washington Daily News,* the White House had to give a little too. "Some of the lines in the show, which cannot be described as pro-Republican," stayed in although the White House wanted them taken out. Also objectionable to the White House, but left in nevertheless, was the anti-war song "Mama Look Sharp."

° These impromptu piano recitals are not always unanimously well received. When the president and vice president spoofed their so-called Southern strategy in a piano duet at the Gridiron Dinner (a prestigious annual men's press dinner to which no women are invited) in March of 1970, civil rights leader Roy Wilkins wrote in the *Washington Post* that he had not been so humiliated since his college fraternity asked him to attend a minstrel show.

President Nixon seemed to enjoy the show thoroughly, even, according to one of the actors, "the bawdy parts."

The food served at Nixon dinners is pretty much the same as when the Kennedys and the Johnsons were in the White House. Jacqueline Kennedy hired a superb French chef, René Verdon, who came highly recommended by New York's Caravelle Restaurant, and put food on a gourmet level not reached at the Executive Mansion since the days of Thomas Jefferson. She also trimmed the menu to only four courses—a soup or fish, the entrée, salad with cheese, and dessert.

Another Jackie innovation was doing away with the formal "U" shaped table of the Eisenhower period, with its massive arrangements of flowers so high a guest couldn't see who was sitting across the table. She replaced it with tables seating 10, centered with delicate, low flower arrangements in the vermeil containers given to the White House by her friend Mrs. Paul Mellon. She stopped segregating the sexes when after-dinner coffee and liqueurs were served, too. Before the Kennedys, male guests joined the president in the Green Room for coffee and cigars while the First Lady took the women to the Red Room.

For a while the Johnsons kept Chef Verdon, then replaced him with Henry Haller, equally expert but less temperamental. They also kept the round tables with their elegantly understated flower arrangements, but President Johnson took away some of the formality of the occasion by refusing to wear a white tie. He and all his male guests wore black ties to every state dinner given during his term of office.

President Nixon went back to a white tie for state dinners. The food is the same, since Henry Haller is a holdover; and though the Nixons use a rectangular "head table" for themselves and their honor guests, everyone else is seated at tables for 10 (occasionally this arrangement is changed to an "E"-shaped table). This is against the wishes of Clem Conger, formerly with the State Department's Protocol Office and now White House curator, who strongly recommended going back to the "U" shape, claiming that the round tables are "night-clubby."

Men and women representing the arts and sciences, politics

and business, the entertainment world and society, came to the Kennedy and Johnson parties. The "Beautiful People" were there, too. Reporters especially enjoyed the newsmaking show business types on hand when Lyndon and Lady Bird entertained. For instance, there was Carol Channing in Rudi Gernreich's yellow bloomer dress at Lynda Bird's wedding. Carol later said she thought that's what people were wearing to weddings. Singer Eartha Kitt provided newswomen with reams of copy when she blasted Lady Bird Johnson and her guests at a "Woman-Doer" luncheon. Mrs. Johnson gave a series of luncheons where she had experts on a variety of subjects speak to a small, select group of women guests. Eartha Kitt was invited to one where the discussion centered on crime control and prevention. After the experts had said their piece, Eartha asked permission to speak: "I think we have missed the main point at this luncheon. We have forgotten the main reason we have juvenile delinquency. The young people are angry and the parents are angry, because they're being so highly taxed and there's a war going on and Americans don't know why. Boys I know across the nation feel it doesn't pay to be a good guy. They figure that with a crime record they don't have to go to Vietnam." Turning to Mrs. Johnson, Eartha said, "You are a mother, too, although you have had daughters and not sons. I am a mother and I know the feeling of having a baby come out of my guts . . . I have a baby and you send him to war, no wonder the kids rebel and take pot, and Mrs. Johnson in case you don't understand the lingo, that's marijuana."

That certainly upset the small, lady-like luncheon, gave the reporters a real news story, and provided comedians with scores of one-liners such as Liz Carpenter's on leaving the White House: "I remember the gay, happy moments . . . moments of warmth and friendship and deep emotion . . . like the day Eartha Kitt came to lunch."

Muriel Dobbin of the *Baltimore Sun* says, "I'll never forget Liz Carpenter following Fran and Helen back to the Press Room, saying, 'I certainly hope you aren't going to give space to that headline seeker.'" Muriel also noted that when Mrs. Johnson made her impassioned reply to Eartha Kitt's outburst,

"It was the first time I ever heard her say anything she hadn't thought out thoroughly first or that Liz Carpenter hadn't written for her."

The Nixon guest lists haven't produced any such newsmakers, nor have they included what "Old Washington" ° and even Republicans think they should. Mrs. Everett Dirksen, widow of Senator Dirksen, described by Clare Crawford of the *Washington Daily News* as certainly not a member of the "no-bra" set, said while discussing White House guest lists at a luncheon at the Embassy of Kuwait, "How can you possibly have the right people invited to the White House when the White House social secretary is a Southern belle who knows nothing at all about diplomatic, congressional and social Washington?"

Traditionally, social secretaries have had a good deal of whatever one might mean by the word "clout." Tish Baldrige had been social secretary to Clare Boothe Luce in Rome and to Mrs. David Bruce in Paris before she took on the job for Jackie Kennedy. Lady Bird hired Bess Abell who is not only the daughter of Senator Earl Clements of Kentucky, a former governor of the state and once a formidable figure in Washington, but the wife of Tyler Abell, son of Mrs. Drew Pearson and a descendant of the distinguished Abell family of *Baltimore Sun* fame. Tyler's father, George, was assistant chief of protocol during the Johnson administration. Both women knew the Washington social scene inside and out. It has not been felt that Lucy Winchester, the present social secretary, knows it to anything like the same extent.

Some Republicans think there's more to the Nixon guest lists than a social secretary who doesn't know the Washington scene. Wauhillau La Hay, in her Scripps Howard column, quotes a Republican senator as saying, "I guess I have blown all our chances to get invited to a White House state dinner. I voted

---

° Few members of "Old Washington" society have been asked to the White House since the Nixons moved in. Georgetown designer Charles Dunham, who has "dressed" some of Washington's most elegant women and who admits he is making fewer and fewer elaborate gowns these days, says the reason is: "Pat Nixon is getting even with the people who snubbed her when her husband was vice president. She isn't asking any of the Washington people to the big things at the White House."

against Haynsworth and the ABM and I'm not committed either way on Carswell." Others who voted against Judge Haynsworth's nomination to the Supreme Court voiced the same complaint. Wauhillau also noted that every senator invited to the state dinner for British Prime Minister Harold Wilson in January 1970 had voted for Haynsworth, and that all invited to the state dinner for West Germany's then-Chancellor Kurt Kiesinger were senators who had voted for the ABM. The very social Republican Senator and Mrs. John Sherman Cooper hadn't made it to a White House dinner during the Nixon administration, said Wauhillau, noting that the Coopers "were strong supporters of Governor Nelson A. Rockefeller at the 1968 Republican National Convention." *

Naturally, the Democrats are amused. At one state dinner, for Australian Prime Minister John Gorton, Senator Edmund Muskie, who was invited because Mrs. Gorton was from the senator's home state, Maine, surveyed the crowd and said, "Coming from my state, I feel right at home." His wife Jane unintentionally dropped the other shoe when she said, "Maybe they are still paying back"—a reference to the unwritten law whereby presidents reward important supporters and large campaign contributors, no matter how uninteresting socially, with a White House invitation.

The Nixons' "paying back" doesn't seem to be all political. They gave a dinner for the Duke and Duchess of Windsor in April 1970, and as Betty Beale of the *Washington Star* pointed out, it was odd that the Nixons, who have never been associated in the minds of the public as international society types, should entertain the Windsors. The reason was: The Nixons owed the Windsors a dinner. The duke and duchess gave a dinner for the Nixons and their daughters when they were in France in 1963.†

---

* Within a few days after the column appeared, the Coopers were invited to the dinner President and Mrs. Nixon gave for the Duke and Duchess of Windsor. They were the only members of congress on the guest list.

† Later Mrs. Nixon's press office announced that the Nixons had met the duke and duchess after Julie had asked her parents to introduce her when she became fascinated with English history several years ago. Clare Crawford pointed out: "It is politically fortitudinous that Julie didn't have a scholarly penchant for fascist leaders—or cannibals."

A story by Marie Smith in the *Washington Post* also confirms the "pay-back" theory. Writing about the state dinner for New Zealand Prime Minister Keith Holyoake, she said, "If the Prime Minister were aware of the financial wealth behind the line-up of 100 guests whose hands he shook he could not have helped being impressed. No less than a dozen of this country's leading corporation presidents or chairmen, many of whom contributed heavily to President Nixon's campaign last year, were there with their wives." And Clare Crawford, of the *Washington Daily News*, pointed out that some 33 chairmen-of-the-board or company presidents and their wives were invited to the White House the night Shakespearean actor Nicol Williamson entertained.

One of the most frequent complaints by newswomen about the Nixon party operation during the early part of the administration was the handling of after-dinner toasts. For the eight pre-Nixon years, with few exceptions, toasts were either piped into the Library for reporters to hear, or the women were invited upstairs to hear them "live."

Following some of the first Nixon dinners, toasts were not given out at all. At others they were taped and played back after the dinner was over. By the time those on deadline got the toasts and phoned in their stories, the entertainment was at least half over. President Johnson, probably as sensitive a man about his image as anyone ever to occupy the White House, didn't stop reporters from hearing the toasts live, even after the *Washington Post's* Judith Martin wrote: "President Johnson told the Prime Minister of Iran last night that it was just as well the American Founding Fathers didn't pick a title such as king, potentate or shahanshah for him. 'I hate to think how our Fourth Estate would react if they had to refer to me that way,' he said. Another problem might have been the president's trouble pronouncing the Persian title. At last night's state dinner, he toasted the 'Sha shah shah.' The Prime Minister came back with a gracious speech about 'LBG.'"

Press gripes about toasts paid off, for a while. Regularly, for months, they were piped into the theater as the president and his visiting head of state gave them. Then at the splendid dinner

President and Mrs. Nixon gave for the Duke and Duchess of Windsor the toasts were not given out; the reporters had to learn from various guests that the former king was still glad that 34 years ago he gave up his throne for "the woman I love." The duke expressed his happiness at being back in Washington and added: "I have had the good fortune to have a wonderful American girl consent to marry me. I have had 30 years of loving care, devotion and companionship—something I have cherished above all else."

Another howl of complaints by the press paid off too. At Kennedy and Johnson parties, reporters joined the dinner guests for coffee and liqueurs, which gave them an opportunity to talk to the newsmakers, even the visiting heads of state themselves. At first the Nixons allowed the newswomen to go upstairs for the entertainment just in time to take seats in the last row after all the other guests were seated—a flashback to the Eisenhower administration. Now, reporters go upstairs right behind what they call the "Second-Class Citizens," guests asked for the entertainment only, and are allowed to mingle for a few minutes.

The first people reporters look for are the President and Mrs. Nixon. Once they see that he is hale and hearty, newswomen check on Pat and what she is wearing. Even reporters like Clare Crawford, who claims "I never mention clothes unless the person is naked," have learned that readers expect to know what a First Lady had on. Everyone agrees that for a woman whose fashion trademark in 1952 was that "good Republican cloth coat," Mrs. Nixon has come a long way and many suspect it was living in New York during those "out" years that did it. Pat Nixon is thin and fragile, an underweight Dresden doll, and some of the reporters worry about her health. Others don't. Some of those who covered Pat when her husband was vice president remember she was just as thin and fragile then. They haven't made up their minds whether her perfect size eight figure is natural or by choice. She certainly doesn't eat much, and when one reporter questioned her about her apparently small appetite, she replied, "I don't want to get fat."

As soon as the Nixons have seen their honor guests to the door and have said good night, newswomen in the pool scatter around as widely as possible to talk to the guests. Since they are the pool, and there are nonpool reporters waiting for the briefing after the party is over, they want to pick up as many newsy tidbits as possible.

Some tidbits are distinctly newsier than others. While the Johnsons were in the White House, they gave a large reception for Democratic women congregated in Washington from all over the country. Wauhillau picked up the following item for her syndicated Scripps Howard column: "Four-month-old Rachel Marie Gordon of Lakewood, Ohio, is going to have something to tell her friends when she grows up," Wauhillau wrote. Then she told how Rachel Marie got hungry and her mother, Mrs. Stephanie Gordon, nursed her as thousands milled around. Wauhillau noted that "The event took place in the main hall of the president's house as the Marine Band, led by imperturbable Captain James King, played 'The Donkey Serenade'—louder and louder."

"It was hysterical," Wauhillau said later. "This Secret Service agent and I were dying of embarrassment. The baby was yelling and the mother whipped out her buzoom and bang! An aide was standing there and we both grouped around her; he turned his back and the band leader, I'll never forget, looked over and the music got faster and faster."

Later in the same story, Wauhillau told about an excited Indianian who yelled across a crowded room to a friend, "Hey, Marge, I've saw her twice. Have you saw her?" Her friend grinned and answered, "No, but I shaked hands with Muriel Humphrey."

Wauhillau likes to stay in the background at large parties, since "you hear funny things, there. At the last Christmas party the Johnsons gave for underprivileged children, I went over and sat down beside a little Negro girl who was holding a brand new doll, a gift from the Johnsons. Her lower lip was down to her chin, and her eyes were filled with tears, and I said, 'What's the matter with you, honey?' She answered, 'I don't want no damn doll, I wants a baseball bat.' "

Wauhillau, who is part Cherokee Indian, is known as the Auntie Mame of the women's press corps and has the kind of gut humor most reporters, male or female, admire. On rare nights when there's nothing important to cover in Washington,

Wauhillau whips up marvelous little dinner parties in her historic Georgetown house where, between working on her ever-present pieces of needlepoint, she dishes up gourmet food ("I love to cook more than anything in this world") and pithy comments about friend and foe alike ("I never knew what an ass she was until she knocked on my cabin door, on one of those wilderness trips with Lady Bird, and told me she needed to urinate. I mean, for God's sake, you can't be a friend of anybody who urinates!"). Wauhillau, who hates to be called by a nickname, started her newspapering in Oklahoma when in high school, "covering everything from rape cases to basketball," and continued through her college years. Later she went into radio and eventually she became an advertising executive in New York. Seven years ago she decided to retire on a little farm in Dutchess County, but one night at dinner her good friends Walker Stone, then editor in chief of Scripps Howard, and Jack Howard talked her into coming to Washington to write a column for them.

Judith Axler, like Wauhillau, looks for the off-beat. When she was writing for the *New York Daily News*, Judy, then 25, was one of the youngest syndicated columnists in Washington. She sprinkled the column, which went to millions of readers, with such items as:

· "Lady Bird, in a low-cut short red dress, took her right foot out of its matching red silk pump twice to wiggle her cramped toes . . ."

· "In case you're wondering, it's perfectly proper to chew gum when greeting the president at the airport. Protocol Chief James Symington did . . ."

· "Indira Gandhi changed her sari eight times during her two-day visit . . . and changed her footwear even oftener. She wears open sandals in many colors and no stockings . . . her toenails are painted bright red . . ."

· "At a White House reception this week one of the guests, glamorous in a long satin gown, felt her horsehair petticoat beginning to slip . . . so she quickly kicked it under the nine-foot-long gilded grand piano. Justice Abe Fortas, who was dancing with Lady Bird, picked it up, asking loudly, 'Whose is this?' then delicately placed the slip on top of the piano. No one has yet claimed it."

· "When Luci took Pat to see the crystal, china, and silver she had chosen, he approved of the designs. But he was appalled at the cost, 'Honey,' Luci is supposed to have reassured him, 'we won't have to buy any of this' . . ."

· "As Sharon Percy walked down the aisle in her long white Mainbocher gown to meet her beaming bridegroom at the altar, there was a tall, dark-haired girl in yellow sitting in one of the pews thinking she might have been in the bride's place. John D. (Jay) Rockefeller IV might have been saying his 'I do' to Lynda Bird Johnson, if she had had her way . . . She invited the young Democrat to the LBJ ranch several times last year to keep her company . . . Later in the fall, Lynda wrote to Jay, asking him to come to Washington to see her. She told him she was lonely, rambling around in the 132-room White House, with her folks off on their trip to the Far East. She said she was just a working girl, hunting for a job, and wouldn't he come and visit? Jay wrote back, kindly and gently explaining that he and Sharon were engaged."

Judy Axler covered Washington society for *The New York Times* after leaving the *News*, and became a free-lance writer when she married psychologist Lester Turner, but is now back on a regular beat for the Jewish Telegraphic Agency and the Israeli News Agency. Her biggest scoop involved ex-movie queen Joan Crawford and the wife of a Supreme Court Justice, and was written while she was still with the *News*.

Reporting on a dinner given by President and Mrs. Johnson, Judy wrote that Kathy Douglas, the fourth wife of Justice William O. Douglas, was seated at the same round table in the State Dining Room as the former queen of the silver screen, Joan Crawford, who, according to Judy, "wasn't acting queenly that night." Before dessert, when a crystal finger bowl was placed in front of the 67-year-old Justice's 23-year-old wife, she was so engrossed in conversation she neglected to pick up her lace doily and parsley-sprigged bowl of water. Miss Crawford reached across three people to lift Mrs. Douglas' bowl and doily from her plate. "That's the way we do it," she said icily. Judy said, "Mrs. Douglas managed a startled thank you. 'That was the first time I'd ever been insulted in Washington,' the still-dazed Mrs. Douglas said later. 'Up till now, everyone has been so nice.' "

Judy's story was picked up by other papers and the Crawford-Douglas finger-bowl incident was a minor splash heard around the world. Miss Crawford vigorously denied the story, but Judy says Kathy herself told it to her a day or two after it happened, while the two were lunching together at the Sans Souci restaurant. Judy, who is about the same age as Kathy, was introduced to Kathy by the Justice whom she had met at a British Embassy party before his marriage, and later Judy was part of one of the groups he took hiking along the C. & O. Canal.

Clare Crawford once summed up Nixon administration parties in *The Washingtonian:* "There is no doubt about it, Washington social life is so dull that if Calvin Coolidge returned he could easily become the Playboy of the Potomac," Clare wrote. She dubbed Nixon society the "Right Society," noting that it did all the right things such as "quoting Norman Vincent Peale and meaning it." She also noted that "black businessmen are in, but black friends are out, not because the Republicans are prejudiced; they just don't have any colored friends." Clare quoted Kandy Shuman Stroud as saying, "The Nixons rigidly practice the mores of the upper middle class. They seem to generate a determined effort to be good."

The Nixon administration was not pleased, but then it's nothing new when Clare is out of favor with people she has written about. She and Judith Martin of the *Washington Post* once teamed up to get a story which upset the White House so much that Liz Carpenter called Clare to accuse her of writing something which might have started World War III.

Clare and Judy were covering the White House party for the

Judiciary in May 1967, when, according to Judy, "Johnson went around telling this story—as you know, he is a blabbermouth—about the night when he sent Navy and Air Force planes to bomb Hanoi, and Luci came in and he told her, 'Your Daddy might have started World War III.' It was the first time we knew that he was aware of what the escalation possibilities might be and of what he was doing. He went on to tell of the restless night he had waiting to hear if the American planes returned."

Continuing the story, Clare says, "Luci told her father to come with her to see her 'Little Monk' friends, so in the middle of the night Johnson and Luci went to St. Dominic's Church to pray and the monks came out to talk to them. The next day all the fighters came back and Luci said, 'See, my Little Monks carried you through.' Judy and I used the story. Well, so did *Pravda.* Liz called me in and she was waving the *Pravda* story and calling me un-American and saying that I might have started World War III."

Though Liz tore Clare apart for writing the story, she didn't say a word to Judy. "I like to think she didn't have the nerve," says Judy.

It turned out that earlier President Johnson had told the Little Monk story to several male reporters covering the West Wing. "There were all these people who said they knew the story," says Judy, "but didn't use it because it might make the president look like a fool. Well, I think it is up to the president not to make himself look like a fool, and if all that stands between the president and looking like a fool is me, then things are in a pretty sad way, right?"

Clare picked up another news-making story one night when she sat next to Governor Nelson Rockefeller at a State Department dinner. The governor told Clare that Hubert Humphrey had asked him to be his vice president. The story had been rumored, but the Democrats denied it, so this was the first time either Rockefeller or Humphrey had confirmed it. Governor Rockefeller also told Clare that the vice presidency ruined Dick Nixon for a while, ruined Hubert Humphrey, and almost ruined Lyndon Johnson. He added that he had told Richard Nixon he didn't want to be vice president because it meant only standing around and waiting for someone to die. Another politician at the table said he thought that Spiro Agnew might be the first man who ever enjoyed being vice president.

Governor Rockefeller told Clare that he thought his candidacy had been ruined by Robert Kennedy's assassination, and that if he had taken on Nixon in the primaries after that, he just would have been paving the way for the nomination of either Lindsay or Reagan, which he would have considered equally disastrous.

Clare graduated from the University of Maryland in 1958, and married a handsome Georgetown University law student, Victor Crawford (now a successful attorney and Maryland state senator), the day after receiving her degree. She immediately started working at the Washington Post and teaching journalism classes at Catholic University. Within a few months the city editor, Ben Gilbert, told her she was "too aggressive to be a reporter" and should look elsewhere for employment. Two jobs later, she wound up at the Washington Daily News where she's been ever since. She won an award for her reporting on unwed mothers—researched while she was pregnant—and her disclosure of the appalling conditions she found have resulted in many changes in the District's maternity clinics. She also investigated the narcotics racket, and another time bought a gun to show how easy it is for anyone to buy a weapon in the District. Eventually the News gave her a column, with the mandate to "go out and investigate Society." She says she has found society people "just as stupid and just as smart as people in low places."

Although she has a regular, three-times-a-week column, and also appears regularly on WRC-NBC news, Clare claims she will never be a great columnist: "I'm not ruthless enough to be great. I don't have the talent for the jugular. I know how to do it, but I don't have the guts. My first inclination is to protect people."

She recalls an interview she had with Rene Carpenter, then the wife of Scott Carpenter, the astronaut, in which Rene told Clare that she and her husband were going to Ethel and Robert Kennedy's wedding anniversary party. Rene said, "I certainly

hope that . . . well, I don't want Bob and Ethel exploiting us."
Clare told Rene, "That's the funniest line I've ever heard. It's
vice versa here in Washington."

Another time, just before the 1968 election, one of Richard
Nixon's law partners, a maritime lawyer, told Clare in great detail what a "wild person Aristotle Onassis was." Clare warned
him that he was now very quotable and shouldn't go around
talking like that.

"I like to write about what really happens, what goes on behind the scenes," Clare says. In a column describing Tricia Nixon's first White House party, a masked ball, Clare wrote: "When
Representative Barry Goldwater, Jr. escorted Tricia down the
grand stairs in the dramatic kickoff of the evening, he was
chewing gum." And, "The tables throughout the East Room,
State Dining Room and Great Hall were covered with spectacular jewel-colored satin tablecloths. The edges of these cloths
were not hemmed, they were pinked."

During another administration, Clare told how the State Department at a swish and stately dinner had the tablecloth
tucked up and anchored with straight pins; and how the White
House had in the ladies' room a pincushion "that your mother-
in-law would criticize if she saw it at your house, but it must be
all right because they had it at the White House."

"I forgot all about it, once I had written it, but God! Months
later we were peeling Liz Carpenter off the ceiling. She not only
didn't like it, she almost lost her mind. She said, 'You don't
come here to the White House to cover the pincushions, you
come here to cover the people.' She was really mad and I kept
saying, 'You've got to be kidding, you've got to be putting me
on.'"

Judith Martin's story about George Wallace being a victim of
White House "discrimination" wasn't one Liz viewed kindly, either. President Johnson entertained the nation's governors, including George's wife Lurleen Wallace, at a White House
luncheon in 1967, and Mrs. Johnson gave a luncheon for the
wives of governors, on the same day, at the State Department
following a ceremony in which each wife planted a tree, in the
name of her state, in a small park alongside the Potomac.
George Wallace was not invited to the president's luncheon

since he was no longer a governor; he was not included in Mrs. Johnson's party because, as a White House spokesman pointed out, he was "not a wife." Judy described in detail George Wallace's lunch in his hotel room and quoted him as saying that no one should be discriminated against because of sex. "I'm against discrimination. It's against the law," George told Judy before he became convulsed with laughter. Liz Carpenter admitted after she left the White House that "not inviting George was one of our mistakes, he got more publicity than we did."

Judy was one of a small group of women reporters President Johnson asked up to the family quarters for a drink following a reception honoring a group of veterans. "He told us about a telephone call he'd just had from Luci. She was in Honolulu, meeting Pat, and then off the record he started telling us all this tremendous business, that he hadn't planned to run for a second term all along, that Mrs. Johnson had in her diary for March 1965 that he wasn't going to run, and that he was going to announce it in 1968. He said that he had never wanted to be vice president and then I said, 'But, Sir, the day before you ran for vice president you were trying to run for president,' he answered, 'But I didn't want that, I was talked into that.'" He spent the whole evening, according to Judy, trying to justify himself, saying that all he wanted to be was majority leader all his life. He even said that Sam Rayburn had written a speech announcing his candidacy for the presidency without his approval.

"I had those two hours with LBJ, in which he supposedly unburdened his heart, but what told me even more about him was when, at another White House party, I saw him standing at the buffet table where there was a big silver tray full of strawberry tarts, and he would take one after another, eat the strawberry and put the tart back on the tray. I thought, 'There's Lyndon Johnson, right there!' No verbal soul-searching he could do is better as a characterization than that."

CHAPTER

6

"In most places in America nobody cares what the upper crust does anymore. Here, because the upper crust is basically political, everyone cares."

Washington, according to diplomats and others who have lived around the world and ought to know, is the most society-minded town on earth, from the point of view of numbers of parties and dollars spent on entertaining. It is, however, a paradox in that the things usually associated with society elsewhere count for very little here. You can have the right ancestors, send your children to the right schools, belong to the right clubs, and still be Nobody in the eyes of the women reporters who evaluate who's "In" and who's "Out." Conversely, your mother can have run a bordello and you can be Alfie Schmaltz from Nowheresville, with dirty fingernails and a wife who calls curtains "drapes" and evening dresses "formals"; but if you are a White House assistant, the press will record your words and hostesses will invite you Everywhere.

The late columnist George Dixon once said that a Washington cocktail party was a place where "you can meet anybody from the 4-H Club's fastest milker to the administration's slowest thinker." (The fast milker will be there because he's from the home state of a powerful congressman who has discovered the easiest way to entertain constituents is to take them to someone else's cocktail party.)

Washington society is based on who makes the news, and those who don't, no matter how socially ambitious, might as well crawl home to Pocatello. Those who have power—elected power, appointed power, "close to the throne" power, and media power—make news, along with an occasional wealthy woman who's willing to devote her energies to collecting people with power.

"If Washington society isn't based on power," ponders the *Washington Post*'s Judith Martin, "How else do you account for a Richard Nixon, a Lyndon Johnson, or a Harry Truman being social lions?"

Liz Carpenter puts it this way: "Washington's a town where a Supreme Court Justice may pick his teeth, but he is still the star at the party because he *is* the Supreme Court Justice."

It is also a place where, though personal stability is essential, the old-fashioned concept of family stability doesn't count, since everything is subject to change all the time, anyway. You can be important Tuesday and utterly unimportant Wednesday, after you have been forced to resign as assistant secretary of pollution. Even Hollywood isn't as fickle as Washington, since there all the stars don't come crashing down at once as they do here every four or eight years.

It is the constantly changing power structure (as Alice Roosevelt Longworth has said, "Washington Society is all come-and-go"), and the absence of the usual guidelines to who's in "Society" and who isn't, that's made reporting for women's pages more perilous, tricky, and influential than it would be elsewhere. Meg Greenfield, now deputy editor of the editorial pages of the *Washington Post* and the only woman among 10 editorial writers, once wrote in the now-defunct *Reporter* magazine, "Although the ladies who compose these columns are not universally loved, they are universally read. In their way they are the fourth-and-a-half branch of government . . ." Both President Kennedy and President Johnson were faithful readers of the local women's pages; President Nixon has told newswomen that he reads them, but the girls are skeptical since learning of the little White House staff group that reads the papers for him, picking out items it thinks would interest the president, compiling them into a daily "paper" which is placed on his desk each morning.

One of the most successful navigators of these treacherous waters of social reporting is Betty Beale, the unquestioned dean of the Washington society scribes, who recently married for the first time at an age she sensibly does not care to reveal. Betty goes to over 500 parties a year, which have paid off for her with such scoops as:

· The engagement of Adam Clayton Powell III, son of Harlem's flamboyant congressman and pianist Hazel Scott, to the socially prominent Beryl Slocum, daughter of the John J. Slocums of Washington and Newport, and a direct descendant of both Miles Standish and Rhode Island's founder, Roger Williams.

· Richard Nixon's purchase of two adjoining houses, one of them from Senator George Smathers, at Key Biscayne, Florida —the third house in the Nixon compound belonging to his good friend, millionaire C. G. (Bebe) Rebozo.

· Lynda Bird Johnson Robb expecting her second child.

· Caroline Kennedy almost drowning in her mother's half-sister's swimming pool when her daddy was in the White House. Betty also told how the then-pregnant Mrs. William Saltonstall jumped in Nina Auchincloss Steers' pool to rescue Caroline.

Betty's home paper is the *Washington Star*, but she also has a Hall Syndicate column in over 100 papers. For over 22 years, she has covered the scene as a nonsmoking, nondrinking, nonnotetaker ("I always think of myself as a guest at a party, and guests don't run around with pencils and notebooks"), handsome, slim, confirmed spinster, though she was suspected of having a poetic (so poetic she won't show anybody his poetry) romance with the late Adlai Stevenson. Once, after a particularly glowing column about his charms, Adlai with his characteristic humor sent her a crystal cat from a New York store which ar-

109

rived with one ear splintered. The two corresponded about its replacement entirely in rhyme.

Then she met George Graeber, a gregarious widower who had been assigned here by Union Carbide as a Washington representative. Most men sent here even by the biggest businesses could spend an assiduous 10 years without ever setting foot in the White House, but within a couple of weeks, Betty had George chatting with Pat Nixon, sipping champagne with all the important Senators in town, and getting to know local celebrities on a first-name basis. "First name only," says Betty pointedly. "Everywhere we went, I purposely garbled his last name so that it sounded like Brabe or Haber. I didn't want some predatory hostess to discover that he was the most desirable bachelor in town in years and grab him for herself. Now I'm paying the price, because nobody pronounces our name right."

Betty's evolution as front runner in the ever-more-crowded field of capital city social reporting reflects the metamorphosis of Washington from a small, somewhat Southern-oriented town where all the Right People knew one another into a large, world-oriented city where the Right People don't matter a lot any more.

She grew up in Old World Washington, going to the fashionable Holton Arms School and then to Smith. Though not technically a cave dweller, since her first resident ancestor was her maternal grandfather, a congressman from Nashville, Tennessee, her credentials are excellent: she is directly descended from Thomas Beale, a vestryman at Bruton Parish Church in Colonial Williamsburg, who was given a large land grant in Virginia by Lord Fairfax in 1640.

She got into the newspaper business via the Junior League, which she joined after graduating from college in 1938. "They put me on the publicity committee, which I hated because in those days I very much disliked writing, and I had to take these releases about their big project, the horse show, around to the society editors. Hope Ridings Miller, woman's editor at the *Post*,° suggested I write a column, since my sister and I enter-

° Hope Miller subsequently became editor of *Diplomat* magazine, and recently wrote an entertaining history of the diplomatic corps, *Embassy Row*.

tained a lot and knew everybody. I was scared to death but I did a sample one, because I felt that if I backed away from this opportunity, I'd never have the courage to take the next hurdle."

The column was called "Top Hats and Tiaras," but Betty's health started flagging—it turned out later she had a salt deficiency—and she gave it up during the war, concentrating on volunteer Red Cross work instead. After she took up Christian Science and got her strength back (to this day, she is a devout Scientist, so much so that she once persuaded a Multiple Sclerosis Association dance committee to change the initials "MS" to mean "Mid-Season" so she could write about it more comfortably), she went to the *Star*, where her "Exclusively Yours" has been as voraciously read by men as by women ever since.

"Growing up in Washington gave me a tremendous advantage," she says, "because automatically when I heard a name, the wheels began to grind and I knew where to place it. Most society writers do not come into this business because of familiarity with the social scene—they've graduated from being copy girls or come from out-of-town—and they can't tell the social climbers who clutter up the diplomatic parties from the people who really matter. I can tell right away who asks me to a party just because she and her husband want their names in the paper, even though they may pretend they don't want me to write it up."

Betty is invited to five or six parties every night of the 365, not only private and charity affairs, but official functions for visiting diplomats, newly appointed officials, outgoing officials, up-going officials, transferred officials, officials officially welcoming other officials, freshly elected members of Congress, and tired old members of Congress celebrating or commemorating something. These are only the parties she tries to cover . . . there are whole icebergs of parties underneath. Yet society in Washington is not sophisticated as is society in other capitals such as Paris, London, or Rome. It is more small-town, though with finer food, fashion, and conversation than you would be likely to encounter in Grand Rapids or Sioux Falls. As writers have noted for years, this is essentially a company town, in which everyone's business is intertwined with everyone else's.

All this is not easy to analyze, and Betty believes that above and beyond reporting as many of these kaleidoscopic events as she can, her function is to inform and instruct. Thus, of the millions of words she has written, she is proudest of a series of three columns she addressed to the new members of Congress in January of 1967:

"Washington society is a pie," she wrote in one. "Not the apple, lemon, or even mincemeat variety, but a pulsating pie. "The nation's legislators . . . comprise one slice of it. The other slices can be labeled: The Administration, The Diplomatic Corps, The Military, The Press, Residential Society, and The Judiciary. The Judiciary is mentioned last because, despite its enormous influence, it is the smallest segment in the social picture. The center of the pie is the president . . . the top man in Washington society. Each slice or segment of the pie points to this center, and from its broad base on the outer rim each narrows down to the leaders who are closest to the White House. Now if you take a biscuit cutter and cut out the very center of the pie—i.e., the points of all segments—you would have the society in Washington that really counts—the inner circle . . . The yen to be in this society is a disease called Potomac Fever, and 'Trying to get rid of Potomac Fever is like getting rid of malaria,' as Adlai Stevenson said once. 'Just when you think it's gone you begin to shake.'"

She let the new Congress know, too, that they weren't to shake hands with the first man they see at the door of an embassy for "He'll be the butler"; issued a warning about social climbers, ". . . when they snow you with attention and invitations, however devastating your charm, they are doing it to promote their own business and social aspirations"; and admonished: "Don't try to corner the grain or the grape market if you want to go around socially . . . almost nobody in the society that counts drinks too much."

Knowing how important press relations are to any elected official, Betty said,

"It is easy to establish good relations with the press if you try the following:

"(a) Level with them. If you can't tell the truth, don't say anything.

"(b) Don't take a fearful or coy attitude toward them. It's an insult to their integrity and they are just as honorable as your colleagues: in many cases more so.

"(c) Don't woo the press with a party for the press only. It looks as if you didn't think they were good enough to associate with your other friends.

"(d) Don't act patronizing toward society reporters. In this city they don't write about canapes and clothes. They can make you far more palatable and personable in print than any of your political pronouncements, and in Washington everyone reads the women's pages to find out what is really going on. . . ."

Nor has Betty been too timid to shake a warning finger at prospective (or incumbent) wives of presidents. Here is a portion of her advice to Mrs. Nixon, in print five days after the latter had received the news that she was to become First Lady of the United States. Pat was to:

"Give regional encouragement to participation in the arts by inviting excellent regional groups from all over the U.S.A. to perform at 1600 Pennsylvania Avenue . . .

"Bring the White House into the electronic age (by televising great events and entertainment) . . .

"Take several [ambassador's wives] on a tour of your, and their, particular interests in America . . .

"Hire a press secretary who is a trained newswoman and whose one idea is to give to the press all she possibly can about the First Lady's activities and hers and the president's social functions instead of trying to withhold as much as possible, as was the case prior to Mrs. Carpenter's regime . . .

"Try to vary as much as possible your guest lists . . ."

Not everybody has such positive ideas. Mrs. Nixon handled the confrontation well. She remained silent, and went about doing things her own way. There's a strong will in that fragile-looking body, and Pat Nixon is one to run her own business.

Betty wrote an open letter of advice to Jacqueline Kennedy, too, in which she suggested that Jackie encourage the arts, vary the guest lists, restore the diplomatic dinners, hire both a press and a social secretary, hold monthly press conferences, change the receiving line from the Blue Room to the East Room, and improve the setting for White House dinners by lowering flower arrangements and turning lights low.

Jackie wrote back a personal letter within a few days, promising: "I have every intention of really trying hard at my new job. You will see—within a year I bet I will have done most of the things you suggested."

When Betty suggested in her column that Tricia Nixon put her hair up on her head and stop wearing it in "Alice in Wonderland style," Tricia told her, "I'll wear my hair short if you will let yours grow long." But Tricia at least partly heeded the advice, for not long afterward she appeared with her long hair pulled back in a much more sophisticated style.

Playing "Dear Abby" to the great is not, however, the meat-and-potatoes of Betty's column. The meat is scoops, such as Ethel Kennedy pushing Arthur Schlesinger and Mrs. Spencer Davis into the swimming pool at the famous RFK dinner which set the final *imprimatur* on the Kennedy administration at play, and the potatoes are the chitchat she picks up night after night as she makes her rounds.

"Embassy people in the main want their parties written up," she says with characteristic matter-of-factness. "It's good publicity, because it shows they are entertaining people who count in our government. They send clippings back home, and invite us to their parties for that reason. Diplomatic news has been a part of my column since the beginning."

With the authority of her unique position, Betty ranks people and when she does they stay ranked. She recently declared that:

"A foreign princess is now the top young hostess in Washington . . . the king of Morocco's 28 year-old sister has definitely established herself as a party giver with imagination and zing.

"The fact that she is the sister of a reigning king doesn't detract either from the glamor of Her Royal Highness Princess Lalla Nezha's hospitality . . .

"Her latest triumph was a hippie party. The wildly attired 50 or 60 guests, most of whom came down from New York, were presented with a handful of fresh flowers—daisies, anemones, and iris—when they walked in. Then they paused by a mirror where there were jars of fluorescent paint to add hippie décor to their faces."

It was tactful of Betty to use the words "top *young* hostess" because up to that time she had so consistently proclaimed the supremacy of the wife of the Spanish ambassador, the Marquesa de Merry del Val, that skeptics believed she was a B. B. invention. The marquesa's fabulous dresses, dazzling jewels, appropriately clever lines had been so thoroughly documented by Betty that when the *Washingtonian* magazine ran a profile entitled "The Remarkable Betty Beale," they puckishly kept reinserting the marquesa's name into a collage of the names Betty most frequently brings into her column.

The marquesa, whose husband has since been appointed ambassador to Japan from Spain, did indeed bring a considerable measure of throaty charm and vivacity to the generally humorless diplomatic scene. Her elevation by Betty to a sort of social Mt. Everest must have amused her quite as much as it did Betty's readers.

Though Betty never says an unkind word about anybody in print (she has a rigid code about this), she is merciless in private. "That social-climbing bitch!" she'll say of a newcomer to the social circuit. "Everybody knows she's been sleeping with every important man who asks her. I'm not going to mention anybody with so little breeding in *my* column!" The decision is usually final: the collapse of one successful annual charity ball is due at least in part to the fact that she refused to mention it at all one year because she considered the chairman an upstart.

Of her principal rival in the society-column field, Maxine Cheshire, Betty has nothing nice enough to say. With the straight face that has made her a first-class comedienne (in the days when the Women's National Press Club put on an annual revue, she always played a starring role), she'll lower her voice to confide, "I don't have anything against Maxine. I don't think she's nearly as bad a reporter as everybody else does."

Maxine got her revenge when Betty astonished Washington by announcing her engagement in her column in January 1969. Maxine wrote, to everybody's surprise, a few congratulatory paragraphs in the *Post*, in which she called George handsome, said she was very happy for Betty, and then suggested that some adjustments might be necessary for George, such as having to spend his evenings at "black-tie dinners where the menu is hand printed in French and there are at least three wine glasses."

Newsweek reported that Betty's counterreaction to this was, "At first I thought she was offering the olive branch, but then my friends showed me all the digs. She doesn't know how to be nice."

Whether Maxine went personally to the composing room, or whether a press-room foreman fond of practical jokes decided to play with the type that night nobody will ever know for sure, but when the write-up of Betty's wedding appeared in the *Post* it contained the following startling information:

"The ceremony took place at Bethlehem Chapel of the National Cathedral, with a reception for several hundred diplomats and socialists at the Sulgrave Club."

Just as Betty is probably the first columnist to announce her own engagement, she may be the first to have described a party of her own in print with the same zestful enthusiasm she brings to other people's. "Martha Mitchell had more dance partners than she could handle that night," she wrote of the dinner dance for 200 she and George gave with the Morse Dials (George's boss at Union Carbide) at the Federal City Club in the spring of '70. "For instance, tall, blond, well-heeled Herbert Klotz, Assistant Secretary of Commerce in the Kennedy Administration, was telling Mrs. M., 'I don't agree with anything you say, but I just love you.'"

The Graeber-Dial party "drew," to use one of Betty's favorite phrases, such a diverse gaggle of celebrities as HEW Secretary Robert Finch, Lynda Bird and Chuck Robb, Gwen, Perle, and Polly, as well as most of the dancing ambassadors and social members of Congress, proving that a key newswoman who chooses to entertain can draw as well or better than 99 out of 100 of the people she writes about.

Maxine's column in the *Post* is called "Very Important People" and some Very Important People indeed feed it the following kinds of information:

· "French President Charles de Gaulle, who restored Louis XIV's Grand Trianon at Versailles for just such an occasion, tried unsuccessfully to persuade President Richard M. Nixon to stay there during his forthcoming visit . . ."

· "President and Mrs. Nixon may have had more than one reason for inviting painter Andrew Wyeth to the White House state dinner last week. Our U.S. Ambassador to Belgium, John Eisenhower, has requested the loan of some Wyeth paintings for the embassy in Brussels."

· "Peter Hurd has done another likeness of Lyndon Baines Johnson that is never going to be exhibited anywhere . . . (a sketch of a horse using the LBJ profile as the animal's posterior)."

· "Senator Chuck Percy . . . won money at the Kentucky Derby by betting on a horse touted to him by President Nixon . . ."

Who, exactly, Maxine's sources are is always a subject of discussion whenever newsgirls get together. Some suspect Kay Graham, president of the Washington Post Company, who is of course invited everywhere and has a vested interest in creating a newsworthy columnist.

Undoubtedly the most controversial woman reporter in Washington (Maxine's critics, according to *Newsweek,* "argue that she is frequently inaccurate"), she doesn't so much cover society as investigate it, perhaps because she once was a police reporter on the *Knoxville News Sentinel.*

Like Rex Stout's detective Nero Wolfe, sitting among his orchids putting the pieces of a crime puzzle together, Maxine sits at her telephone ("I almost never get material at a party") gathering bits and pieces of gossip for her column. She seldom bothers with people on the purely local scene, except for such revelations as that Margot Hahn (the wife of the Republican chairman of the City Council), is making a preparation called "saucy mustard" in Mrs. Arthur W. Gardner's kitchen. Maxine calls people all over the world (she has said that her telephone bills run as high as $25,000 a year), and turns up some remarkable scoops, many having to do with real-estate transactions, income-tax returns, or financial deals:

· "Philanthropist Mary Lasker's foundation gave the White House's Elizabeth Carpenter $3,000 in 1966 to subsidize 'press hospitality' for Lady Bird Johnson's trip to Big Bend National Park." Maxine said Mrs. Lasker hoped the money would guarantee maximum news media coverage for the event and that the check was listed by the tax exempt Albert and Mary Lasker Foundation for that year under "civic and miscellaneous contributions." (Snapped Liz' husband, newspaperman Les Carpenter, "And part of the money went to install Johnnie-on-the-spot toilets along the Rio Grande for the use of reporters, including the one from the *Washington Post*.")

She revealed that a foundation financed by Schenley Industries' Lewis Rosenstiel had contributed more than 1 million dollars to establish a separate foundation honoring FBI Director J. Edgar Hoover. She also detailed the financial history of Dick Dickerson, husband of NBC commentator Nancy Dickerson. Her disclosure of Dick's finances shortly followed his resignation as president and executive officer of Liberty Equities Corporation, eight days after the Securities and Exchange Commission had suspended trading in the company's over-the-counter stock. Maxine noted that Dick was a "man with high White House connections when Lyndon B. Johnson was president," and that he "began his rapid rise in the autumn of 1964."

Maxine defended herself against those who cried "foul" (for her attack on a colleague) in an interview, saying that the information on Dickerson's difficulties had first appeared on the financial pages, that the story was both a newsy and fascinating account of a man's rise to power through influence and that there was no malice in her reporting.

Nancy, a former "close friend" of Maxine's, is said to have declared both Maxine and the *Post persona non grata*. But as Maxine told *Newsweek:* "My first responsibility is to my column and I have no loyalty to anyone else . . ." And in an interview with *Life*, she said: "The problem of society reporters has been that too many of them have cared more about their friends than their paper."

Hers is a different approach from that of her rival Betty Beale, who says that "No hostess with a grain of sense invites a reporter to a party who will sabotage her or her guests in her column the next day. To use someone's hospitality to hurt is self-destructive to a columnist. It closes doors. There are certain private things about everyone that shouldn't appear; I do not believe that is withholding news."

The two do agree wholeheartedly on one thing: they are not friends. Liz Carpenter loves to tell this story about them:

Life magazine was doing a story on the two of them and wanted to photograph them at a White House party. Betty and Maxine were both dressed to the nines, and highly sensitive to the fact that they were being covered as competitors. They didn't want to be photographed together, and stayed on opposite sides of the room. Both spent the reception hour vivaciously and ostentatiously in action. "There was no time," says Liz, "when the photographer couldn't have caught either one in a good pose. But the photographer knew that the key picture would show them together. He found a red velvet circular sofa in the China Room, which he immediately dubbed the love seat, and asked me if I could get the two of them on it." Liz did, "simply because by this time I had gotten so carried away by the whole project, it was amusing me and all the newswomen who were there. I just told them that they were both to come and sit on the velvet seat." They took their time getting there, outplaying each other, prima donna fashion, and finally they sat down on opposite sides. The photographer needed a wide lens to get them both in. "They wouldn't move closer together, and each tried to catch whoever was passing by in conversation so she would look like as if she was the one pursued. I don't think either one spoke to the other during the entire evening."

Maxine, one of the very few women with children (four) who has made it as a well-known Washington newspaper woman, is married to former United Press newsman Herbert Cheshire, who's now with McGraw-Hill. They met in Knoxville where Maxine, who was born in Harlan, Kentucky, went after going to the University of Kentucky, Union College in Barbourville, and the University of Tennessee. Along the way she won some beauty queen titles.

She came to Washington when Herb was transferred here, and got a job with the Women's Department of the *Post* where she did general assignment reporting until she started her column four years ago. There's no doubt that the column, which is syndicated in some 150 papers, is well read . . . gleefully when she takes out after someone the reader doesn't like, and furiously when the reader is the victim.

Kandy Shuman Stroud wrote in *Women's Wear Daily* that Maxine "is best described as the columnist who came to dinner . . . and probably never will again. Many of Washington's portals bar her entry. The Joseph Alsops cut her off their invitation list ages ago. Perle Mesta grits her diamonds at the mention of Maxine's name, because she once accused Perle of trying to upstage Ted Kennedy by giving a dinner party at the same time as his."

Pointing out some of Maxine's "goofs," Kandy tells about Maxine reporting "the British ambassador standing on a chair shouting gauche phrases to UPI wives in the British embassy, when in fact, his excellency was not even in town at the time"; and when Maxine said Ethel Kennedy brought pink silk sheets to Georgetown Hospital when she had Rory, her eleventh child, a story denied by all principals.

Maxine explains the pink silk sheets: "They deny it by saying the sheets were not 100 per cent silk. They may have been 60 per cent silk and 40 per cent Dacron. But I know from my sources that it was true."

Actually, the sheets were neither silk nor silk and Dacron. They were Porthault linen, which any of the Beautiful People will tell you are far more chic, and even more expensive, than silk.

Kandy Shuman Stroud, who has a few critics of her own, looks like one of the Beautiful People her paper loves to write about. She's chic, in her twenties, has a full mane of streaked blonde hair falling around her shoulders, and wears designer clothes—mini, midi, or maxi, whichever is IN at the moment—in size eight. Her boss, Lloyd Schwartz, Washington bureau chief of Fairchild Publications (*Women's Wear Daily,* plus three other dailies, four weeklies, a magazine and an audio-radio service) has what he calls a peculiar system of rating Washington newspaper women: "It's on the hardness scale, some are too hard and I like feminine women. I don't think just because you are a reporter and a woman that you have to be hard as nails. I rate them one to ten; one is soft, beyond five you are at the danger point. Kandy is soft."

If he means by "soft" looking feminine, acting like a lady, and speaking in a low, fashionable voice, he's right. But reporters competing with her on a story know they're up against a tough, hard-working reporter.

So does President Nixon. The night he escorted Golda Meir, Israel's prime minister, to her car after a state dinner in her honor, Kandy, along with other newswomen, was standing beneath the north portico at the White House. The president had said good night to his guest and started back up the steps when Kandy called, "Did you give her the jets?", a reference to the rumor that the purpose of Mrs. Meir's visit was to convince President Nixon the United States should sell jet planes to Israel. President Nixon threw up his hands and started to walk away, then turned back and said, "She makes quite a case."

Pat Nixon, too, might have run to the dictionary to recheck the definition of "soft" after reading some of Kandy's comments in WWD about her during the campaign:

"There's no denying her [Pat's] stiffness. Sometimes when Dick is speaking, she looks as though a laser beam couldn't melt her expression or her rigid posture, but some call it discipline. Others say it's because she's heard the same old speeches a hundred times, so she just tunes out.

"Pat and Dick seem to ignore each other. There's little obvious communication. They don't talk at rallies. She stays in the background, greets the people, signs autographs. If they are together, he does the talking. After all, they don't call him 'the Boss' for nothing."

Kandy had a big strike against her when *Women's Wear Daily* sent her to Washington in January 1968. The Johnson administration was furious with the paper, which had not only published details of Luci Johnson's wedding dress before release date (WWD said they got the description by good old *Front Page* sleuthing; the White House barred all WWD reporters from the wedding, saying WWD got copies of its "hold for release" description from other reporters). WWD had also made many uncomplimentary remarks about the "Birds" in a series of aviary stories about Lady Bird, Lynda Bird, Luci Bird, Lyndon Bird, the Bird House, Mama Bird, Baby Bird, Papa Bird, and so on. It also had carried the uncomplimentary two-page spread on Liz Carpenter titled "Loud Liz, the National Mouth," less than two months before Kandy checked in.

"I was terrified to call the White House," Kandy admits, "and Liz was very cold." Actually, she didn't have to spend too much time in or around the White House while the Johnsons were there. The campaign started and she, at various times, traveled with the McCarthys, Kennedys, Humphreys, Rockefellers, and Nixons, as well as covering both conventions, handicapped with a just-below-the-knee cast on a leg she broke skiing. "I wore that cast for over nine months—for a while it was up to my hip—and still had to keep up with all the other reporters. Consequently I wound up with Bobby Kennedy pushing me through the crowd, saying, 'Look out for this lady,' Ev Dirksen leading me around by the hand, and even Richard Nixon saying, 'Here's the lady with the cast.'"

Kandy married a handsome young doctor, Frank Stroud, in early 1969, though Bess Abell, then social secretary to Lady Bird Johnson, tried to discourage the marriage. Kandy wrote an article calling the appointment of Bess's husband Tyler to be chief of protocol "cronyism." A few days later when Kandy and Frank, then her fiancé, were at a party given by Nancy Dickerson, Bess told Dr. Stroud, "If I were you I wouldn't marry Kandy. She's a woman who turns on other women and writes about their husbands." Frank, who is doing his military service practicing pediatrics at the Navy Dispensary, ignored her advice and the two, with their baby daughter, live in a tremendous "pure Victorian" Georgetown house—where they entertain the capital's bright young people at elegant little dinners. Kandy reports such things as:

· President-elect Richard Nixon asking a woman who had reserved the Plaza Hotel grand ballroom for a wedding reception for her daughter to change the date since it was the same as the one Julie Nixon had chosen for her wedding. When the woman refused, said Kandy, the Nixons had to change their date.

· David Eisenhower wanting to serve in the Navy rather than the Army.

· Rita Hauser, Nixon's glamorous appointment as U.S. delegate to the U.N., giving up her seat at a White House state dinner for Golda Meir to "a Jewish man from Milwaukee who had raised such a fuss when he wasn't invited." Rita skipped the meal and came in for the entertainment only. Kandy didn't know it at the time, but the man from Milwaukee, an important Republican fund-raiser, was upset because, through a White House mistake, another Milwaukee man with the same name received the invitation which should have gone to the loyal GOP party member. The delighted "wrong" man accepted and attended.

Kandy is a fine example of how an energetic young woman can till the Washington vineyard, and there could be 12 of her at work without the surface of the society picture being more than scratched. As Kay Graham, publisher of the *Washington Post*, says, "In most places in America nobody cares what the upper crust does anymore. Here, because the upper crust is basically political, everyone cares."

Syndicated columnist Betty Beale chats with President Lyndon Johnson at a White House state dinner for the Emir of Kuwait.

Mrs. Richard Nixon is interviewed during the 1968 campaign by Washington newswomen (left to right) *Wauhillau La Hay,* Scripps Howard; *Isabelle Shelton,* Washington Star; *Nan Robertson,* The New York Times; *and Mary Wiegers,* Washington Post. COMPIX *Below, Marianne Means, columnist for King Features-Hearst Newspapers, interviews President John F. Kennedy in his White House office.* UPI *for* HEARST HEADLINE SERVICE

NBC's Nancy Dickerson and other members of the White House press talked informally with President Richard Nixon at a White House screening and dance given by Mrs. Nixon for Washington newswomen.

The President's telephone was hastily covered by a Secret Service agent, to keep newswomen from seeing the private numbers, the day Mrs. Nixon took women of the press on a tour of RMN's private office. Standing (left to right) are the Secret Service agent (unidentified), Pat Gates, U.S. Information Agency, Mrs. Nixon, Trude B. Feldman, Jewish Press (looking at flag), Isabelle Shelton, Washington Star, and Helen Thomas, UPI.

Tricia Nixon, elder daughter of President and Mrs. Nixon, explained to Marie Smith, Washington Post, the changes First Lady Pat Nixon had made in the yellow oval room of the White House, when Mrs. Nixon invited newswomen to see the newly redecorated family quarters. Back of Tricia is Angele Gingras, Bell-McClure Newspaper Syndicate; in the background are Winzola McLendon and Ann Wood, New York Daily News; and to the right of Marie Smith are Ymelda Dixon, Washington Star, and Barbara Furlow, U. S. News & World Report.

Walking through the ground floor corridor of the White House are Betty Beale, Washington Star; Kandy Shuman Stroud, Women's Wear Daily; Tricia Nixon; and Ymelda Dixon, Washington Star.

Syndicated columnists Malvina Stephenson and Vera Glaser (left and right) have a fast interview with the talkative Martha Mitchell and her husband Attorney General John Mitchell, at a Washington party. REPUBLICAN CONGRESSIONAL COMMITTEE PHOTO

Taking notes at a press briefing held by First Lady Pat Nixon's staff director are (left to right) Marikaye Presley, Dallas News; Hazel Markel, Palm Beach Life; Vera Glaser, Knight Newspapers; Fay Gillis Wells, Storer Broadcasting Co.; Frances Lewine, Associated Press; and Helen Thomas, UPI. In the background is Sara McClendon, El Paso Times.

A broken leg didn't keep Kandy Shuman Stroud (right) *of* Women's Wear Daily, *from covering the 1968 Presidential primaries. Here she is talking with Mrs. Robert Kennedy whose late husband was campaigning for the Democratic Party's nomination as a Presidential candidate.* FRANK DIERNHAMMER, WOMEN'S WEAR DAILY

Clare Crawford, Washington Daily News, *stopped to interview her former classmate from the University of Maryland, Connie Stuart, following a press briefing in the White House theater. Connie is now staff director to First Lady Pat Nixon.* LOU HOLLIS, WASHINGTON DAILY NEWS

During the Johnson Administration, Liz Carpenter (standing by mantel) held press briefings in the White House library.

Barbara Coleman (kneeling) interviewing Mrs. Lyndon B. Johnson, aboard a plane, for the "Here's Barbara" television show, during one of the First Lady's frequent trips. Liz Carpenter, Mrs. Johnson's press secretary, is standing behind her. Below, Shirley Elder, who covers the Hill for the Washington Star, and a newspaper colleague interview Congressman John Anderson of Illinois (in foreground).

Free-lancer Anne Chamberlin with Senator Edward Brooke of Massachusetts at the Valco Aluminum Smelting Plant in Ghana where she followed him to get material for a Cosmopolitan profile.

"Covering the Hill is just like covering the State House, there's the same bull, only it's on a broader scope."

A lot of reporters much prefer covering the Hill to the White House. They like the variety of dealing with 535 separate princelings instead of the same old king day after day. To others, it's a frightening assignment, because the closer one gets to the U.S. Congress, the further away it goes. It appears on the maps and charts to be connected with the rest of the city, and the constitution claims it is the third branch of government. But on closer inspection it turns out to be an entirely separate world referred to locally as "the Hill."

The geography seems sensible and orderly enough, rather like a medium-size college campus: a stately parade of buildings, surrounded by lawns, curving walks, formal gardens, and perpetually filled parking lots.

To the north are the two Senate office buildings—the Old SOB, as wags love to call it, which has majestic high ceilings, a noble marble staircase, and splendid ornate committee rooms; and the New SOB, which looks like a bleached marble box, with low ceilings, slippery floors, small windows sealed shut, stale air, peculiar acoustics, and other technological improvements.

It takes an Old, New, and New New office building, to the south of the Capitol, to shelter the 435 members of the House of Representatives. The two older buildings are scaled to comfortable proportions. The New New, or Rayburn Building, looks rather like the Dalai Lama's palace in Tibet. It is a shocking waste of the taxpayers' money and it appears that there are a lot of financial shenanigans connected with it to boot.

Although the late Capitol Architect, George Stewart, who was not an architect at all but an engineer, kept telling Congress that the Capitol building itself would collapse if they didn't add four dining rooms, two cafeterias, two auditoriums, a batch of conference rooms, offices, storage space, and several acres of fresh marble to the West Front, it looks steady enough to the naked eye. The sheer weight of the cumbersome machinery of government might collapse it far more rapidly than nature could.

There is also a teeming life underneath all this, including small open subway trains to whisk the members from their offices to their respective chambers in time to vote or answer quorum calls. (When the last Senate subway was dedicated, one of the orators of the day called it the "Swift Chariot of Democracy.") There are several layers of garages, and miles of subterranean passages filled with old furniture, stationery stores, snack bars, cafeterias, and even a hairdressing establishment.

Most congressional offices resemble the stateroom scene from the Marx Brothers' *Night at the Opera*. Newspapers, file folders, letters, and pamphlets are piled in the chairs, on top of the file cabinets, on the rug, on the desks, in the IN boxes and OUT boxes. Each senator and congressman manages a patch of office space behind closed doors entirely to himself, but when he wants to venture out into the world, or even down the hall to the men's room (if he hasn't one of his own), he has to fight his way through a coat closet, past the mimeograph machine, around the office coffee pot, and across the knees of half a dozen secretaries and assistants, all of whom seem permanently locked in conversation over big console telephones with light-up buttons that look like mini-computers. If there is a sofa in the outer office, it usually contains three constituents in shirtsleeves, two cameras, a ladies' tote bag, an umbrella and a home-town telephone book.

It is pounded into everyone's head in political science courses that the real work of Congress is accomplished in committees. It also goes on, if you know where to look, in party caucuses, telephone calls, chance encounters in the cloakrooms, informal meetings in the various "hideaway offices" scattered among the nooks and crannies of the Capitol, and at certain tables at certain hours in the various private dining rooms.

When Congress is in session, the House meets at noon, and there is a lively moment while the clerk reads the roll as though he were calling hogs at a country fair. There's a great surging turbulence of people coming and going, shouting "Here!" when they hear their names and thumping each other on the back.

Next thing, nearly everyone has vanished into thin air. From the gallery one face can't be told from another. Apparently they want it that way. The guards treat anyone pulling a pair of opera glasses out of her purse as if she were sneaking out a hand grenade. Glasses are against House rules—along with amplifiers, microphones, and tape recorders. It would be a help to reporters if the Congressmen all wore numbered jerseys, like football players.

The Senate is not quite so confusing. There are fewer senators to keep track of, and they sit at assigned 1819-style desks each equipped with an inkwell, a penholder and a glass shaker filled with blotting sand.

Armed with a seating chart, the reporter can at least try to recognize the names and number of the players. The trouble is that 50 per cent of the time they are visiting around at other senators' desks, and 90 per cent of the time they aren't in the Senate chamber at all, except for a quorum call or a vote.

It is odd to watch some lone Senator standing at his desk delivering a moving speech on a crucial subject affecting the destiny of our planet to a rapt audience of one *Congressional Record* reporter, taking flowing shorthand notes in black ink. What few other Senators there are on hand appear to be using their time to answer mail.

Speaking of the *Congressional Record*, in spite of its reporters' diligent shorthand notes, it doesn't exactly print what everybody said in the House or Senate. Each Senator and Congressman is allowed to "Revise and Extend" his remarks to express what he wishes he'd said, rather than what he actually did say. So, unless a reporter's hearing is sharp, her pencil fast, and she happens to be in the gallery precisely at the right moment, the spice of the day's debate in its true form sinks forever without a trace the instant the words are uttered. What senators mostly want removed is their insults to one another, some of them pretty spicy.

If the Hill is a kingdom separate from the rest of Washington, the House and Senate are sub-kingdoms, and each senator and congressman rules over a mini—occasionally maxi—kingdom of his own. Even the young Senate pages, as LBJ protégé Bobby Baker illustrated, can grow up to run a considerable dukedom.

The reporters who cover the Hill have their own seniority system. Some of the old hands are like a third branch of Congress and more than once they have played a considerable part in starting congressional investigations—or even initiating legislation. Not too long ago Sanford "Whitey" Waltzman, a reporter for the *Cleveland Plain Dealer*, got so involved in a bill authorizing the Pentagon to check contractors' books for possible overcharges that by the time the House passed it he was calling it "my bill." It was. He had privately urged certain congressmen to introduce it, and kept nudging them to see that it moved along until it reached a vote.

The daily papers, wire services, photographers, TV, radio, and magazines each have their own "galleries" in both the House and Senate side of the Capitol. These are not only a set of assigned seats overlooking each chamber, but also offices with desks, the ubiquitous leather couches, telephones, and a few employees who keep track of mail, releases, speech texts, and messages to call the office.

There are reserved press tables in the House and Senate dining rooms. At certain times reporters are allowed on the floor of both Senate and House, and the rest of the time they can send in notes to call members off the floor for a chat.

Only a handful of women have managed, after a hard fight, to become full-fledged Hill correspondents. There were 50 accredited correspondents to the Capitol in 1850, all male, until a determined newswoman from the *New York Tribune*, Jane Grey Swisshelm, appealed to President Millard Fillmore for his personal help to break down the press gallery's "no female" rule. Few followed Jane (perhaps because Mary J. Windle, an accredited reporter during the Civil War, was thrown into prison by Lincoln as a Confederate spy) until World War II, which, as pointed out earlier, was the springboard into journalism for many women, there being so few men left in the city rooms.

Even then, though women were allowed in the press gallery, it was not without discrimination. They didn't have a rest room, and the press gallery's standing committee, made up of newspapermen, wouldn't let them have one. The women argued that the men had a "men's" room, so why shouldn't they have a "ladies" room? The standing committee was adamant. Led by May Craig, correspondent for several Maine newspapers, the women did an unprecedented thing, which was to ignore the committee and take their case directly to the Senate Rules Committee and the Speaker of the House. The problem of the ladies' rest room was brought before the full membership of both houses which voted overwhelmingly in favor. Incidentally, Mrs. Craig (known to millions of TV watchers as the reporter in the flowery hat who was always recognized at press conferences by Presidents Eisenhower, Kennedy, and Johnson) pulled the same thing on the Air Force. When she was going to Europe to do a story on the Army, she insisted that a ladies' room be set aside on one of its B-29s.

Even today, equal as women are, men are more so. There is something intractably male about the Hill set-up. As a female threads her way through the main press gallery, she feels she has wandered unbidden into a murky enclave of dark leather, old cigar butts and spittoons, an enclave in which she looks faintly out of place. There is a sort of locker-room rapport between the newsmen and the senators and congressmen they cover, full of jokes and knowing references that escape her understanding unless she's hung around that locker room a long, long time.

Nonetheless, there *are* a few women who have found success and happiness on the Hill. Some of the ones who stand out are:

Marjorie Hunter of *The New York Times*, Liz Wharton of UPI, Shirley Elder of the *Washington Star*, and Norma Milligan of *Newsweek*.

By the time they've learned enough to be good at the job, none of the women reporters on the Hill are exactly teenyboppers any more; the basic physical requirements are strong legs to carry them from offices to hearing rooms to the Capitol and back without a heart seizure, the digestive system of a horse— even congressmen's wives have begun to complain about the high cholesterol, low protein, and zero charm diet dished up to their husbands in the House restaurant—and a knack for surviving without sleep.

As Norma Milligan of *Newsweek* says, "During the thirties the famous ad was that you'd walk a mile for a Camel cigarette; well, up here, we'd walk five miles for a congressman any day, if he's making news. I wear out a pair of shoes a month just tramping between the House and Senate office buildings."

The daily gallop chasing news around the Hill reminds one again of college—except that some days all the classes seem to meet at once. There is even a system of bells in all the buildings when the Senate and House are in session, so that when the members are not on the floor they'll know they should dash over for a quorum call or a vote (different bells for each). A typical scene takes place in the Senate dining room when the buzzer rings for a vote and half the people in the room drop their forks and dash off—the senators rushing out to vote and the other Senate staffers rushing to the nearest telephone to make sure "their" senator has heard the bell, and to remind him what the vote is about.

Marjorie Hunter of *The New York Times* adores the Hill. "I prefer the House to the Senate," she says. "It is more of a challenge, and also you have easier access to people. It is group, rather than individual, politics. The Senate is one hundred personalities, while on the House side there are far more Indians than chiefs."

She covered the North Carolina Legislature for her hometown paper, the *Raleigh News and Observer*, for six years, and spent ten with the *Winston-Salem Journal* before coming to Washington at the invitation of her editor, who had taken a job with *The Times.* He subsequently went back to take over as publisher of the Winston-Salem paper, but by that time she was hooked and couldn't bear to leave. In her opinion, covering her state legislature was invaluable training. "Understanding the basic nature of democratic politics, which is to say compromise between opposing forces, can best be accomplished on the state level, because when it's national, although it's the same in principle, it's vastly more complicated."

Marjorie has had her share of scoops covering the Hill; two that stand out irritated President Johnson very much. One involved his poverty program. President Johnson had a task force working to draw up legislation for the program when she was told, by one of those mysterious sources, exactly what was going to be in the legislation, and wrote a story about it. Later Pat Moynihan, then an LBJ administration official and now one of President Nixon's trusted advisors, told her that President Johnson "had a fit, and the only thing that saved my job was assuring the President that I didn't know you."

Another Marjorie scoop was the news that President Johnson had decided to name Hubert Humphrey as the person to pull together all of the Great Society's domestic programs. Someone told her, and naturally she used it. President Johnson was "furious. He thought Hubert had blabbed," she says.

The New York Times is an unusually liberal paper when it comes to giving leeway to its reporters. As the aristocrat of the newspaper world, it can hire anybody it wants to, talk to anybody it wants to (as Arthur Krock abundantly demonstrated in his memoirs), and print anything it wants to. Just as it carries no frying chicken ads and few routine crime stories, it loftily disdains to report an event just because it happened. To be interesting enough for the *Times*, a story must be interesting in Hong Kong, New Delhi, and wherever else the sun sets on the *Times'* worldwide empire.

Thus Marjorie's first task when she arrives at the House press gallery every week-day morning that Congress is in session, after having read the whole of the morning *Times* (Washington circulation 10,000 of the most influential people in town), is to decide what is worthy of her paper's attention. On any given day, there are a dozen or more committee hearings on both the Senate and the House sides. Some hearings with potential news might fizzle out like a flat bottle of champagne; others produce unexpected fireworks.

She tries to drop in on as many of the committee meetings as possible, but says the only way to get a really good story is to talk to the congressmen in private to find out what's on their minds. Then she can write the background if there's going to be a fight. Background and in-depth stories is what the *Times* wants.

While the House and Senate, which convene at noon, are calling the roll, Marjorie grabs some lunch and figures out the agenda for the afternoon. By three o'clock she has called her office to tell them what she expects to make her big story for the day. If Congress is especially busy, she might write two stories.

Asked if it is a disadvantage being a woman on the Hill, Marjorie is one of the few who says "no," though it must be remembered that being with *The Times* gives her a special status. "In some ways I have a terrific advantage. There are so many men that it's confusing for a senator or a congressman to remember what paper everybody represents. They can find the *Times* just by looking for 'that blonde woman.' And it makes a big difference to be known when you want to find out something in a hurry."

Shirley Elder, who covers Congress for the *Washington Star,* doesn't totally agree. "There's no girl up here who's a real confidante of the great or near-great, simply because men find it so difficult to be buddy-buddy with a girl." Shirley, an iconoclast at heart (or rather, the sort of person who dares tell the emperor he has no clothes on) has wanted to work on the Hill since she first came to Washington from Seattle some 15 years ago. "The White House beat is considered the peak of jobs in Washington, but I think it's a great bore because all the news is funnelled through the White House press aides. For all its prestige, the White House press corps relies essentially on canned news. Here, we get our own news, and generally straight from the horse's mouth."

An attractive single girl in her thirties with a filing-cabinet mind, Shirley, who is now the *Star's* senior reporter for the

House, (she covered District affairs for them for several years), also finds the House more interesting than the Senate. She credits the difference to the House's five-minute limitation on debate. "It forces them to think quickly and speak concisely. In the Senate, they can drone on and on. Also, House members are more intimately involved with legislation, whereas Senators rely on their staff members to do the bulk of their legislative work, so are seldom as closely in touch with what is going on."

A typical day for Shirley begins between 9:30 and 10 A.M. in the House press gallery, where she figures out which committee hearings will provide the best stories for her afternoon paper. The name of the game is picking the right hearing. Two events that Hill reporters on the House side normally cover are Republican Leader Gerald Ford's press conferences following the weekly meetings of congressional GOP leaders with the president and Speaker John McCormack's daily 11:55 meeting with the press in his office.

"Not that it is any loss to miss McCormack's press conferences," says Shirley. "He is old and creaky, and though he's supposed to be a leader, I find him a classic example of a follower. Old-timers recall that when he was majority leader [just one step down from Speaker], he was effective. But those years of strong Democratic leadership from the White House seem to have softened him. He has a great memory, though, for every favor he ever did for anyone, and feels betrayed if a colleague forgets those favors and balks."

Shirley illustrates her point with this story: Congressman Sid Yates of Illinois was defeated in one election, thus breaking his line of seniority. When he was re-elected two years later, Majority Leader McCormack just winked, and simply added all Yates' service together so he could still have a suite in the new Rayburn office building. When Yates voted against the leadership on the bill to extend the 10 per cent surcharge on income taxes, one of McCormack's top aides was heard to mutter, "That's appreciation for you. And after all we did to get him his beautiful new office."

When McCormack announced in the spring of 1970 that he wasn't going to run again, Shirley wrote the *Star's* front-page story on it with relish. Privately she said, "The Speaker's post is hard to give up. Not the least of the perquisites of the office is the $40,000 a year doorkeeper who follows behind the Speaker as he goes to the House floor each day and brushes the dandruff off his suitcoat."

Reporters also try not to miss the daily ritual known as the "one minutes." Formally, it is called the "morning hour," and though it rarely lasts an hour, it is a period of time right after the House convenes at noon when the members can talk about anything they want, so long as they don't hog the floor longer than one minute. Often, these talks produce nuggets of news, or hints of something bigger to come. The only trouble, from a reporter's point of view, is that they're so hard to hear.

"Some Congressmen are such mutterers they can't be understood even when they use the mike," says Shirley. "I often wonder whether the American public would elect some of the guys if they could see them at work. There are some you can't talk to after midafternoon, because they may already be drunk. One Marylander regularly attends House sessions, but seldom hears anything because he's asleep. Two soft old white-haired gentlemen from New England always sit together and almost always nap. Sometimes you can't tell whether they're dozing or not."

After the morning hour comes the quorum call, which is simply a reading of the roll but, for 435 names, takes half an hour or so. This is when the reporters go to lunch, either at the table set aside for them in the restaurant or, when the weather is nice, under a spreading elm tree on the Capitol lawn. While picnicking, they stare at the tourists (who are staring at them), and listen for the bells that call the House to order. If invited by a congressman, they eat in the members' dining room (beer, but no Bloody Marys). Occasionally, they go to the "Rotunda," the "Monocle," or one of the other jammed, expensive restaurants within walking distance of the Capitol where lobbyists and constituents take members of Congress or their principal assistants and/or girl friends. Most of the restaurants are conveniently dark and noisy, with piped-in message systems so a member can be called over the loudspeaker if he should have to hurry back to the floor for a key vote. It doesn't look well to miss too many of those, and at least one Democrat, Senator Proxmire of Wisconsin, boasts regularly of his nearly 100 per cent voting record.

Reporters devote the afternoons to catching up with what they missed in the morning, and trying to find out what's going to happen tomorrow. The best place to start is the Speakers' lobby, which is just off one side of the House chamber and is open only to congressmen, the press, and a few staff people. During roll calls, House members can be snagged as they arrive to answer their names. If they slip by, the doorkeepers will ask them to come out into the lobby to talk to reporters, who then have a chance to quiz them about their activities in an informal, relaxed setting.

Speakers' lobby interviews are useful for keeping track of the running story, like Rep. Richard D. McCarthy of New York's continuing battle with the Defense Department over the production, testing, and storage of germ and nerve gas weaponry. On any given day, McCarthy is quite likely to have fired off a letter to Defense Secretary Melvin Laird, or to have gotten a reply from an earlier letter. Also, when congressional reaction to something—presidential statements, the war, taxes—is needed, the speediest way to catch members is in the Speakers' lobby.

Inevitably, reporters get to know and like some congressmen better than others. Some are so obscure that no one in the press gallery can recognize them. But there are many stars. Shirley says of these: "McCarthy has a nicely balanced sense of humor that keeps his crusades in sensible perspective. Andy Jacobs of Indianapolis can be a real old-style comedian, and he even looks a little like one of the Smothers Brothers. Edith Green of Oregon is competent and hard-working. She, too, has a sense of humor—that's an essential. Missouri's Richard Bolling is brilliant and knows as much about House inner workings as anyone.° John Moss of California, John Brademas of Indiana, and Henry Reuss of Wisconsin are earnest and dedicated. In due course, you learn to approach each one differently."

Most are cooperative with the press; only a few aging Southerners see the papers as a consistently hostile force. "They're peddling their own point of view, always, so it's the reporter's job to sort things out and try to differentiate between truth and wishful thinking."

° Congressman Bolling's book, *House Out of Order*, is considered to be required reading for anyone covering the Hill.

Norma Milligan gets to the Hill at about the same time as Shirley, but since she works for a weekly magazine, *Newsweek*, she has time to drop by the periodical gallery to pick up the *Congressional Record* and to finish the morning papers. She goes to House Minority Leader Gerald Ford's meeting with the press, then rushes back to the Senate in time for the "dugout session"—the 15 minutes the press is allowed on the Senate floor before the session begins. "You stand in the well of the Senate and wait until Mike Mansfield, the Majority Leader, and Minority Leader Hugh Scott come to their desks. If Sam Shaffer, *Newsweek*'s chief congressional correspondent, is there, he will take one and I will take the other. If he's not, I try to listen to both. If there is a big story, whatever Mansfield says about it he will say at the dugout session."

The minute the buzzer sounds, all reporters have to get off the floor, some to head for the press gallery, others to hearings and press conferences.

One of the trends worth watching on the Hill these days, according to Norma, is a political generation gap. "Before 1968, most of the committees were controlled by the conservatives, because the South was consistently Democratic for so long. Today a new coalition is emerging. There are young men on both sides of the aisle who are challenging the old system."

Norma, who is in her forties like most of the "name" newswomen, grew up in Heavener, Oklahoma (population 2,200). In about 1945, after attending the University of Oklahoma, Norma came to Washington, took a Civil Service exam, and landed in the Veterans Administration as a stenographer. After a year, Norma couldn't "stand it any more," and an employment agency sent her to Ernest K. Lindley, the Washington bureau chief of *Newsweek*, who was looking for a secretary. He told her she looked too thin. Norma, who is still a size six, replied, "I've always heard that it takes a lean horse for a long race." She got the job.

After nine years, she made the jump from secretary to reporter and covered the White House social scene during both the Kennedy and Johnson administrations. She was a "pool" reporter for the Luci Johnson–Pat Nugent wedding and was assigned a spot 15 feet from the altar in the Shrine of the Immaculate Conception behind a palm. But, she says, "The real emotional experience of my life was a hike through the giant California redwoods with Lady Bird Johnson."

Being a woman reporter on the Hill, those who cover it say, is not too different from being a man reporter. Eileen Shanahan, who covers financial affairs for *The New York Times,* says her news sources assume she knows what she is doing simply because she is working for the most influential paper in the country. Margaret Kilgore, who covered the Hill for UPI until December 1969, when she was assigned to Vietnam, says covering the Hill is just like covering a state house: "There's the same bull, only on a broader scope."

Correspondents for the smaller papers around the country have a different role to play. They are supposed to watch their own home-state congressional delegations, and therefore seldom need to pry information from a stranger. Nina Auchincloss Steers, correspondent for the Chattanooga, Tennessee, *Times,* is one of the most beauteous of these. A half-sister of Jackie Kennedy, Nina has the flair for clothes, the charm, and the aristocratic disdain for the mundane that characterizes the family. In addition to reporting once a week on the activities of the Tennessee delegation for her paper, she is finishing a biography of the late Senator Gore of Oklahoma. It took a good deal for Nina to close the credibility gap, but she has done it with an intensity and a seriousness of purpose which have convinced the men she writes about that she's not just another one of the Beautiful People amusing herself with politics.

Barbara Kober is one of the very few reporters assigned to the Hill for the women's angle only . . . for the *Washington Star's* women's section. She covered the United Nations for Hearst, the White House for the Carpenter News Service, and Embassy Row for the *Star* before going to the Hill where she says 75 per cent of the Washington news can be found.

"It's easier to find out what the president is doing or thinking by going to Capitol Hill than to the White House," she claims. "Legislation often rises and falls on the waves of the president's support or opposition. But when I want to find out how the administration feels about a proposed bill, I don't ask the president's press secretary, I find a faithful news source on Capitol Hill."

Barbara keeps tabs on women members of Congress, wives of congressmen, legislation concerning women, and picks up such scoops as an exclusive interview with Mrs. Adam Clayton Powell, when Congress coaxed her up from Puerto Rico to testify about the salary checks her congressman husband made out in her name, but which she said she never received.

Barbara is blonde, pretty, and looks like "the girl next door." Her sense of humor is her most outstanding feature. At a dinner in her honor, she made the following comment: "The story of my life is being where the action isn't. I was at the White House when Soviet Premier Khrushchev was pounding his famous shoe on the United Nations' table, and at the United Nations when President Kennedy was assassinated."

Barbara would like to go back to the old days when there was a "leg man" and a writer. "I'm a writer, but a lousy reporter. I'm basically timid and hate bothering people with questions. I'm a poet and if I had the guts to do it, I'd quit and start on my own." She does admit that she enjoyed having President Kennedy call her by her first name, dancing (three times at one party) with President Johnson, and being one of the first to interview President Eisenhower the day after he left office.

"There is a great need in this profession for women who care enough, are dedicated enough to take the time to be professional," she says. "It is no longer possible for reporters to be hacks." As for the people she covers on the Hill, "There isn't a perfect member of Congress, but I also don't know a completely stupid, completely dishonest, completely disinterested or completely bad one, either."

In addition to reporters who concentrate entirely on the Hill, there are several women who are highly knowledgeable about Congress, even though their work keeps them poking about in nooks and crannies all over the rest of government.

Esther Van Wagoner Tufty, known as "The Duchess" because of the imposing blonde braids she wears around her head like a coronet out of a Holbein portrait, has her own bureau representing some 300 papers in New York State and her home state of

Michigan, where her brother Murray D. Van Wagoner was Democratic governor at the time of the Franklin D. Roosevelt New Deal.

She spends 75 percent of her time on the Hill, "because anything of interest to my papers is bound to filter through the offices of the senators and congressmen. Once I get wind of it there, I go out and track it down." She is the only woman to have been president of the Women's National Press Club, the American Newspaper Women's Club, and the American Women in Radio and TV, and perhaps the only living woman to have gone overseas as a war correspondent in World War II, Korea, and Vietnam, where she was one of the first reporters to be shot at in a helicopter and the first woman to interview wounded soldiers aboard the Navy hospital ship *Repose*.

Perhaps the best known, outside Washington, of any of the women manning their own bureaus is Sarah McClendon, famous as a fearless interrogator of presidents at their televised news conferences. Among her many electrifying salvos was her question to President Eisenhower about which policy decisions Vice President Richard Nixon had helped to make. Many think Ike's reply that, if given a week, he might think of some, may have cost Nixon the 1960 election.

She has also demanded how 400 acres of cabbages, about to be plowed under, could be gotten to the people of Appalachia, who had not had anything green in their government-subsidized diet for six months . . . why widows were being allowed to lose their homes in transactions in which the Federal Housing Administration's policies helped to fleece them . . . why troops were sent to Lebanon without consent of Congress . . . why each member of Congress was not sent copies of the president's speeches (that oversight was corrected instantly) . . . why "two well-known security risks" were allowed to reorganize the State Department. The president—John F. Kennedy—asked her for their names, she told him and the ensuing uproar has scarcely yet died down. Lawsuits were threatened, and Sarah was barred from using a State Department telephone. Sarah is unrepentant. She believes what she learned in journalism school—that being a reporter is "a public trust."

Recently she upset a Nixon press conference when she asked:

"Mr. President, would you please tell us when you are going to make some real, honest-to-goodness changes in personnel in these bureaucrats who have been in power through many generations who are still wasting the taxpayers' money and making errors on the war and policy and promoting their friends, who are unqualified, to high jobs? I refer particularly to the office in the Pentagon of Assistant Secretary of Defense Barry J. Shillito." President Nixon replied: "I don't know the gentleman, but after that question I'm going to find out." Evidently, as it turned out, the president had forgotten appointing Mr. Shillito, a Johnson administration appointee, to his Defense Department job in February 1969.

The reactions of Sarah's fellow reporters to her techniques range from fascination to outrage and horror. *The New York Times* and the *Washington Post,* among others, wrote irate editorials against Sarah following the Shillito question. On the other hand, NBC's David Brinkley pointed out on the evening news that "Sarah's questions are often useful . . . press conferences lose their usefulness if reporters are afraid to ask ugly questions." Once, after she wrote a note of apology to President Eisenhower, fearing she had asked him too sharp a question, Ike wrote a friendly note back, saying, "no apology was needed."

Sarah was born in Tyler, Texas, and graduated from the University of Missouri School of Journalism in 1931. She has operated her own Washington news bureau since 1946, sending a regular column and other news stories to clients all over the South and Southwest as well as doing almost daily radio broadcasts for a South Carolina station. She cheerfully admits that her independent spirit has cost her several jobs. She tries not only to be a reporter, she says, but also "to perform some public good" in her work by being "a clarifying, revealing, simplifying, humanizing person, even at times a sort of catalytic agent who makes news for others and sometimes for the whole country as well as getting her own story."

A case in point was the time, during the Johnson administration, when she asked Secretary of Defense Clark Clifford if President Johnson knew before he announced the bombing halt in North Vietnam that the South Vietnamese would not go along. Secretary Clifford took 25 minutes to outline details of what happened in the White House leading up to the announcement, and to acknowledge that this was the case.

"And yet," Sarah points out, "this was the obvious question to ask and no one else was asking it though the conference had gone on for some time." Her technique is always to ask the key question, "the thing about which people want to know at the time. How odd it is that many other reporters do not. Some Presidents may come away from conferences wondering why no reporters ask the obvious questions."

Sarah gets very much put out with anyone who thinks her questions are planted by others: "Nobody ever gives me questions. I have people calling me long distance wanting me to ask things for them and I tell them I have my own questions; they are mine, and I take responsibility for them. Sometimes newspapermen walk up and want me to ask a question, saying, 'I don't have the nerve.' Many times women have far more courage than men."

Along with asking questions of presidents, Sarah continues with her investigative reporting and turns up many firsts. She was the first to find out that President Johnson had turned down the portrait Peter Hurd had painted of him. It was printed in one of her Texas papers and picked up by one of the wire services, but didn't cause a ripple until a large metropolitan paper printed it. Only then did it become a great story, with Johnson's opinion of the painting, "The ugliest thing I ever saw," becoming one of his most widely quoted remarks.

Sarah also had the first story about Bobby Baker, secretary to the Senate Democratic majority leader and protégé of Lyndon Johnson, who later lost his job after he was accused of being involved in "wheeling-dealing" scandals.

"Somebody gave me this and I thought it was too big for my little Texas papers alone, although I sent it to them. Since it was national news I was on the telephone all weekend trying to market it. The *Des Moines Register Tribune* and the *Chicago Tribune* told me that there couldn't be anything to it or their man in Washington would have had it. The *Washington Post* wouldn't use it. Finally that dear, sweet North American Newspaper Alliance took it. NANA had it on the wire when I got a telephone call from Walter Jenkins (then an aide to President Johnson) saying my Texas paper had called to tell them at the White House what was in the story. Walter ordered me not to print it. I told him not to treat me like a criminal because this story was too big to hold back. Clark Mollenhoff (then with the Cowles publications, later an aide to President Nixon and now back with Cowles) told me, 'I won't have anything to do with it because when you stir dirty apples you get dirty.' Later he and every damn person in the world jumped on it."

The Bobby Baker story wasn't the first one she wrote that irritated LBJ. When he was in the House, she once angered him so much he cornered her and shook his finger in her face. "I shook my finger right back and said the story was true and that I was not going to be anyone's henchman, that I was going to be an honest reporter. Johnson wants someone he can trust who will always write his side, and this is what he had with some Texas reporters."

Mentioning Texas reminds Sarah of the way some editors and publishers think they should staff their Washington offices during different administrations: "With Johnson, there were quite a few Texans added. They brought in a lot of fresh, beautiful women when Kennedy came in. Now that Nixon is in, the editors are sending a lot of strange new men." Hard as it would be to document this statement, it probably has some truth to it, since Sarah is known for her bulldozing accuracy.

By and large, she likes the Hill. "I had read so much in *Life* and *Time* and other magazines making fun of Congress that I figured all of them were crooked politicians and that they weren't capable and I was prepared to have no respect for them. But when I started on the Hill, I began to learn about these people and how they work, and now I see how many of them try very hard, or have limitations and try to overcome them. I also see what long hours many of them work and how sincerely many want to make the system better, and what high and lofty ideals some of them have. I also see some who are crooked and some who are no good. But the more I observe how it works, the more respect I have for Congress, individually and collectively."

Sarah is founder and director of the McClendon Press Briefing group, which she started some six years ago because she thought (1) women did not have the same access to news sources that men did, (2) it would help make women better reporters by giving them more ease and confidence. "We need more women reporters to ask questions because women are good at that. I've been to many press conferences that were pretty dull because all the questions were asked by men."

Editors and male reporters (even many newswomen) didn't take the McClendon Press Briefings seriously at first. Reporters were assigned to them only if it was convenient. Then came the J. Edgar Hoover briefing.

Sarah arranged in November 1964 for the FBI director, who wasn't prone to giving interviews, to meet with women reporters in his office, where he surprised all of them by talking for almost three hours on a variety of subjects, dropping such pearls as, "Around Philadelphia, Mississippi, law enforcement is practically nil and many times sheriffs and deputies participate in crime," and his opinion that the Rev. Dr. Martin Luther King Jr. was "the most notorious liar in the country" when he claimed that FBI agents in Georgia would take no action on civil rights complaints.

Few metropolitan papers sent reporters to the briefing. Fortunately, the *Washington Post* sent Elizabeth Shelton, a top-notch reporter who for many years was night editor of the *Post's* women's section (no small job on a paper that remade its women's pages right along with its city, national, and world pages until long after midnight). Elizabeth, called "Dottie" by her friends and no relation to Isabelle Shelton of the *Star*, took the whole three-hour McClendon Briefing down in shorthand and was able to supply not only her own paper, but the wires as well with such other Hoover observations as:

· It was not the FBI's business to guard anyone, including protecting of the president and "wet-nursing" those who "go down to reform the South."

· There was police participation in crime in several Midwestern cities.

· The FBI director was "in violent disagreement with the bleeding hearts who want to raise the age of juvenile delinquency to 21. I believe it should be down to 16."

· It is the responsibility of the home to set an example for young people and parents should be charged damages for the trouble their offspring cause.

· Justices of the Supreme Court should be in the "bleeding hearts" class for ruling that a prisoner must be arraigned within 24 hours and cannot be held for days on suspicion of crime.

· The Warren Commission report on the assassination of President Kennedy was "a classic piece of Monday morning quarterbacking."

All of it made front-page news around the country, and from then on, the McClendon Press Briefings have been well attended.

When the briefings first started, Helene Monberg, another reporter who has established an independent news kingdom of her own, helped Sarah so much that the briefings were known for several years as the McClendon–Monberg Press Briefings, although Helene insists she was merely a helper because she thought the briefings such a great idea.

The granddaughter of a Danish railway engineer who came to Leadville, Colorado, in 1887 to seek his fortune in the silver mines ("which he never found, but he was a great guy, God love him"), Helene has moved through the news business like a one-woman tornado. For her, the Hill is a way station on the path to higher things. "I came to the realization a long time ago that things don't happen in this town on the Hill. The Hill is a woman. The Hill can't initiate. And Congress so badly needs to be reorganized.

"It can't seem to get its show on the road. The decisions aren't made there. Certainly not made there in the 60s under dynamic leadership like that of Jack Kennedy and Lyndon Johnson as president, and as will be provided in his own much quieter way by Richard Nixon."

Helene wants to go where the action is without wasting much

time on the Hill, where she says stories aren't "meaningful" enough. She prefers doing natural resources subjects in depth—stories such as water development. In 1965 she started a weekly "Western Resources Wrap-Up" which covers everything from the implications of the current Negro migration to the West to a review of J. K. Galbraith's *The New Industrial State*. She says it has been "a marvelous success."

Her 76 newspaper, radio-TV, and newsletter clients in 14 states are the "cream of the cream," she says. For "Wrap-Up," she has no assistant, no copying machine, and does all the work, including mimeographing, herself. She is the example *par excellence* of the engaged journalist—or the idealist rampant. She puts her muscle where her heart is. "For many years I have been involved right down to the gut on water projects. You're laying down your water supply for the future and these stories are the most fascinating, toughest, in some ways most frustrating, in some ways the most glorious type of writing you can do . . . if I'm known for any one thing it's my water stories. This is a hard slugging business in an arena where you get to know people and they get to know you, and you hope that you stand up well in the circumstances."

Helene says she gets "further and further away from politics because political decisions are so damn superficial and that's one reason there is such a mess in this country. I tend to work more and more in the economic field. You are working there more in the realm of fact. I think politics are going to come closer and closer to the honest decisions made in economics."

She works seven days a week—except during the World Series. She travels four to six weeks out of the year and is in a freedom of the press battle about twice a year. "When the chips are down you have to see that the First Amendment is polished up for the guy that comes after you. I'll leave no stone unturned to win a freedom of the press battle. I just finished a Freedom of the Press battle with the Public Land Law Review Commission. I can't imagine 50 years of age being so much fun—by then you're supposed to be dead!"

"President Nixon said a man who leads must assume great self-assurance even if he doesn't have it."

Few Washingtonian newswomen could be called fashion plates, but by and large they are trimmer, slimmer, and better dressed today than 30 years ago when members of the corps sloshed around in raincoats and Aunt-Jennie-type shoes. Credit for changing the appearance of women in the press, making it better looking and younger looking, goes to the newcomers in the media, the television girls, though Liz Carpenter says, "The broadcasting girls gave a new look to the press, but I don't know that they improved its quality."

Members of the writing press, seeing that many of their TV sisters were selected for their looks, rapidly went on diets, tinted their hair (most chose a blonde shade), started paying attention to their clothes and, incidentally, lost the name "newshens." Eve Edstrom, the *Post*'s award-winning expert on poverty, tells how wearing the right suit one day helped her: "I had tried and tried, but couldn't get recognized by President Kennedy at a press conference. Then the day of one conference, I was walking by Garfinckel's when I saw this spectacular 'hot' pink suit in the window. I bought it instantly and wore it to the conference. President Kennedy recognized me and I asked my question."

Undoubtedly one of the TV women who spurred the writing press to glamorize itself is NBC's Nancy Dickerson. After President Kennedy had delivered his famed inaugural address on a bitter cold January noon in 1961, the first public words he spoke were, "Thank you, Nancy." After President Johnson's inaugural, the first words the public heard from him on TV were, "Hello, Nancy." With Richard Nixon it was a shade different. As the White House limousine drove up to the Capitol steps, Mr. Nixon nudged President Johnson and said, "There's Nancy," with which they both walked up to her NBC mike and disclosed what they'd been talking about on the way from the White House. Nancy had the scoop: first they talked about dogs, then President Johnson gave Mr. Nixon some advice. Nancy's getting used to that sort of treatment from presidents.

She's also used to having scoops leaked to her by high government officials. Nancy was in country clothes, walking in the woods with her children when a call came (from an unidentified source) telling her that Secretary of Health, Education and Welfare Robert Finch would announce the next day the immediate halt in production of any foods containing the artificial sweetener cyclamate. Nancy immediately got dressed, dashed into town, and went on the 6 P.M. news show. All evening rival networks told the story, prefaced with "Nancy Dickerson of NBC reports . . ." Nancy explains that "the papers and other stations attribute the story to you only when they think it might not be true. This is to cover themselves in case you've made a mistake."

By any standard one applies, Nancy is one of the nation's top news correspondents and television personalities. A *Variety* poll named her one of TV's "Top Ten Gabbers." She dresses impeccably in clothes designed for her by such top fashion names as Geoffrey Beene and Courrèges. She lives at Merrywood, Jackie Kennedy's childhood home, a country mansion with a sweeping view of the Potomac River. She has an ex-movie actor husband, three teen-age daughters of his by a previous marriage, and a couple of photogenic blond sons, ages seven and five. She dined at the White House frequently when President Johnson was in office, and was the first newswoman invited to a state dinner under President Nixon. Her parties are packed with political, and sometimes theatrical, stars. Nancy arrived in Washington in 1951 fresh from teaching third grade in Wauwatose, Wisconsin after graduating from the University of Wisconsin. Her assets were brains, good looks, charm, and a large pinch of self-discipline. Thirteen years later, at the Democratic Convention of '64 in Atlantic City, President Johnson was to step off the plane at the Atlantic City airport to announce the news, via Nancy over NBC, that he had chosen Hubert Humphrey to be his vice president. Needless to say, the other newspeople who had travelled from Washington in the plane with him were more than mildly infuriated.

To understand Nancy's meteoric rise to national fame requires realizing that glamorous women are something of a rare commodity in Washington: that's one reason why not only the city but the nation went wild when Jackie Kennedy was First Lady. Sweet, earnest, and well-turned-out as Mrs. Nixon may be, nobody could accuse her of possessing that ineffable charisma that turns on the media and the voters. Mrs. Agnew is the very prototype of the supermarket-going American housewife. Most wives of senators and congressmen are so harassed trying to manage the children and the household while Dad campaigns, flies home to make speeches, or answers the questions of constituents that only a few like Joan Kennedy, Lorraine Cooper, wife of Senator John Sherman Cooper of Kentucky, or Nouala Pell, the wife of Senator Claiborne Pell of Rhode Island, would look at home in the pages of *Vogue* or *Harper's Bazaar*. Wives of foreign service officers are kept so busy packing or unpacking their household effects they scarcely have time to get their hair done between moves. Washington is just not a suitable backdrop for the Beautiful People; it is a city primarily of desperately hard-working men and, as the saying goes, "the wives they married before they were important."

So when a handsome young brunette with big brown eyes and a honey voice arrives on the scene, it is not too surprising to discover her standing out in the crowd. John F. Kennedy and Henry (Scoop) Jackson were two of the first congressmen Nancy met when she went to work for the Senate Foreign Relations Committee. Then Republican Senator Ken Keating of New York, now our ambassador to India, took Nancy under his wing. Soon Nancy had met Everybody who was Anybody in town. She met then-Majority Leader Lyndon B. Johnson, too, and on February 22, 1960, the day Nancy became the first woman TV correspondent for CBS, LBJ and Mrs. Johnson gave a party for her in his Senate chambers. That date was something of a milestone in Nancy's life, since the Johnsons invited the president of CBS and all the other important officials of the network. Of course no one was about to miss a party given by the Senate majority leader.

Her first TV assignment was covering the civil rights fight in the Senate, which was led by Lyndon Johnson and has, as Nancy says, so drastically altered the course of American history . . . even LBJ's severest critics on the Vietnam war concede that his narrow victory on civil rights was a triumphantly shining hour. It was during her time on the Hill that she also got to know many of the Republicans now in power: Defense Secretary Melvin Laird, then a congressman from Wisconsin; Gerald Ford, now House minority leader; and the then-Vice President Nixon.

"Mel Laird was one of the first people to be nice to me when I came here in the fifties—after all, we were both from Wisconsin," Nancy says. "So it seemed natural for us to have a party for him and Barbara when he became secretary of defense. I wanted him to get to know some of my friends, and some of the columnists, better."

"And I wanted John Sherman Cooper, the most universally respected and loved Senator in town, because he is the leading opponent to the ABM—he was adorable and got up and sang an old Kentucky song—to get together with Laird, because they couldn't disagree more on ABM, but they have to get together on it someway, somehow."

The Lairds arrived early at Merrywood, and while going over the guest list Nancy mentioned that Henry Kissinger, the president's principal assistant on foreign affairs, was expected. "He couldn't possibly be coming, because he's in Florida with the president," said Secretary Laird. "You must be wrong." He picked up the phone, called the Signal Corps, and indeed Kissinger was at Key Biscayne.

"Oh, dear," said Nancy, "What'll we do for an extra man?" With which the secretary of defense called the Pentagon (it was now ten minutes to eight) and asked the secretary of the Navy and former governor of Rhode Island, John Chafee, what he was doing for dinner. Chafee said he had planned to drop by the apartment of Assistant Secretary of State William Macomber for an informal supper on his way home.

"I asked him to come to my house instead," says Nancy. "So he rushed home, got into a black tie, showed up about 8:15 and was the hero of the evening, not because he had taken Kissinger's place but because everyone here was so pleased by his decision about the *Pueblo*." Secretary Chafee, that day, had announced his decision not to punish Commander Lloyd M. Bucher or anyone else connected with the *Pueblo* seizure off the coast of North Korea. "Punch Sulzberger, the editor of *The New York Times*, and Bennett Cerf, down from New York, were as impressed as I was by the final handling and disposition of the *Pueblo* case."

Marie Smith reported the dinner in the *Post*, noting that Nancy said Secretary Chafee had "saved her life" when he withdrew his acceptance of the invitation to the Macombers to come to her party instead, which caused *New York Times* columnist Russell Baker, one of the wittiest men of our time, to dash off the following commentary: "Shortly before party time on Thursday night, the whole Washington social structure began to totter at its peak . . ." He quoted Marie's account of the dinner, including Nancy's quote, "He saved my life," adding:

"Who, you will ask, will save the Bill Macombers? The *Post* is silent on this point, which is too bad, because it takes us to the best point of the story. After Bill Macomber learned that he was faced with imminent social ruin . . . he made a series of calls for help.

"Senator Fulbright took mercy on him, called Carl Marcy—chief staff man on the Senate Foreign Relations Committee—and urged Marcy to save Macomber's life. Marcy agreed, but to do so he had to withdraw his acceptance of an invitation to a scrabble party and beer drinking at the Dun Giffords.

"Gifford is on Senator Kennedy's staff, and when he heard that his social future was threatened by the Marcy withdrawal he swung into telephone action. Rowland Evans, a syndicated columnist, agreed to help and telephoned Robert Novak, another columnist, with an urgent plea for him to drop everything, think up some seven-letter words containing Q, X, and J, and get right over to Gifford's.

"Novak was the hero of the evening at the Gifford house. No one even objected when Novak made 'exquaje' on the scrabble board and scored 97 points . . ."

Once again, Nancy was a perfect example of a newswoman who creates her own news. Not many, however, have the backing of a financial Prince Charming. Dick Dickerson is an enterprising real-estate speculator as well as the developer of Merrywood, where he has several clusters of modern, imaginative townhouses selling in the $150,000 price range. According to columnist Marian Christy of the *Boston Globe,* he is a "tycoon." Whether or not that's so, he is successful enough to provide his wife with a maid, a cook, a nurse, a gardener, a butler, a Rolls Royce, and other luxuries which rival diamonds for the title of a girl's best friends.

Nancy leaves the house every weekday morning at 7:30, having breakfasted with the children and done her isometric exercises. When she arrives at the studio, she has her hair done while she reads the wire copy ("I have a pact with Mr. Avon of Saks Fifth Avenue that we won't say a word"). On the days she has her nails done she catches up on magazines because "you can't read newspapers when you're having a manicure as there isn't room." After she's discussed with her producer what's going on the morning news show, there's just time to write and rehearse her five-minute segment before going on the air at 10:25. "That may seem like an undue amount of preparation for a five-minute show, but we all find we need that much time." After the show is over, she starts working on her twice-weekly "political column of the air."

Nancy believes these syndicated shows, which she calls columns (one-minute-and-a-half of news analysis rather than straight news), are the wave of the future for TV. "It is a whole new writing form, almost a geometric problem it is so concise. I wish I had more chance to use words, but I don't think anyone on TV is good enough to hold an audience much longer than that." Nancy figures that every time she goes on the air, she has an audience of at least 5 million people, "and I want to prepare as much as possible so as to look foolish as seldom as possible."

Sometimes she has to fight skeptical bosses to get one of her startling scoops on the air. She had just come back from Europe, where she had found the British more interested in Senator Eugene McCarthy's views on our Vietnam policy, as expressed on the Foreign Relations Committee, than people in Washington. She talked to him for an hour and a half in his office, and he told her he was prepared to use any normal party processes he could to change Democratic party policies. When she asked the gut question, i.e., whether he would go so far as to lead a "dump Johnson" movement, he answered, "If we have to, we will do that, too."

Elated at having gotten a scoop, Nancy went back to NBC to write the story for the "Today" show, only to get the word back from New York that this was not news, and would she please write them a little something about style or class in the Capital.

"I was furious. I knew this was the news story of the year, and I went down the hall and did it for local TV, and it inadvertently got on the cable to New York and the editor of the night news led with it." The president of NBC News heard it and called Washington to say he wanted to lead the "Today" show news with it. She was home asleep when she was called to come down right away to tape it, and at first she was so mad she refused. Needless to say when she heard who'd made the request, she had no choice but to drive into town at dawn.

Nancy often takes news contacts to lunch either at a restaurant such as the Sans Souci, the Rive Gauche, or the swank 1925 F Street Club, to which she belongs, then spends the afternoon on the Hill tracking down a leading figure like Foreign Relations Committee Chairman William Fulbright. "It can take all afternoon to have a private conversation with a key figure, but if you're talking about something as delicate as what our ABM policy should be, you can do much better in person than on the phone." After all the years she has covered the Hill, she finds nothing quite as exciting as listening to a personality like Senate Majority Leader Mike Mansfield explain what he is trying to do, knowing it is her job to translate what he said to the vast television audience. "I like putting on the record the reasons behind the news, which is what I'm trying to do in these syndicated columns. And I know I'm closely watched because once when I suggested that it might be time for J. Edgar Hoover to retire, that maybe no man should amass that much power over so many years, I got great masses of mail accusing me of being a Communist, a filthy liberal, all sorts of things."

Nancy's television career started when she persuaded the then-Speaker of the House Sam Rayburn to give her a private interview, something male correspondents never had been able to get him to do. "I called the Speaker at his apartment and asked him if I could please interview him about the future of Congress, what was going to happen, etc. He always liked young people, was very fond of girls, and was particularly lovely, nice, and gentle with me, so he grunted (he was always gruff), but said, 'Come in tomorrow.' When I got there with all the paraphernalia, camera, cable, and all, he said he would be interviewed by me, but not by all that 'group'. When I explained that I had to have the crew, he was utterly charming."

Her last question was, since it was the speaker's birthday, "What is your birthday wish?" The speaker answered, "I hope I'm right back here next year." Nancy replied, "I hope I'm right back here next year, too." Nancy was asleep the next morning when the producer of the Walter Cronkite show, which had carried her interview with Rayburn, called to say, "My God, you've got to go on every night!"

She has an uncanny knack for being in the right place at the right time. She had never met Governor Spiro Agnew of Maryland when she called to ask him what he was doing to support Rockefeller, and lo and behold he was preparing to open up the national Rockefeller headquarters the next day, so she interviewed him for her program, which meant that in Miami, when he was chosen to be the vice presidential candidate, there was Nancy, one of the few reporters who had ever so much as met him, able to go right on the Huntley-Brinkley program armed with the facts.

Though most of her stories are acquired on the shoe-leather circuit, the evening slipper circuit can be productive, too. It was at her own dinner party that she learned, from someone in Kennedy's administration not long after he was inaugurated, about his plan to change the entire command system of the Pentagon. The next day, she went to see her guest in his government office ("I have never in my life used anything I learned at a party without at least calling to check") and asked if it would be all right to broadcast what he had told her. This was a Friday afternoon, and the president, followed by most of the White House press corps, was aboard a plane to Hyannisport for the weekend when he got word that she had broken the news. As soon as they landed, the reporters had to meet with the president to get the story, which he had not planned to release until Sunday.

"This is one example," says Nancy, "of why women's page reporters have an inside and factual knowledge that many other reporters don't, but I don't think it's fair to your guests to have them worrying all evening about how something they say is going to be recorded in print. I have many reporter friends, but I always expect them to adhere to the same rules I do." Actually there are few instances of newswomen "doing in" an official with information they have gleaned at a party. It's more generally the opposite: a few years back, a much-respected Cabinet officer who was master of ceremonies at a large charity ball stood up, in a state of obvious inebriation, to address the gathering of nearly 1,000 ticker holders. After 15 minutes, he was persuaded to sit down, and because it was totally unprecedented and out of character, not one word about the incident appeared in the extended press coverage of the ball the next day.

According to Nancy, the last thing you do when you are sitting next to a president at dinner is to ask him a question which will obviously make news. "You talk about subjects which are of mutual interest, period. Eunice Shriver once warned me that there are certain things you just don't say to a president. I can remember during the 1964 campaign arguing with President Johnson on the plane for hours, and a member of the staff telling me he had never heard anyone from the press argue with him like that before. I discovered about LBJ that he absolutely could not stand to have anyone disagree with him, whether you were a reporter or a king, teacher, plumber, or woodsman. It was psychologically necessary for him to try to persuade everyone to agree with him. I therefore never got into a discussion unless I had an awful lot of time, so that we could have a real dialogue."

Nancy was not only the first reporter President Kennedy spoke to after he was inaugurated, but the last one when he was still president-elect. It was so icy cold that January day in 1961 that the wives of the dignitaries and many of the VIPs were taken into the Rotunda while waiting for the inauguration ceremonies to begin. When the time came for the swearing-in, it took longer to reassemble them than anyone had anticipated, so Nancy and JFK made small talk for 10 minutes. "He was obviously nervous—I wouldn't say fidgeting, but he was anxious to get the show over with. Then when it was over, he was so exuberant that he didn't even wait for Mrs. Kennedy, he just came rushing off the platform and I said, trying very hard, as all of us did, not to call him 'Jack' any more, 'Congratulations, Senator.' Fortunately, at that point, nobody had been calling him 'Mr. President', so he didn't think anything of it.

"When he said 'thank you, Nancy' it went booming out on all the networks, so I wrote him a note apologizing for my mistake, and telling him his thanks had been duly noted by the people I work for." Shortly afterward, she received a letter written on the light green stationery used by presidents for their personal correspondence: two handwritten pages including the statement, "I will be glad to give a coast-to-coast endorsement for you at any time, and hope you'll do the same for me," signed "Jack." This letter, postmarked January 21, 1961, is one of her most prized treasures, not only for its sentimental but its monetary value. Kennedy signatures are worth more than even Lincoln's or Washington's now, because his secretaries signed most of his letters after he became president. Nancy has letters, on green stationery, from LBJ and RMN, too.

Nancy's tastes in political persuasions are catholic, to say the least (she is a Catholic, by the way). Every year, she and her husband Dick go down to Senator Harry Byrd's picnic on his Berryville, Virginia farm . . . a holdover from the old-fashioned hoe-down complete with cider, fried chicken, music, and speeches his late father used to give annually for his Senate colleagues and other friends. "It's great fun because you see both conservatives and liberals there, and Gretchen Byrd's hospitality is so superb and Southern."

Last year, who should turn up (the luck of the Irish, again) than the president and Mrs. Nixon. "I talked to him about how he seemed to be so relaxed about everything he was doing, and he said he was glad it appeared that way, because a man who leads must assume great self-assurance even if he doesn't have it, and even his hands must seem relaxed and confident. Then we talked about how since he has become president there have been studies done of his hands at his news conferences . . . whether they had been in his pocket too much or he should hold them behind him more."

"I've never seen such a cool president as Nixon was that day," she says, adding that she demonstrated to him how Jackie Kennedy held her own hands in public.

Nancy is always travelling around the world (she had the only exclusive interview with Mrs. Nixon during the around-the-world 1969 trip; President Nixon telephoned to thank her after seeing the broadcast and wound up talking to her for 25 minutes, "about many, many things"), and one of her favorite memories is of Lady Bird Johnson's famous trip down the Rio Grande.

She studied speech at Catholic University (you can't say things like "you know," on television) and thinks being a success in her field requires a combination of knowledge, background, and acting ability. "It takes a good actor years just to learn to walk across a stage, and I think it is short-sighted on the part of the networks not to take news correspondents someplace for a month and teach us how to communicate."

Anybody who can make the following statements with authority surely cannot have a communications problem:

· "One of the worst things that happened to President Johnson was inheriting people like Walt Rostow, whose judgment was very poor. It was sad for the president, and sad for the country. Dean Rusk was a noble man who did his job as best he knew how, but I feel his escalation policy on the war was very wrong."

· "I see profound changes in President Nixon. Some say he is not a man of great humor—this is no time for a sense of humor anyway—but I think he really has read this book about the theory of positive mental attitude, and while you can't put him yet in the category of the 'greats' in the White House, just having gone to the depths he has been in and then rising to the heights where he is now proves he is a man of parts. Chancellor Adenauer used to say that a man is measured by the degree of his adversity."

· "Any conversation with President Kennedy was a challenge, whether it was about who was the most beautiful woman in the world, or the best professor at a university, or the best ambassador. You never relaxed your mental processes with him, because he loved all the best things, the most intelligent men and the best wine and the best ideas and the best execution of them, and as always with the Kennedys there was no hesitation about asking you a direct personal question."

Eugenia Sheppard, one of the nation's top Beautiful People chroniclers, lists Nancy along with Mrs. John Sherman Cooper, Ethel Kennedy, the Marquesa de Merry del Val, Perle Mesta, and Jane Pickens Langley as one of the Washington hostesses whom "no one ever refuses."

Nancy doesn't like that image of herself as a social figure. "I find all that stuff about the lap of luxury I live in mortifying," she says. The hard-working Nancy probably is more the real Nancy than the social gadabout. On May 8, 1960, she broke the true story behind a major plane crash in San Francisco: it had been caused by the first murder of a pilot in midair in commercial aviation history. "Nobody else had the story," she says, "so I got full credit for getting it first. There's a credibility gap when you're a girl, but once you've proved yourself, I think you have a tremendous advantage, even if it's just that most men are still somewhat startled to find a woman who knows their business as well as they do."

Although Washington doesn't have another woman TV personality in Nancy's league, there are many women here in radio and television now, not only in the girl-type talk shows,° but on news spots, too. For instance, the head of the radio-TV network Triangle Stations, Incorporated, in Washington, is Ann Blair, who had a background in reporting for a radio musical station before starting her news behind the news for Triangle eight years ago. Caroline Lewis was a reporter at the *Washington Post* when WTOP-radio-TV coaxed her into joining their news team. As Peggy Stanton, a handsome brunette who was a White House correspondent for ABC-TV until she married Congressman William Stanton of Ohio, says, "Everyone in radio and TV wants a woman, nowadays. It's like having a Negro—token integration." The stations are finding out that some of these women are doing excellent jobs.

Another is Marya McLaughlin of CBS, a blue-eyed, redheaded Irish girl whom a male colleague calls "the best humor sophisticate I know." Her name has been linked romantically with Senator Eugene McCarthy and gossip columnists have predicted a forthcoming marriage. She usually covers the Hill and flies around the country—or out of it—with presidents, but her most recent coup was getting an interview with Martha Mitchell, the outspoken Southern wife of Attorney General John Mitchell. This was only a few days after the November 13–15 Moratorium, and Mrs. Mitchell frankly said that her husband compared the antiwar demonstration to the Russian Revolution. She added that her husband had said many times that "some of the liberals in this country, he'd like to take them and change them for the Russian Communists."

All the news media had a field day with that story. Finally one woman wrote that the attorney general was muzzling his wife, but another asked him about it at a party and he said that Mrs. Mitchell could go on television, radio, or anywhere else and say anything she wanted to say, "as long as she says it in Swahili." Mrs. Mitchell told reporters at a later party that she

---

° The daytime talk show in Washington takes on a special dimension because of the daily presence of experts from around the world. Betty Groebli, whose show "Frankly Female," won the TV-Radio Mirror award for 1970 for "Outstanding Programing in Radio Broadcasting," has one of these.

actually was studying Swahili. The episode gave Liz Carpenter a good line for her "State of the Union Message," delivered at a Women's National Press Club party in her honor on January 20, 1970, one year after she and the Johnsons left the White House: "I tried to be a good member of the Silent Majority, but I just wasn't up to it," says Liz. "I felt frustrated the whole time—like Martha Mitchell with a mouth full of novacaine."

Mrs. Mitchell, whom Jean Powell of the *Washington Star* describes as a woman who "speaks softly and carries a lot of tongue in her dimpled cheeks," has turned out to be the most quotable ° member of Nixon's official family:

· At a party given by Sidney and Evelyn Zlotnick she told her dinner partner, Republican Senator Charles Percy, "It's liberals like you who are selling this nation down the river to the Communists."

· She told one reporter that life in Washington was "Quite a comedown . . . We're not living on the same means we had in Rye, N.Y. I think the government should give us free housing. We'll be happy to go back and make some money."

· *Time* quoted her as saying: "Anytime you get somebody marching in the streets, it's catering to revolution . . . my family worked for everything. We even had a deed from the king of England for property in South Carolina. Now these jerks come along and try to give it to the Communists . . ."

· She infuriated Congressional wives and made headlines when she went on a lobbying spree for Judge Clement Haynsworth, the Nixon nominee to the U.S. Supreme Court. Blonde, aggressive Martha Mitchell telephoned some Senate wives and staffers and is said to have threatened to "go on national television and defeat" the senators in their re-election bids if they didn't vote for the confirmation of Judge Haynsworth. Nobody knows how many senators she scared, and the majority voted

° Attorney General Mitchell is quotable, too. When asked if his wife had recommended a woman for nomination to the Supreme Court, the dour-faced John Mitchell answered, "Only her."

against and killed the confirmation, but she did anger a lot of people. One outraged Senate wife told Isabelle Shelton of the *Star* that Mrs. Mitchell had even used "vile and nasty" language in her calls. Most wives refused to talk about Mrs. Mitchell's lobbying, but Mrs. J. William Fulbright said for the record: "She called me. It startled me and made me a little angry. I told her I didn't like being lobbied, that I didn't try to run my husband's affairs. But she kept going on for 30 minutes. She said she'd been calling people like that for three days. I have never, in all my life in Washington, had a Cabinet wife or any other wife call me and lobby me for my husband's vote."

The press first heard of Mrs. Mitchell's unorthodox activities when an irate Senate staffer hinted at it to two or three newswomen. Even with a tip from such a reliable source, the story was hard to confirm at first since no one would admit having received a call from Mrs. Mitchell. Two days after the first leak, Sarah Booth Conroy broke the story on the front page of the *Washington Daily News*. Isabelle Shelton's story came out the next day with quote after quote from Senate wives. One, recalling that Mrs. Mitchell had said during her TV interview with Marya McLaughlin that the attorney general would like to change some of America's liberals for Russian Communists, said: "I'd like to suggest we just trade HER for anybody."

Martha Mitchell again made front-page headlines after the Senate refused to confirm the nomination of Judge G. Harrold Carswell to the Supreme Court. She called the *Arkansas Gazette* at 2 a.m., urging them to "crucify" Senator J. W. Fulbright, a Democrat from Arkansas, who had voted against the confirmation. "It makes me so damn mad I can't stand it," Mrs. Mitchell told the *Gazette*. Senator Fulbright, ever the Southern gentleman, said that Mrs. Mitchell had a right to her views, although he did note that "she is a little unrestrained in the way in which she expresses herself."

Barbara Coleman is a fragile-looking blonde whose TV show, "Here's Barbara," was seen only locally until September 1969, when she started broadcasting it coast to coast. She recently formed her own company, Coleman Enterprises Incorporated, which syndicates other television shows as well as her own.

Talking to the soft-voiced Barbara, one is apt to think her shows are all calm and pleasant peeks at the social side of Washington—at a reception given by President and Mrs. Nixon at the White House; at the Spanish Embassy during a black-tie dinner; at a supper-dance given by Perle Mesta for Ethel Merman. But her manner is deceptive. Barbara is apt to show up (on camera) in the surgical department of Children's Hospital, recording a heart operation on a nine-year-old girl; at a prison where she spent four days posing as an inmate and later returned to film her story.

One of Barbara's shows made history several days after it was on the air. She had the last interview with Mrs. Martin Luther King before her husband was assassinated, and Barbara says, "I had a premonition, so I asked her if she felt for her husband's life, and she said yes she did but that she was very philosophical." The night Martin Luther King was killed, the network ran Mrs. King's answer over and over again.

She interviewed Norman Dacey, author of *How to Avoid Probate*, who left the studio saying, "I didn't come down from New York to be insulted by a dizzy blonde." Barbara had spent the evening before the interview with a group of lawyers who helped her frame her probing questions.

Heads of state, members of Congress, Cabinet members, embassy wives, high government officials all show up on Barbara's show at sometime or other. Discussing some of the people she has interviewed, Barbara says: Mrs. Johnson "is the most disciplined woman I have ever seen;" Perle Mesta "is one of the most interesting women in Washington, she seems at times not to pay attention, but she has a truly sharp mind and it's remarkable the way she can maneuver people;" Mrs. Agnew "had no preparation for this job, but she is completely unflappable, no matter what you ask her;" Joan Kennedy "seems so much more outgoing now, she doesn't even talk in that soft voice she used to;" Mrs. Nixon "has a great deal of warmth which doesn't reach the American people because she is so surrounded by Madison Avenue experts."

Fay Gillis Wells of *Storer Broadcasting* is the only woman covering the White House on a daily basis for radio and television. She is also a survivor of President Johnson's four-and-one-half-mile walkathon around the White House South Lawn on a hot day in August 1965. She has a medal to prove it.

The Democratic Convention was going on in Atlantic City the day President Johnson, trailed by members of the press, walked and walked around the South Lawn, discussing everything except the one thing they wanted to know—who would be his running mate during the coming campaign. Finally, the forced march was over and the president asked the three women who survived—Helen Thomas of UPI, May Craig of several Maine papers, and Fay—into his office to receive one of the LBJ commemorative medals.

Another newswoman who was rewarded for walking with LBJ was Grace Halsell, a reporter for several Texas papers. Grace tells about it in her book, *Soul Sister*. President Johnson saw Grace in the crowd of reporters trailing him on one of his walks around the South Lawn and called to her, "Come over here, you are the prettiest thing I ever saw." He telephoned her the next week and hired her as a staff writer. She stayed at the White House for three years.

Fay is a pioneer aviatrix and an experienced foreign correspondent. In 1964, her newspaperman husband Linton opened the Storer Broadcasting Company's Washington bureau, and Fay became its first White House correspondent, the job she has now. Wherever the president goes, Fay goes. She was one of the few women who followed the Nixons on their around-the-world trip in 1969. When asked to compare President Johnson and his relationship with women of the press with President Nixon's, Fay answers: "I guess Nixon has been so busy getting his ducks in a row he hasn't had time to make friends with the press; he seems to be leaving that up to Herb Klein (his communications director) and Ron Ziegler (his press secretary). He is so different from Johnson. You were overwhelmed by Johnson; his Texas hospitality completely engulfed you. President Nixon has led an entirely different life. He's always cordial, but with Johnson you were kissing cousins. I can't imagine Nixon kissing one of us." Neither, one might add, can any other woman reporter.

Peggy Stanton, when covering the White House for ABC, also found Lyndon Johnson a hospitable president to cover. "One day after a parade for an Arabian king, LBJ dropped his guest at Blair House and then motioned to Helen Thomas and me to get in the limousine with him. So here I was, sitting in the bubble-top with the president, the Secret Service, and Helen Thomas. The crowds were there and when they waved the president said, 'Wave.' So Helen and I waved. Those people will be asking themselves for 25 years who was waving at them."

Now that Peggy has given up her career for life with her congressman husband and their baby daughter, Kelly, she says she has often thought about the news profession and wondered if it is really a good one for women.

"I would recommend it only to the very strong—physically, emotionally, mentally, and most of all character-wise. Because there are pitfalls all around you," Peggy says. "There is a natural hardening factor for women in reporting because they see so much more; I often wonder if it isn't more than a woman should see and hear of the dregs of humanity, if she is to maintain her sense of values and sense of proportion about life. A woman is essentially good and idealistic and naive and she loses most of her naïveté in the reporting world, and how do you balance that off with femininity? And there are the temptations, a lot of things offered, as a way to get ahead. But a woman cannot be a news reporter and get along on chemistry; she has to use her brains and writing ability—otherwise she is just going to appear a fool. I have seen too many bitter and hardened. I went into it because I wanted to do something really worthwhile, I wanted to contribute, I wanted to be where the action is, I wanted to see history happen, and to watch the people who make it happen. But at first you don't realize that if you watch the people who make history happen you will watch a lot of things about them you wish you had never seen."

"Nobody cares how you get a story, you are just supposed to get it."

Just as everything from sex in movies to college students' attitudes toward education is changing, so is the role of Washington's women's pages. Though they haven't confined themselves, for many years, just to food, fashion, weddings, anniversaries, and debuts, as have many papers in other cities, they are still going through a period of self-examination and self-doubt. The *Star* has changed the name of its society section to Women's World, the *Daily News* has incorporated its women's news into a new section called Portfolio, and the *Post* has virtually eliminated women's pages altogether with its year-old section called Style, a sort of daily magazine combining what used to be "For and About Women," with the arts, theater, travel, and other features deemed to relate to the leisure time of both sexes.

Readers familiar with the Washington scene found it odd that a section such as the controversial Style, which at first almost completely ignored women's news, should appear in the *Post*, since it is owned by a woman, Katherine Graham.

The story of Kay's life would make a fascinating novel. When she was growing up, it was not any easier being Jewish in Washington than anywhere else, and she was in the shadow of her mother, the formidable Agnes Meyer, philanthropist and "women doer" supreme. After Kay married Philip Graham, a devastatingly charming young lawyer with a sharp wit and a sophisticated eye for the ladies, her self-confidence wasn't bolstered much, either. Like many shy women, Kay retreated into the world of babies, bridge, and books, letting her husband have the spotlight.

When Phil died after a tragic illness, the National Cathedral was jammed with sympathizers. What was going to happen to "poor Kay," the retiring widow with the four attractive children? It turned out that being on her own was the best thing that could have happened to bring out Kay's latent business and social talents. The famous Truman Capote *bal masqué* in her honor at the Plaza Hotel in New York a few years after her husband's death symbolized her transformation inwardly and outwardly: Cinderella may not have found another prince, but she had certainly found the glass slipper. Now, she is well dressed, at ease in any crowd, and radiant with success. She personally supervises all the operations of the *Washington Post* Company, which includes *Newsweek* magazine, radio and television stations, the Paris edition of the *Herald Tribune*, a partnership with the *Los Angeles Times* in a news syndicate, and many other properties. Much to the discontent of its readers who are conservative-oriented, the *Post* has pioneered in championing the poor and the underprivileged, running long series about slum landlords, ghetto loan company practices, rats, and other blights on modern urban life which few major papers even ten years ago paid serious attention to.

From the time Kay took over the *Post* in 1962, she started making changes, the biggest coming in 1965 when she made Ben Bradlee, the chief of *Newsweek's* Washington bureau, managing editor, and then executive editor. Helene Melzer, a night women's editor at the *Post* before going to the *Wall Street Journal,* writing for the *Washingtonian* magazine, told how Bradlee quickly took command, first with format changes, then by adding a number of young Ivy League types and subtracting over-

65 veterans. He completed his takeover, she said, "by bringing in a cadre of his own kind of newspapermen as assistant managing editors in the various editorial sections." Eventually he got around to the women's pages and decided the thing to do about them was to abolish them altogether, and create the new Style section. In this, he had the wholehearted backing of his employer, Kay, and the trend-setting move was made to the consternation of some readers, the delight of some, and the glee of the *Star*. Gwen Dobson said her paper's circulation jumped markedly when the *Post* cut out its coverage of women's news in depth.

"I don't think in this day and age that women's interests are different from men's," says Ben Bradlee. "I think it's insulting to infer that they are interested only in recipes, lovelorn problems, and where Mrs. Merriweather Post° danced last night." Be that as it may, the *Post*'s women's pages, under former editor Marie Sauer, were read by men as well as women, especially diplomats and high government officials.

Her reporters scooped not only rival papers but the *Post*'s own news section so often that Al Friendly, then managing editor, more than once tore into the newsroom crying, "When World War III is declared, *Washington Post* readers will learn about it by reading our women's section!" When the then-city editor, Ben Gilbert, developed ulcers, women's page reporters felt their party-reporting was, if not totally, at least partially the cause.

Discussing Miss Sauer recently, Helene Melzer said, "She was a hard taskmistress to whom no assignment was impossible and from which no reporter dared return storyless. Such pressure occasionally drew tears from reporters; it often reaped hostility; but it always earned respect. For she was a pro as a newspaperwoman. Her staffers, whose alliance varied and changed almost daily, could always shred her with criticism in the snack bar.

° Mrs. Post, the Post-Toasties heiress, is one of the world's richest women. Her Washington estate, Hillwood, a showplace filled with priceless art and jewels, many formerly owned by European royalty, was deeded to the Smithsonian after, according to gossip, the Eisenhower Administration turned down her offer to give it to the government as a residence for the Vice President.

But they also wondered if the constant tension and turmoil wasn't intended to make them work better; most of them claimed that if they could work for Marie Sauer, they could work for anybody, anywhere."

But, as Helene points out, Miss Sauer did not fit in Ben Bradlee's reorganization plan. She retired, and gone in the *Post* is the voyeur aspect from the women's pages; gone the sense of participation, over one's morning coffee, in the swirling social life of the city. Where Mrs. Robert Low Bacon might have been pictured pouring tea to help save Venice from sinking into the Adriatic Sea, now will be found such down-to-earth articles as one by reporter Phil Casey on how the zoo goes about cleaning up its animal refuse, long perorations by Nicholas von Hoffman on the beauties of the hippy life or the evils of "What's-His-Name," as he calls the president of the U.S. in print (God only knows what he calls him in private), or blanket coverage of the Woodstock rock and pot festival by B. J. Phillips, who is one of the best examples of the *nouvelle vague* newswomen. At the advanced age of 23, she has been kicked off her Griffin, Georgia, high-school paper for saying "the sky wouldn't fall in if we integrated the schools," and virtually invited to leave the *Atlanta Constitution* for putting "heat on" the Atlanta police and the Georgia Power Company. "I don't like being such a tiny cog in this huge machine," she says of working at the *Post*, "but at least being here at the center of the world I can see the bankruptcy, the deception, and the corruption that are the root of things for myself. All those unresponsive cats up on the Hill and all over town in the government agencies and even in the White House drive me right up the wall."

According to one *Post* editor, the feeling among the hierarchy is that "the old type women's section is on its way out, because women are people, too, and just as interested in the hard news as men. We have over 400,000 daily readers and over half a million on Sunday, so we don't want to write for the Perle Mestas * or the small group that goes to diplomatic parties, but for the general public."

Style was launched in January 1969, with a male editor, and

* Perle Mesta canceled her subscription to the *Post* soon after Style was launched.

Kay Graham says that at first it "went a bit overboard in the liberal egghead department, such as when we ran two reviews of the same book on one day, but that was to be expected. Now we are redressing the balance.° But you know where I'd like to see Style go? I'd like it to have no hard news, so that if the Secretary of State addresses the Women's Republican Club, it's *news,* not *women's news.* We've all just got to get away from this idea of a sex separation."

Though Kay isn't totally in sympathy with the Women's Liberation Movement ("They scream too loudly") she thinks its message is a valid one. "Opportunities for women have been much more limited than any of us realized until recently, certainly than I realized until I started working in the business. There's a parallel to the Black movement, in that nobody really cared until the problem was brought forcibly to the world's attention. I think every thinking person is aware of it now, and it's resolving itself."

Presiding over the Style experiment now is Elsie Carper, who was a newsroom reporter for the *Post* for many years, then took over the personnel department at the request of Phil Graham, who was so grateful he made it possible for her to buy *Post* stock, at a price only a fraction of its present value. Elsie had gone back to reporting, this time covering the Hill, when tapped to edit Style. Single, hardworking, an outspoken advocate of equal opportunity for women in journalism, and absorbed in her job, Elsie has found the task of finding a balance between Society coverage, Old Style, and the new conglomeration in which Society is sandwiched somewhere between a review of *I Am Curious-Yellow* and an abortion series is not easy to handle. As a start, when she took over, she began sending her reporters around the nation and the world far more than formerly. Mary Wiegers went to Houston to interview the wives of the astronauts, Dorothy McCardle flew to Palm Beach to write about Mrs. Joseph Kennedy and attend a party Marjorie Post gave for the Duke and Duchess of Windsor; Margaret Crimmins

---

° When Kay Graham mentioned that she would like to see more party coverage in Style, a male editor dutifully sent a reporter to cover a high-school prom, much to the amusement of *Post* reporters who, for years, had been covering Washington VIP parties.

covered the Paris and Rome fashion openings; Judy Martin wrote a series on the first crossing of the new *Queen Elizabeth;* Merle Secrest, whose forte had always been in-depth interviews with visiting personalities in the art, theater and literary worlds, now spends a lot of her time in New York, talking with people like Eleanor Steber of the Metropolitan Opera and Ted Mann of Circle-in-the-Square, or covering the Antoinette Perry Theatrical Awards, an event the *Post* would have been unlikely to send a reporter to in pre-Style days. Maxine Cheshire writes almost as much about New York these days as she does about Washington (it was she who reported that some letters of Jackie Kennedy's to former Deputy Secretary of Defense Roswell Gilpatric had been stolen from his New York law office and were about to be sold at auction). It appeared for a while that, like many Washingtonians, the *Post* had decided that Washington Society was too complex a matter to be grappled with, and that the only answer was to get out of town as frequently as possible. But in early 1970 the *Post's* top management took another look at Style, and as Kay Graham said, decided to redress the balance. Tom Kendrick was dispatched from the State Desk to become Style's managing editor, and Mary Wiegers—a bright, pretty, under-thirty reporter—was made an assistant editor in charge of everything known as women's news, society, fashion, food, family living, and features for and about women. Mary's first changes were in the paper's social coverage. She beefed up the night party staff, putting the *Post* again in competition with the *Washington Star*, whose pages have informed the reader right along every afternoon just which parties would have been the right ones to be at the previous evening.

Gwen Dobson, the *Star's* women's editor, has 19 reporters working for her in addition to columnists Ymelda Dixon and Betty Beale. A native of Alexandria, Virginia, she must have been the youngest women's editor in the country when she stepped into the job on the *Alexandria Gazette* at 17. She got out of it as fast as she could and became the *Gazette's* reporter at the Fairfax County Courthouse. Gwen considers it her job at the *Star* to cover the White House and the First Family ("any sneeze, cold, trip, dress, or hair-do"), the 116 diplomatic missions or embassies, the Cabinet and the Congress and how they live. "I would like to do more on residential society, but you generally find that anybody who is wealthy, secure, and Old Family prefers not to be in the paper."

There's also a whole new generation of newspaper women who don't care about covering the Old Families. As Gwen puts it, "I have a terrible time getting my younger reporters to cover society events . . . they all want to write about Junior Village, our indigent children's home, or abortions or something equally activist. I have three, Toni House, Mary Margaret Flatley, and Mary Anne Dolan, who are in their twenties and create a tremendous generation gap for me, in that they'll be troopers and go to an embassy party or some such where I assign them, but they really don't want to because they'd much rather be out covering some new movement. The thing that worries me about it is the getting away from objectivity. You can't be proving a point and be a good reporter at the same time."

All of Gwen's "girls," as she calls them, have something in common, though: "They're ladylike, competitive, jealous and aggressive, and they have to be because if they are going to be shrinking violets they are going to have their brains beat out here in Washington. Nobody cares how you get a story, you are just supposed to get it."

The aggressiveness and rivalry in the Washington women's press corps constantly amazes out-of-town newswomen who come here to join it. Helene Melzer, the wife of Leo Melzer of U.S.I.A. and former women's editor of the old *Los Angeles Mirror,* bluntly says, "It's a competitive jungle."

The above traits aren't new for women reporters here. Probably the most aggressive Washington newswoman on record was the belligerent gossip Anne Royall who got an interview with President John Quincy Adams by the simple expedient of sitting on his clothes while he was bathing in the Potomac and refusing to leave until he talked with her. Today, the Secret Service would keep a reporter from obtaining the bare facts in such a way, and a good thing, too, since many reporters would surely try.

Back in 1951, the now-defunct *Washington Times-Herald*

asked several newswomen if they thought members of their sex more aggressive as reporters than men. Liz Carpenter, then writing for eight southwest Texas papers, said, "They definitely are. Men like to avoid arguments, while women don't mind controversy. Women have had to work hard to get where they are in the newspaper business, so they are not cowed by anything." Betty Beale, answering the same question, said: "I think that women probably are more direct and aggressive than men. One thing about a woman—she knows what she wants."

Bonnie Angelo's resolve to get a particular story in 1960 may have changed American history. Would John Fitzgerald Kennedy have won the election if he hadn't made his famous speech to the ministers' meeting in Houston, Texas? That's one of those "ifs" Richard Nixon must have asked himself many times. Kennedy decided to make that speech after seeing a story written by Bonnie, now a correspondent for *Time* magazine, then a reporter with *Newsday*'s Washington Bureau.

There were many undercurrents about the religious issue during the 1960 campaign, so when a group of ministers meeting in Washington to discuss this issue refused to let the press in, "it just whetted my appetite." Other reporters accepted the ministers' promise to hold a press conference after the meeting, but not Bonnie: "Such secrecy is no way to get a reporter off a story!"

She found a back entrance to a little room above the meeting site where a sound engineer would have been sitting had the meeting been "on the record." It was large enough to hold Bonnie in comfort and she listened to everything that went on, taking notes—first in a notebook, then later on every available scrap of paper in her purse—for over three hours.

Afterward, the ministers held their prearranged press conference, but according to Bonnie: "What they said at the press conference wasn't at all what they had said in the meeting, which was very ugly and bigoted."

Norman Vincent Peale, a friend of the Nixon family and the minister who performed the ceremony when Julie Nixon married David Eisenhower in December 1968, was the leading figure at the 1960 meeting, says Bonnie, noting also that her reporting of his part in the proceedings ended her friendship with the Reverend Peale.

"Kennedy was on a whistle-stop tour in California when my story was given to him, and that is when he determined to make the Houston speech, to tackle the religious issue head on to show how much of this plotting against him was going on. What happened then is history. What I did might be called snooping, but I call it getting a good story," Bonnie says, "and it is the scoop I take the greatest pride in."

A graduate of the University of North Carolina, Bonnie is married to Harold Levy who headed the *Newsday* Washington Bureau when Bonnie was there, but is now the special assistant to John W. Gardner at the Urban Coalition. They have a nine-year-old son, Christopher. "Running a household and being a reporter takes an enormous amount of organization, and organization is not what I like best," says Bonnie. "I sometimes feel as I drive toward my office that one set of problems recedes as I pass Western Avenue (a dividing line betwwen the District and Maryland), and another set looms, with the reverse at night."

Getting the beat on other reporters is not one of Bonnie's problems, because her fine stable of contacts sees to that. She had the national beat on the story that Carl Rowan, the Negro columnist, was being appointed director of USIA ("The White House called and begged, 'Just give us six hours before you announce it'"); that John Glenn was going to announce (the first time) that he was running for the Senate; and that the Russians were sending their "space woman" here for a propaganda coup ("I had guidance from a space fellow on that").

Bonnie is a pretty brunette, so small she was able to take the part of Caroline Kennedy and ride a child's tricycle on stage at a Women's National Press Club party. She has always lamented her size, but it was because of it that she got one of the most interesting assignments of her career. She became a pool reporter for the wedding ceremony when Lynda Johnson married Marine Captain Charles Robb, because Liz Carpenter decided that details of the actual ceremony, as it took place in the East Room, must be recorded for history. A platform with small wing-like panels had been erected for the altar and for the bride and groom to stand on. Liz figured a small reporter could kneel in one of the wings to watch the expressions of Lynda and Chuck, and Bonnie was the only one who could fit in the space.

"I was in a new dress for the occasion but nobody saw me," Bonnie recalls. "I was shepherded in before anyone arrived and I had to take off my shoes and kneel through the whole ceremony, peering through a slit in the sheet. Only the pupil of my eye was exposed. Lynda and Chuck were only three feet from me—from there I got the smiles, the wall-to-wall dimples, the touching smile duly reported by the press, all through the sheet."

Another reporter small in stature, but Napoleonic when after a story, is Myra MacPherson of the *Washington Post*. Myra will look you right in the eye and "sincerely" tell you she doesn't believe in reporters flying under false colors, that they should always identify themselves as being members of the press, because it wouldn't be fair to talk to a potential news source without letting him or her know everything being said was in danger of winding up in print. Yet when faced with not getting her story, or else posing as someone she wasn't, Myra joined Judith Martin, also of the *Post*, in a revival of *Front Page* reporting to get the details of the Nixon-Eisenhower wedding reception.

They didn't go quite so far as the late Bess Furman when she put on a Girl Scout uniform and crashed Mrs. Herbert Hoover's White House party for the Scouts, scooping her colleagues with a note-by-note account of the event, while the Scouts serenaded the First Lady. But Myra and Judy—both married, both mothers of small children—posed as college girls to crash the wedding reception at the Plaza Hotel in New York.

Later their paper published their "thank you" note to Julie Eisenhower, in which they told how Judy, Wellesley '59, and Myra, Michigan State '56, got past the Secret Service and local police (they followed a bridesmaid from the ladies' room, chatting with her all the while), and about the two boys from Amherst ("You girls go to Smith?") who gave them their admission cards so the girls could get back in after leaving to call "mother" (their editor), then publicly apologized to Julie for upsetting her when they asked her where she was going on her wedding trip. "We got the distinct impression, from the long look you then gave us," wrote the party crashing reporters, "that it was time to leave; your mother's press secretary thought so, too."

Both thought being thrown out made their story even better. And a bonus, says Myra, was seeing Pat Nixon totally relaxed: "She was dancing and blowing kisses to everyone."

Another wedding Myra covered (without crashing) was reported by her "like it was," while other society writers were describing it in straight wedding coverage style:

"Adam Clayton Powell III, son of Harlem's flamboyant congressman, and Beryl Slocum, daughter of the socially prominent Newport and Washington John J. Slocums, were married yesterday in St. Mary's Chapel of the Washington National Cathedral.

"After a 4 P.M. traditional short ceremony, during which the bride and bridegroom exchanged rings and a polite kiss, the couple walked solemnly down the aisle. So did the bride's father, a direct descendant of Miles Standish, and the bride's mother, a direct descendant of Rhode Island's founder, Roger Williams.

"But the irrepressible Powell strode down the aisle with a beaming grin, slapping old friends on the arm. Powell, a Baptist minister, seemed as much at home in the National Cathedral with its tapestry and candlelight and Gothic architecture as he does in his own church, Harlem's Abyssinian Baptist."

After describing Powell's long black robe and his conversation with the press outside the Cathedral, Myra covered the reception in the Slocums' Georgetown home which "included certainly one of the most varied guest lists in that exclusive community."

There were the "New England accented, socially prominent people who have four addresses," Powell's Harlem friends, and entertainment-world friends of the groom's mother, pianist Hazel Scott.

"Powell," wrote Myra, "told one woman the secret of making

good Stroganoff, smiled pleasantly as he was introduced to another and slipped in an occasional 'Keep the faith, baby.' "

She noted that when a friend said, "Man, you must be hot in that robe," Powell whispered roguishly, "I ain't got nothin' on underneath." To another he said, "I rent it [the robe] out for Halloween."

Myra, who was a copy girl on the *Detroit Free Press* and a reporter with the *Detroit Times* before coming to Washington, worked for the *Washington Star* and *The New York Times* before going to the *Post* ("You improve financially everytime you move"). Between jobs she took time off to have two babies. Her husband is Morrie Siegel, the sports writer and TV newscaster, and she says that from the first their marriage would have been doomed if he hadn't been a newspaper man.

The day they were married, while on the way to Williamsburg, Virginia, on their honeymoon, Myra had her groom stop the car several times on the highway so she could make calls from along-the-roadside telephone booths in order to line up clearance to cover the Beatles the day she was to get back.

After covering the Beatles and writing and filing her story, she got home at three thirty in the morning, and "in the old tried-and-true tradition, I took off my shoes and unlocked the door, to find Morrie was sitting there, slumped in a chair. He looked up and said, 'Damn it, this isn't the way it's supposed to be. *I'm* the one who should be coming in late.' "

The desire of Washington papers to broaden the scope of women's pages beyond the usual sugary fluff of most society sections has produced a corps of women writers who go to every event, no matter how trivial, looking for a news story. Sometimes they succeed.

· Gloria Ohliger, former women's editor of the *Washington Daily News* and a lover of horse racing, was out at the Laurel Race Course for the running of the International Race when she spotted FBI Director J. Edgar Hoover, also a devoted racing fan. Gloria asked Mr. Hoover a few questions between races, then got the scoop that Mr. Hoover would be glad to stay on the job if Richard Nixon asked him (this was five days after Nixon was elected), and that there was "no question about the evidence" against James Earl Ray (the alleged assassin of Martin Luther King); he also added that Ray's new attorney, Percy Foreman, was "one of the cleverest."

· Helene Melzer of the *Wall Street Journal* broke the story that Martha Mitchell, the attorney general's wife, was allergic to pot. Mrs. Mitchell told Helene about her allergy, which had kept her at home for two days with puffy eyes and swollen cheeks, when the two were touring the Philadelphia mint with a group of Washington women. Mrs. Mitchell's experience with pot was perfectly legal since she whiffed it while on a visit to the Bureau of Narcotics. An agent put some marijuana leaves in a pot and ignited them to demonstrate to the group of Cabinet wives that marijuana had a distinctive odor.

· Joy Billington of the *Washington Star,* while covering a routine embassy dinner given by Ivory Coast's Ambassador Timothee Ahoua and his pretty wife, Germaine, learned that three nights before the South Vietnamese Ambassador Bui Diem had joined the peace demonstrators in the November 15th Moratorium. He said he joined the 250,000 demonstrators to get a "feel of the people" by "mixing with the masses." The ambassador was with the throng, which included some carrying North Vietnamese flags, for over an hour. He told Joy that the rhetoric was much as he expected.

· A *Post* reporter was covering a small dinner party at the home of Washington Attorney Sylvan Marshall and his wife, Mara, when General Earle G. Wheeler, then chairman of the Joint Chiefs of Staff, discovered one doesn't have to be on the Hill to testify at a Senate open hearing. Senator Vance Hartke confronted the general, in front of the Indian ambassador and a former president of Panama, about his stand on the war in Vietnam. The general finally told the senator, "You politicians make wars, we of the military only fight them." He added that if "this war is lost, it will be lost in Washington, not in Vietnam."

· Marie Smith of the *Post* was up on the Hill working on a story when she dropped in on Senator John Kennedy to see if he was going to a deer hunt the Senate Majority Leader Lyndon Johnson was giving at the LBJ ranch. No, he wasn't, answered the young senator because his wife, Jacqueline, was expecting a baby. Marie had the scoop about Jackie's pregnancy. A few months later, Caroline Kennedy was born.

Clare Crawford, while at a White House party, heard Senate Majority Leader Mike Mansfield say that about once a month he and President Nixon breakfast alone at the White House. Senator Mansfield, who did not breakfast à deux with LBJ, a member of his own party, said that he and President Nixon "discuss everything, and I have found the president most accommodating, courteous, and understanding. We have our differences. He, of course is interested in the Democratic votes. But he never presses me."

Elizabeth Shelton of the Post, while at the National Archives looking over the galleys of the third edition of its magazine, Prologue, spotted a heretofore unpublished historic letter. It was written by a nine-year-old fan to President Franklin D. Roosevelt in 1935: "I like the stamps you sent me very much and the little book is very useful. I am just starting my collection and it would be great fun to see yours which mother says you have had for a long time. I am going to frame your letter and I am going to keep it always in my room. Daddy, Mother, and all my brothers and sisters want to be remembered to you." It was signed, Bobby Kennedy.

Washington's fashion and food writers are news oriented, too. So although Washington doesn't have any nationally known fashion designers, and as any gourmet knows, it's rare when one gets a really great meal in any public eating place here, the fashion and food coverage is widely read throughout the world.
Nina Hyde of the Washington Daily News says: "Fashion starts at the White House. Front-page news makes front-page fashion. If a woman is going to be in the public eye, other women are influenced by what she wears—witness the Jackie Kennedy hat and Mrs. Johnson in her Adele Simpson clothes."
Nina could have mentioned Mamie Eisenhower's bangs, too, only she is so young she probably doesn't remember what Ma-

mie's short, tightly curled bangs did to the nation's coiffures.

A pacesetting fashion writer, who covered the European shows regularly years before either the *Post* or the *Star*, papers with much larger circulations, sent their fashion editors abroad regularly, Nina thinks Mrs. Nixon, too, will have an impact on fashion. "She started in timidly, and she has timid advisors, but she is coming around," Nina says. She thinks Mrs. Nixon certainly would like to be more bold, fashion-wise.

When covering a luncheon, wearing a St. Laurent pants suit, Nina went up to Mrs. Nixon and the First Lady linked her arm through hers. "You look great," she said, and "you make me so jealous, I can never wear pants."

Nina replied, "Mrs. Nixon, you would look divine in pants."

Then Mrs. Nixon told her about a party the Nixons gave in their Fifth Avenue apartment, not long before coming to the White House, when a woman guest wore Pucci pants and "curled up on the sofa with her legs underneath her all the time." When the party was over Mr. Nixon turned to his wife and asked, "Is that the latest thing, those pants?" Pat said it was. "Well," Mr. Nixon firmly said, "no one in my family will ever wear them." And no one in the family does.

A political science major at Smith, Nina worked for *Women's Wear Daily*, then for Tobe, a fashion consultant firm, before marrying Washingtonian Lloyd Hyde.

One of the most exciting fashion stories Nina has covered was one she helped create. She was a planner of the first fashion show ever held in the White House. On March 1, 1968, the best of American fashion—from the top fashion designers of both the East and West Coast—went on the runway in the State Dining Room following a luncheon Mrs. Johnson gave for the governors' wives. On the committee, too, were the fashion editors of Washington's two other papers—Eleni of the *Star*, and Dorothy LeSueur of the *Post*.

Eleni, who is married to the *Star's* managing editor, Sid Epstein, and Nina don't agree on the Washington woman's fashion image. Nina says "there is an awful lot of safe dressing here." To prove her point, she mentions that 27 women wore the identical dress to the 1969 inaugural ball and 13 wore identical dresses to the symphony ball the year before. All 40 dresses were from

Malcolm Starr, whom Nina calls "the savior of Washington since his evening dresses sell for only about $200 and they have a good but safe look."

"I'm tired of that cliché about Washington women being dowdy," Eleni says. "The transplants who come here with each new administration might start that way, but they quickly shape up once their figures and faces start appearing in the newspapers. In fact, we'd be sued if we did before and afters." She usually gives a woman six months to "get the message" and finds they usually do.

Eleni has written about almost every woman making news here. During an interview with Mrs. John Sherman Cooper, one of the most sophisticated women in Washington, Eleni discovered that the Senator's wife did not learn her fashion savvy at her mother's knee. When Lorraine Cooper was a young girl in Paris, her mother sent her to Lanvin's. "The *vendeuse* educated me," Mrs. Cooper told Eleni. "She taught me why certain things were not good, and what to do with my hair. She showed me how everything should go together in a wardrobe—I remember a color combination of almond green and tobacco that was a dream." Eleni also learned that Mrs. Cooper frequently buys white dresses and then dyes them another color at a later time.

Marian Burros' food columns in the *Star* are generously sprinkled with recipes for Mrs. Melvin Laird's "Easy But Good Chicken," Mrs. Claire Chennault's "Princess Omelet," "Meatball Stroganoff" as served at the home of Senator George McGovern, the White House chef's "Yam Purée," and even an ancient recipe for "Corsey's Crock" (a potent punch made with rum, brandy, whiskey, and spices) which she got from Samuel Kirk Millspaugh whose Samuel Kirk silver company, based in Baltimore, has made silver for such people as LaFayette, Jerome Bonaparte, the Philadelphia Biddles, and the New York Astors.

Her counterparts at the other Washington papers don't take Marian's newsmaker-plus-recipe approach to food writing. Ann Crutcher, food and women's editor at the *News*, dishes up delightful historical theses about the food she's telling one how to prepare, and then lets her readers know how to go about eating it. Elinor Lee of the *Post* leans more toward openly nostalgic recipe columns where one finds such calorie-laden gems as "Aunt Alice's Own Salad Dressing," Aunt Alice being a deceased relative-in-law of Georgetowner Mrs. Robert F. Evans.

Marian spends most of her time in Washington's VIP kitchens, including the one at the White House. She once ate a state dinner (for Canadian Prime Minister Pierre Trudeau) in the kitchen with Swiss-born Henry Haller and Heinz Bender, the pastry chef, serving her. When the chef served the Bernkasteler Doktor, a German Moselle considered one of the finest of its kind imported to this country, it was sour. "The next day it would have been vinegar," Marian says. Since she was served from a bottle which had been opened upstairs, and from which more than half had been served, it's evident that more than one guest had had his glass filled from the same bad bottle. She hopes the prime minister wasn't one of them.

The Trudeau dinner wasn't Marian's first White House story. "I had two delicious scoops which drove Liz Carpenter right up the wall," she says. "No one was supposed to know that the cake for Luci Johnson's wedding had eight layers and was eight feet tall, because the White House felt there was something *nouveau riche* about having a cake that big, and even later when Luci had to stand on a platform to cut it, they wouldn't tell how tall it was. When I found out it upset them terribly—almost as much as it upset them when I found out that Lynda's cake was being made at the Greenbrier Hotel in White Sulphur Springs, West Virginia, and was being carried by the Secret Service over back roads to Washington. They had to take out the back seat of a cadillac to put the cake into it. At first the White House denied my story, then put a release out on it themselves."

A Wellesley graduate (she majored in English), the wife of an engineer, and the mother of two—a boy 14 and a girl 9— Marian is co-author of four cookbooks with her long-time friend Lois Levine: *Elegant But Easy, Second Helping, Freeze with Ease,* and *Come for Cocktails, Stay for Supper.*

Discussing the kitchens of some of Washington's best-known people, Marian says:

"You wouldn't think you could get in trouble with these food stories, would you? Mrs. Melvin Laird (wife of the secretary of defense) will never talk to me again. I quoted her when she said—she is very friendly and quite casual—that when she has guests she greets them at the door and says, 'You all go on downstairs and drink.' "

· "Pat Mosbacher (wife of Chief of Protocol Buz Mosbacher) says her husband thinks the reason seasonings were put on food in the old days was to kill the bad taste; so they use only salt, and a minimum of that."

· "Mrs. Percy [the wife of Senator Charles Percy] has a marvelous Chinese cook; he can cook anything. But when she wants to entertain at a small elegant dinner she has him cook Chinese dinners. When you take pictures at the Percys' they won't let you take any pictures showing a window or a door, because of what happened to the senator's daughter."

· "The Marquise de Merry del Val was so nice I didn't write this story about the Spanish Embassy. They make the most glamorous dishes—quails in birds nests, mousse *de fois gras*, soufflé *amandes*—all very well; I walked into the kitchen and saw all these things that had taken days to make and right beside them were cans and cans of Pillsbury refrigerated rolls, which the cooks were rolling furiously."

Many Washington newswomen also have discovered that writing about the capital's VIPs can be lucrative for free-lancers.

One person whose tax installments must be rising in a delirious spiral is Frances Spaatz Leighton, a most prolific "ghost," although with her shoulder-length, teased, reddish-blonde hair and dynamic outfits she is far too colorful to be confused with a transparent wraith.

While holding down a full-time job as Washington correspondent for a Sunday supplement published by Metropolitan Sunday Newspapers, Frances turns out other people's behind-the-scene stories ("I'm just hung up on living other people's lives") faster than most writers do full-length magazine pieces. More than one has hit the best-seller list, the latest being Mary Gallagher's memoirs about her years as Jackie Kennedy's secretary.

"My idea of a dream assignment through the years was to write about Jackie Kennedy and it happened! I used to work in the same building as Jackie when she was a newspaper woman and my idea of an ultimate book was to do her story. Unfortunately I do not have the last part, since she married Onassis. But I did learn a little sidelight that didn't get into the book. Even in Georgetown Jackie was so used to having a nursemaid from the very beginning that on the Nanny's day off, before the other maid arrived to take the Nanny's place, Jackie was desperate to have Mary Gallagher stay, because she'd ask, 'What if the baby needs changing?' She didn't know how to change the baby's diapers. I think that is so delightful that Jackie was so unused to being a mother, that she had never learned to be a mother."

Sarah Booth Conroy is a full-time reporter for the *Washington Daily News* but moonlights (at $100 per story) for *The New York Times* women's pages, writing features and covering special parties such as White House state dinners, especially newsworthy embassy parties, and the annual pet show at Ethel Kennedy's Virginia estate where the only phone available for reporters is in the men's room alongside the swimming pool where "the men kept coming in and out and were most surprised to find a woman there, on the phone." Sarah also writes articles for such magazines as *Ladies' Home Journal*.

At the *News*, she is art critic, feature writer, and occasionally a hard news reporter, but usually for events involving the arts. She is the wife of Foreign Service Officer Richard Conroy who's on loan from the State Department to the Smithsonian in the International Activities Department, where he helps arrange explorations and exhibits. This fits in nicely with Sarah's interest in writing about arts and crafts.

She recently scored a coup when she got an exclusive interview with Mrs. Richard Helms, wife of the director of the Central Intelligence Agency, and revealed that the CIA chief and his new wife read spy stories to relax, never go to cocktail parties and never stay late at dinner parties so he will be "in a fit state to make a decision" when the telephone rings at three or four in the morning; that Mrs. Helms never wears pants suits because he doesn't like them; and that she had signed a two-year contract with the Smithsonian Institution to be on their Radio Smithsonian staff. Cynthia Helms told Sarah she took the job because she wasn't good at ladies' luncheons since she "never could find any clean white gloves."

One of the wittiest and most imaginative of the Washington free-lancers is Anne Chamberlin, a blonde and slim Vassar graduate whose travels range from Israel for *Vogue* to Ghana for *Cosmopolitan*, with stops in Washington to dash off such uncharacteristic but lucrative fluff as what the new Republican wives like to serve for dinner (for *McCall's*).

Anne Nevin Chamberlin majored in French at college, then specialized in roaming abroad for *Life* before joining the staff of *Time* in Washington. She worked for the *Saturday Evening Post* as a roving correspondent until its sad demise and has been on her own ever since. A blue-blooded Brahmin whose grandfather, Ethelbert Nevin, composed "The Rosary," "Mighty Lak' A Rose," and "Narcissus," Anne was very much at home with the Kennedys and their entourage during the JFK presidency, and the results of her observations of high society here were recorded in a barbed article in *Esquire* called "Love in Washington":

"It is ironic that a town designed by a Frenchman and populated by a vigorous army of men and women in their prime—all of whom lust for success and know the delights and temptations of power—should be such a miserable place for love," she wrote. "They seem to have used so much energy advancing their careers at the office that they find it more interesting to continue jockeying for position among their fellow power drivers for the evening than to entertain the ladies."

She then told the story, which must have given many a bachelor-in-demand a sense of *déjà vu*, of the evening when a particularly assiduous new suitor walked a female guest from a dance to her car. "You're absolutely marvelous," he whispered into her ear after a kiss. When she told him she liked him too, he replied, "Then call me."

Anne has mixed feelings about the joys of being on one's own. "The day you walk out of the cozy cubicle you have occupied as a correspondent in the Washington Bureau of a prosperous magazine and set up shop as a free-lance writer is one of life's heady moments, and you should savor every whiff of it," she says.

Not the least of the hazards of being self-employed is what she calls "your warm new relationship with the Internal Revenue Service." With no withholding from a salary, your income tax payments come as a ghastly surprise four times a year, and it's a shock to realize that you forgot to keep a record of those taxis, bundles of paper, and long-distance calls for your deductible business expenses. "I've got the chit for a seven-*centime* chair in the Tuileries, a 13-cent notebook from Tel Aviv and a ten-cent bridge toll in Bangor, Maine. The library that inherits the Chamberlin papers falls heir to a rich lode of notes to myself reading: Logan Airport toilet, ten cents."

Washington is reputed to be a journalists' paradise, and Anne agrees that it is, especially coming here from France, where a reporter ranks somewhere between a "*clochard*" (street bum) and a "Corsican narcotics pusher." But she finds a world of difference between being a member of the working press and an independent writer.

There's the matter of accreditations: For instance, Senate and House passes expire with each session of Congress. "For a while, as long as the man at the door remembers your face, you can still join the convivial lunchers at the Press Table of the Senate Restaurant on Pecan Pie Day. But pretty soon you get asked: 'Who are you *with*, Miss?' and he's not referring to your luncheon companion. So if current events are your main interest, get used to observing them in fragments through the legs of some police horse, instead of from the press bleachers with the rest of the gang."

But she does find landing assignments easy. "All you have to do is write about a Kennedy. Don't lose hope if you don't happen to be one of Jackie's most intimate girlhood friends or her former personal secretary. Every now and then the editors will want some fringe Kennedy story, like 'How Much Ethel Kennedy Pays Her Cook,' or 'Memoirs of JFK's Navy Dentist.' If you think you can make the big time with a witty study of the Smithsonian Bug Collection, or A Morning with the Reconstituted Milk Tasters in the Agriculture Department Basement (my own field of expertise), or even A Girl's Guide to Anti-Ballistic Missiles, you'd better move back to Moose Jaw.

"In addition to which, it's a mistake to suggest an article in the first place. If *their* idea doesn't pan out, it's not half as much your fault as when *your* idea is a dud."

However hard it may be to make a living as a free-lancer, it certainly can be a way of meeting the Right People. Sue Sheehan, the young (Wellesley '59), vivacious wife of *New York Times* correspondent Neil Sheehan and a Washington-based member of *The New Yorker*'s "Talk of the Town" staff, pulled a real coup in May 1970, when she managed to do what most sensible reporters would have thought impossible: to write a piece about Jackie Onassis for *The New York Times* (Sunday) *Magazine* without being repetitious, awestruck, or nasty.

"Jackie wouldn't let me interview her," Sue says, "but in retrospect I'm glad she didn't, as I was able to see her entirely as others see her, without my own reactions getting in the way. The important thing is to get the okay from the press secretary, in Jackie's case Nancy Tuckerman. Without that, people like artist Bill Walton, a close friend of hers, would never have had me for tea and scones and very high-level gossip. That's all this sort of piece is, you know: legitimate gossip."

Sue did get in touch with some one hundred friends and acquaintances of Jackie's, ranging from historian Arthur Schlesinger, Jr., to former social secretary Tish Baldrige Hollensteiner, "who wasn't very helpful because like so many of the Kennedy entourage, she has a vested interest in preserving the Camelot image." She was startled by how cooperative 99 percent of them were . . . all, in fact, but Michael Forrestal, a former frequent escort and dashing man-about-town who refused to see her. "I could almost tell which men had been sort of in love with her. A film came over Roswell Gilpatric's eyes whenever he mentioned her name. . . . I think it's an asset being a woman when you're trying to get at the truth about people. What man could play so dumb as innocently to ask another man, 'Do you think Jackie actually has a *sex* life?'"

Another of the most successful newswomen-turned-free-lance is Judith Viorst. She writes delightful books of poetry (*It's Hard to Be Hip Over Thirty and Other Tragedies of Married Life*) at the same time that she tosses out brilliant think-pieces for the *Washingtonian* magazine and articles for *McCall's, House and Garden* and *Redbook.*

Until the *New York Herald Tribune* folded, Judy was its Washington correspondent covering the social beat. "I would not find it at all interesting as a 'civilian.' If you can go to a party as a reporter and with justification eavesdrop on conversations, butt in and ask people questions and get them to say things that you are much too well bred to ask them about when you are not a reporter, then it is a lot more fun."

Although she enjoyed many things she covered, Judy doesn't think she is constructed to be a newspaper person, claiming it isn't her pace. She likes to have time to write a story properly, and the pressure of daily deadlines disturbs her.

She writes the first draft of all of her stories in longhand, which is another reason she doesn't care for newspapering. "I covered the 1964 Democratic Convention for the *Herald Tribune,* and had to file my stories down in their newsroom in the basement of Convention Hall. But I had to write in longhand and who ever heard of writing a news story with a pad and pencil? I was terrified that they would find out, and as a matter of fact my husband * kept saying, 'This is a disgrace.' So I would write the story in my hotel room and come down to the newsroom and say, 'I have to do my story, may I have a typewriter?' I'd put a pile of papers, with my story already written, by the side of the typewriter and start pounding away. They'd think, 'Oh, boy, she really can knock out a story.'"

Judy chose to work at home, writing children's books and articles on married life, making her beat the domestic scene, because she found the newspaper business too inflexible. "You have to be on the scene when you're working for a paper. I remember covering the International Ball the night my son An-

---

* Judy's husband is Milton Viorst, author of *Fall From Grace,* the story of the Republican party's identification with the Puritan ethic, and *Hostile Allies,* the story of the relationship between President Franklin D. Roosevelt and General Charles de Gaulle.

thony had the croup. I left him with the baby-sitter with all kinds of instructions, and it was the definition of hell and everything that was wrong with being a working mother. I was there with those luxurious satins and feathers while I had a kid at home, choking."

As Anne Chamberlin summarizes the free-lance situation: "I keep telling myself, especially on summer weekends, when I'm wondering if I can wrestle a new ribbon into my Olivetti without getting strangled in its coils, and all the rest of America is out frolicking in the swimming pool: Free-lancing may not be all Fun. But it beats working."

10

"This is a town where shrimp-bowl intrigue is apt to be very newsworthy."

With all the embassies here giving national day celebrations (except for the Germans who have no national day), receptions in honor of visiting dignitaries, luncheons, dinners, fashion shows, and concerts, a reporter on the embassy beat can be pretty choosy. Barring the presence of a head of state or a well-known artist as the honor guest, embassies are usually covered according to their social desirability. This is a nebulous quality hinging on the tastes and inclinations of the ambassador and his wife, the current relations of the country with the U.S., and the amount of publicity generated.

Former French Ambassador Hervé Alphand's devastating blonde wife Nichole, made the French Embassy so much the place to go during the Kennedy administration that invitations to her soirees were, next to the White House's, the most coveted in town. She charmed everybody, and her ability constantly to dream up something new to promote France—she turned the christening of a new French Line ship in New York into a benefit for Family and Child Services of Washington, for example—created such an enormous amount of publicity it must have been at least partly responsible for Hervé's promotion to second in command of the French Foreign Office. He, too, made news, most notably at a private dinner given for Adlai Stevenson, then ambassador to the U.N. and in Washington for consultations. When the hostess meekly asked whether she might seat Adlai on her right, since he was the guest of honor, though Hervé outranked him, Ambassador Alphand replied, "Absolutely not. If you do I shall have to leave. I am representing President de Gaulle." The flustered hostess quickly rearranged the seating, creating a confusion which definitely livened up the party. Ambassador Alphand's remark could not have hurt him back in Paris. Evidently, a *Post* typo in a story about Mme. Alphand didn't either. The reporter wrote, "Madame Alphand wore bouffant black." It came out in print, "Mme. Alphand is bouffant black." The late Philip Graham, then publisher of the *Post*, was so delighted he sent copies to all his friends in Paris.

An embassy's social standing, as rated by reporters, is fluid, but a few generalizations can be made:

· Britain and France are always on top of the social heap although France temporarily slipped during the peak of Charles de Gaulle's anti-Americanism. Congressman Thomas M. Rees, a Democrat from California, during that period said, "If there were a black market in invitations, one Spanish would be worth one and a half Kuwaits, and a Kuwait would be worth five French . . . It's been a tough year for the French." The Alphands' successors, the Charles Lucets, less party-oriented than the Alphands, weathered the situation with Gallic aplomb.

· Russian parties are always blanketed by the press, not because the parties are gay, but because of the power of the Soviet Union. A reporter's principal challenge is to size up the political climate by noting the rank and station of envoys from other countries. U.S. officials boycott them when the cold war is momentarily icy but make a point of showing up when there is a visible thaw.

· Among the other Western European countries, Spain and Italy head the list when they have vivacious ambassadors (and wives), as both do now. Currently Portugal is fashionable, too. Finland was quite important, socially, when Ambassador Rickhard Seppala and his vivacious wife were here, although Mme. Seppala did upset a group of society writers when she asked them over for dinner and insisted they try out her new sauna. The women, freshly coiffed, took off their fancy cocktail dresses and bravely, if reluctantly, went through the whole sauna routine: hot steam room, cold shower, circulation whipped up by hitting themselves with sprays of birch leaves, and another cold shower. Mme. Seppala expressed regret that there wasn't any snow to walk through from the steam room to the showers, as in Finland. The reporters expressed a vast relief.

Reporters aren't the only ones who encounter hazards at embassy parties. Pretty Ann Hand, wife of LBJ's Chief of Protocol Lloyd Hand, was served an unfamiliar appetizer at the Tunisian Embassy, a pastry with a slightly cooked egg inside. As Ann bit into it, the runny yolk dripped down inside her décolleté dress. "She had to sit there and mop up," reported another guest who had fortunately been warned by her dinner partner to lean over her plate.

A visiting head of an Arab country was entertaining John F. Kennedy at his embassy when bowls with leaves floating in them were placed in front of each guest. Thinking it was a finger bowl, President Kennedy started to dip his fingers in it when the frantic chief of protocol caught his eye. Kennedy stopped just as the Arabian lifted his bowl to his lips and started drinking.

· Ireland and Israel and Greece always "draw" because of their large ethnic representation in this country, though opposition to the military government in Greece now is keeping some guests away. When Arthur Goldberg was a member of the Supreme Court, his position was considered a plum for the Israelis, just as Vice President Spiro Agnew presumably enhances the status of Greeks.

· Among the Latin-Americans, Argentina and Brazil are the traditional leaders, but the Peruvians often top them. When Enrique Tejera-Paris and his ravishing wife Pepita were here, Venezuela eclipsed all other Latin American embassies in desirability. Pepita scored a coup when Lady Bird Johnson, then the First Lady, came for lunch. Lady Bird, though, almost precipitated an international incident when she liked the dessert so much she asked for the recipe. Mme. Tejera-Paris graciously sent it around to the White House. But it didn't work; either some ingredient was missing, or had been added. Were the Venezuelans deliberately trying to keep the secret of their marvelous *quesillo* from the Americans? No, but the cook was. Even with a spy staked out in the embassy kitchen watching as ingredients were put into the bowl, the true recipe was impossible to get. Finally a threat was made: some say Mme. Tejera-Paris told the cook she would be sent back to Venezuela, while others say she threatened to remove the cook's name from a Venezuelan food story scheduled for publication in a national magazine. Within hours, Mrs. Johnson had the correct recipe.

· Among the Far Eastern embassies Japan and Nationalist China usually command the most attention; Eastern European embassies for the most part are pretty dull, although there are occasional flashes. Traditionally, the Arabs and Africans, in that order, have followed the Eastern Europeans. Then came the idea of featuring native fare.

In the old days most embassy entertaining was French, or pseudo-French, and whether it was *réussi* or not depended on how well it was done. Syndicated columnist "Suzy" recently led with "If you can't make it to Spain, *hombre*, the next best think is to go to a party at the Spanish Embassy in Washington, *ole!*" She could have written almost the same lead about most of the 116 (at last count) embassies in Washington. The up-to-the-minute thing is native dress, foods and wines, art and entertainment. The Indians wear saris and serve spicy hot curries; dinner at the Korean Embassy can take two hours, consisting of dozens of specialties succeeding themselves on tiny grills in front of each guest; the British serve strawberries and Devonshire cream on the Queen's birthday, and have dished up the Beatles as entertainment on another occasion; the Royal Burundi drummers and Watusi dancers, complete with spears, performed at a Burundi reception; Cardin showed his *haute couture* at the French Embassy; Mstislav Rostropovich and his wife, Galina Vishneyskaya, a soprano, performed at the Russian Embassy; and the Japanese Embassy, with a real tea-house in its well-manicured garden, where tea actually is served, is probably the most exquisite miniature homeland of them all.

The first to make native fare desirable were the Arab nations, previously low on the women reporters' social list. They started their ascent on the social ladder right at the time when the French, under the Alphands, and the British, with Lord and Lady Harlech, were so in favor with President and Mrs. Kennedy.

Credit for putting Arabs on the Diplomatic Row map goes to Jackie Bengelloun, the sophisticated, bright, and comely wife of the then-Moroccan Ambassador Ali Bengelloun, now director general of Morocco's largest industry, phosphate. After Jackie poured so much money and care into producing spectacular parties, other Arabs followed suit, and soon society writers were going into verbal ecstasy over Arabian food, clothes, décor, entertainment, and hostesses. Judith Martin of the *Washington Post* told how it happened:

"It was really the native bit that did it. Whole lambs pushed steamship rounds from the buffet tables. Baklava replaced *petits fours*. The coffee was the kind that made your eyeballs tingle, or it was omitted in favor of mint tea." She told how guests sat on cushions on thick-carpeted floors, eating cous-cous with their well-manicured hands, wore caftans (usually the gifts of the hostess), found jugs of French perfume tucked into their dinner napkins, and watched entertainment which was a mixture of Arab and mod. "A tired diplomat could lie back and watch a belly dancer undulate—all while fulfilling his official obligations. A Cabinet minister could enjoy the latest in head-shattering teen-aged bands without ever stepping into a discothèque . . ."

The same article says the Arabs suddenly stopped wanting publicity on their parties because, what with the belly dancer and other many-splendored things, "The picture and word about the good life in Washington flashed back to Arabian capitals.

Diplomats began to fear the loss of job or entertaining allowance from the government officials who disapproved of 'the image'—or who got jealous and wanted to be ambassadors to Washington themselves."

Soon the Moroccans didn't have to worry about the image back home. Ahmed Osman, husband of Princess Lalla Nezah, sister of the king of Morocco, was sent to take over the ambassadorship from Bengelloun's replacement Ahmed Laraki, who was sent home to be foreign minister after only 18 months in Washington. The king gave him only eight days to pack and say good-bye.

But the swinging parties at the Moroccan Embassy still were kept under wraps for a while. Abdeslam Jaidi, the embassy press attaché until early 1970 when he went to New York as consul general, said, "We stopped inviting the press because the guests, especially the politicians, didn't like it. The reason we had coverage in the first place was that it was the fashion in Washington to have parties reported. And we wanted the American public to be aware of Morocco. But if you get a bad press, and if your guests don't want to come back, we thought 'why?' "

"When we stopped asking the press, we discovered some of our guests were telling them what happened, much of it wrong. We have eliminated those people from our guest lists."

As an example of the "bad press" they and their guests received, the Moroccans quote a column written by the *Washington Post's* Maxine Cheshire, who was not present on the particular evening she describes:

"The Moroccan Embassy put aside Washington's Green Book social list and thumbed through outdated back issues of Photoplay to come up with a guest list for Saturday night. There was a Hollywood contingent that looked, someone said, 'Like Mme. Tussaud's waxworks'—many there USED TO BE somebody."

Some of the used-to-be's listed were Merle Oberon, Ann Sothern ("used to be several dress sizes smaller") and Micheline Lerner, who, Maxine reported, "ignored the hostess' place cards in order to sit next to her date." This offended Washington socialite Joan Gardner, who "lectured Mrs. Lerner severely on the niceties of social deportment."

Blonde Joan Gardner, the wife of Arthur W. Gardner,

whose father was ambassador to Cuba under Eisenhower, was described by Maxine as being "one of those behind-the-scenes, seldom-publicized powers who terrify social climbers in Washington." According to Maxine "the late John F. Kennedy was one of the few people with nerve enough to challenge her. Once, after he got into the White House, he demanded: 'Who does she think she is, that she can decide who's in and who's out?'" Dynamic Joan, the Washington editor for *House & Garden* (strictly a part-time job) and one of the city's outstanding wits, is actually not so formidable as she seems. But she does have a network of close friends which makes her one of the best news-getters in the city.

Judith Martin of the *Washington Post* is the first to admit that, when covering the party beat, she was far from welcome by many of the people she was assigned to cover.

"The Kuwaitis even declared me *persona non grata* when their emir was here," she gleefully reports. "An awful lot of people think they can buy you with a dinner or a bottle of Scotch sent around to the house, and since there *are* a lot of people they can buy that way, they're really stunned when somebody doesn't react. The Kuwaitis had courted me for years—there were hints of trips, all those dinner invitations, and oh, God! the bouquet they sent when Nicky was born, you wouldn't believe it, all pink and blue and about 30 feet wide and the nurse could hardly carry it into the room. Then to their surprise, when they gave these decadent parties, I wrote about them like it was. Others were writing about how terribly charming and elegant it all was."

Judy wrote such things as: "Hubert Humphrey wandered into the Kuwait Embassy's Arabic splendor like Tom Sawyer exploring a Rudolph Valentino set . . ."

In an earlier story she mentioned the "pillowed splendor known informally as 'the seduction room' . . ."

The "seduction room" is what the Kuwait ambassador calls a 200-year-old Arabian room which was lifted out of a palace in Damascus and transferred—carved cedar panelling, oriental carpets, urn-shaped glass chandeliers, soft pillows, low divans, and all—to the Kuwait Embassy on Tilden Street. It has the cushioned comfort reminiscent of the Arabian Nights, though it is almost certain that nobody in the supremely behavior-conscious diplomatic or official world has ever so much as contemplated an actual seduction there.

"When I wrote about these things," continues Judy, "it upset them terribly, because it had never occurred to them that if they invited a working reporter she would run around reporting on exactly what she saw."

Judy was assigned to cover the emir when he came to pay the last state visit of the Johnson administration, but the Kuwaitis wouldn't let her come to their party for President Johnson, declaring her *persona non grata*.

The *Post* kept Judy assigned to the state dinner at the White House, over which the Kuwaitis had no control, and Judy's greatest triumph was standing in the entrance hall of the White House, the first person to greet the Kuwait ambassador and the beauteous Mme. Al-Ghoussein.

They weren't pleased with her story about the White House that night, either. "I tried to cover that dinner with all fairness, but something happened that I would have written about anyway that was terribly funny. They had some musical comedy entertainment and President Johnson tried to get the emir to clap along. The emir was confused, poor soul, and kept looking around the room, and Johnson was poking him in the ribs, carrying on, clapping his hands and stamping his foot. The poor emir felt etiquette obliged him to stamp his little fat foot, and I wrote about it."

The Moroccans stopped asking Judy to their parties, too. The straw that broke the camel's back was a story she wrote accusing the king of Morocco of walking out on then-Vice President Humphrey.

It seems that the king had wanted to give a party for the president, but the State Department said it wasn't possible since the king wasn't on a state visit. The Moroccans were so sure the president would not fail to come if the king gave a party that they went on with it. "And when they heard that President Johnson really wasn't going to be there, and the vice president was coming instead, the king walked out," says Judy.

The Moroccans vigorously deny Judy's story, saying the king

did not know the vice president was coming. According to Judy, she heard the Secret Service agents talking via their walkie-talkies" and when they got the word that the vice president was on his way, they passed the information along to the king. He left immediately."

Later, when she wanted to see the Moroccan's new heavily carpeted, many-pillowed Arabian room, Judy was refused entrance. She got in later with fellow members of the Wellesley Club who were taking a tour of the embassy. Judy says, "When I walked in with my little white card pinned on my shoulder, saying 'Judith Martin, '59' the Moroccans almost fainted."

The Arabs weren't the only ones to feel the bite of Judy's caustic reporting. When during the Johnson administration it was decided that the press couldn't attend a particular White House reception except to watch the guests being received (it had been customary to let at least a pool of reporters mingle with guests during receptions), Judy wrote, "Relations were strained at the diplomatic reception which President and Mrs. Lyndon B. Johnson gave at the White House last night. The president handled diplomats from around the world with hugs and handclasps—but all the while, a knot of hostile people stared at him from a few feet away. Communications had broken down between the White House and the press, all over the Blue Room floor . . . The reporters, who normally dress appropriately for White House parties and who think of themselves as behaving like ladies, were furious. They wore street clothes to the black-tie reception and politely but repeatedly declined glasses of champagne which were offered to them. 'I'll never eat or drink another thing in this house,' said one veteran White House reporter."

Judy, who started working at the *Post* as a copy girl during vacations while going to Wellesley, is married to Robert Martin, a brilliant National Institutes of Health doctor. They spend several weeks each year in Spain, following the bullfights, which doesn't surprise any of Judy's colleagues since she's the *Post*'s most ardent Hemingway buff.

After several years of covering diplomatic row and White House parties, Judy was shifted to an assignment which, loosely, might be called critic of the contemporary scene, which is just where her enemies say she should be, since "she always criticized everything anyway." But admirers of Judy's satirical and witty style thoroughly enjoy such observations as:

· A complete review of the movie *Sappho Darling:* "In *Sappho Darling* at the Plaza Theater, Yvonne D'Angers shows off her silicone injections to a character named Sappho Anderson. The rest of the movie's overdone, too."

· On Richard Burton's former wife, Sybil: She "looks like a grey-haired teen-ager of about forty."

· When President Nixon welcomed the astronauts back to earth: ". . . . he called the span of the moon trip 'the greatest week in the history of the world since the Creation.' Only a comparison with the creation of the universe could make traveling in it seem a small achievement. Even the president's most loyal, conservative, middle-American supporters must have winced."

· On covering a Marlene Dietrich press conference: "I spent the 50s being in love with Ernest Hemingway . . . and Ernest Hemingway's idea of a woman was Marlene Dietrich. Monday night I went to see her in the hope of learning something." Then, after describing Miss Dietrich's rudeness to an old couple who timidly approached to say that they had always admired her, Judy said: "I'm glad I never met Ernest Hemingway."

Embassy parties aren't just fun and games for reporters. As Liz Carpenter once said, "This is a town where shrimp-bowl intrigue is apt to be very newsworthy."

Rice bowl intrigue is newsworthy, too. Especially when a reporter like Ymelda Dixon picks up, in casual conversation, a story such as: Anna Chennault, widow of Lieutenant General Claire Lee Chennault, went to Vietnam in 1968 to talk to Premier Ky about delaying the peace talks in Paris to help Richard Nixon win the election. Ymelda, widow of humorist George Dixon, who writes a column, "Your Date With Ymelda," for the *Washington Star,* was at a Korean party one evening when she overheard two guests discussing Anna Chennault. As she recalls the conversation, one guest asked, "Where is Anna?" Another said she was in Vietnam. Still another asked why. The answer was, "She went to talk to Ky about not saying anything before the election." It was just ordinary Washington party chitchat, but in print it didn't take long to come to the attention of the State department.*

Ymelda had another story about Mrs. Chennault which has left the mysterious but powerful Republican hostess quite cool toward her. When a friend of Anna's told Ymelda that the General's widow had spent over $300,000 on her penthouse at the Watergate Apartments, where many key Republicans maintain their chichi apartments, Ymelda wrote about it. "Anna called to tell me that when she got home from New York, there was an Internal Revenue agent waiting on her doorstep to inquire about this huge sum of money," she says.

Madame Chennault was also upset with Ymelda when she wrote that Mme. Ky was complaining, at one of Anna's parties, about Americans being so materialistic. "There she was in Italian silks, talking about going to New York shopping, wearing all those jewels, and talking about American materialism," says Ymelda. "I wrote it. Naturally it upset the South Vietnamese."

Mrs. Chennault has also been immortalized in print by Sally Quinn, one of the *Post* Style section's most competent new young writers. "I know it's unfashionable to talk about communism," Sally quoted Mrs. Chennault as saying at a luncheon given in her honor on Capitol Hill by Mrs. Strom Thurmond, "but the young people are being influenced by propaganda from other parts of the world . . . they don't understand that the people in Viet Nam are fighting for freedom." Republican Senator Milton Young of North Dakota gave Anna her ultimate accolade, according to Sally: "If there were more Americans like Anna Chennault, this country would not be in the shape it's in now."

Ymelda covers Washington society in general, embassy parties

* Later, Theodore H. White, in his book *The Making of the President—1968*, reported that Vice President Hubert Humphrey knew of Mrs. Chennault's activity, but refused to reveal it in the campaign because he was convinced Richard Nixon had not approved or known of her actions. Mr. White also said that the Nixon staff was furious when it learned what Mrs. Chennault had done.

in particular, and admits with characteristic honesty that even for a society reporter she overdoes it on the Spaniards. "One of my daughters lives in Spain, so I knock myself out for them." Ymelda's other obvious prejudice is for the Eugene McCarthys. Right up until the day Senator McCarthy left home, Ymelda was regularly devoting space to how her good friends Abigail and Gene wouldn't dream of breaking up this Catholic marriage made in heaven. Her friends haven't dared tease her with the thought that had she printed fewer protestations about the loving couple, the senator, who is famous for his puckish quality, might not have felt driven to prove her wrong.

She got into the news business via an unusual route. George Dixon, the late political humorist, was something of a practical joker as well as one of the cleverest of satirists. He made his wife famous by constantly getting her name wrong on purpose in his column, or else attributing remarks to her as a ventriloquist does to his favorite dummy. She also is the daughter of the late Senator Dennis Chavez of New Mexico, so that her political and social connections in Washington formed an intricate spider's web. Shortly after George Dixon died, people started suggesting that Ymelda go into the newspaper business, and finally a friend who was working at the *Post* talked her into it. "I submitted sample columns and Marie Sauer, then the women's editor, said that I would have to leave this alone and that alone because it was Maxine Cheshire's territory, so I called Gwen Dobson, women's editor of the *Star*, and invited her to lunch. She called back to tell me Newbold Noyes, the editor-in-chief, had told her to take me to lunch at the Sans Souci, and I knew right away I was in. Part of the deal was reporting social events over the weekends, when the others would rather not work. I love this job. I work like a dog and don't make much money, but Gwen says all reporters are egomaniacs, and I like being a fish in this pond."

Occasionally a hostess will ask a society reporter to come before dinner for cocktails only. Ymelda refuses to drop in on any party before a dinner to which she is not invited. "I'd feel like a servant if I did." Once Mrs. Felix Schnyder, the wife of the Swiss ambassador, invited Ymelda to stop in for cocktails, and she replied: "Mrs. Schnyder, since you are a very lovely person,

I want to tell you that you are making a terrible mistake. If you expect decent coverage, you must ask the reporter for the entire evening."

She hates cocktail parties, and says no news comes out of them, but feels she must go in order to meet people to call on later. "I don't hate dinner parties, in fact I like them. I'd like them a lot better if, as a member of the press, I didn't get such dreadful dinner partners."

One reporter covering the embassy circuit full time is Dorothy McCardle, a silver-haired veteran reporter with more verve and energy than many a beginner one-third her age. She is calling her autobiography, if and when she writes it, *Crime to Caviar*. It's certainly a fitting title. She first won recognition covering such stories as the Lindbergh kidnapping and the Bruno Hauptmann trial, and now she gets scoops, such as Agnew blaming Chief of Protocol Bus Mosbacher for Pompidou's difficulties in Chicago, doing the embassy beat for the *Washintgon Post.*

After covering the White House during the Johnson administration, Dorothy was switched to Embassy Row when the *Post* decided it had to change its image with foreign diplomats if it ever wanted to be invited inside an embassy door again. It couldn't have pleased the embassies more.

Over 20 of Dorothy's 45 years of reporting have been spent covering society, and she's especially simpatico with the diplomatic community since her husband, Carl McCardle, a free-lance writer, was an assistant secretary of state for four years of the Eisenhower administration. Dorothy can dig out a news story at any party without rattling the bones of the skeletons in the closets, and as far as is known, Jacqueline Kennedy is the only person who ever has been furious with her for something she wrote. That was when she revealed that the then White House curator, Lorraine Pearce, had slapped Caroline's hands one day when the child touched the antiques.

Landing her first newspaper job at the *Philadelphia Inquirer* in 1924, Dorothy covered crime and disasters until 1948 when Carl was sent to Washington to head the *Philadelphia Bulletin's* bureau. She free-lanced for a while, and then for 15 years wrote a "Mirrors of Washington" column for NANA until she finally joined the *Post* staff in 1960.

The debut of Mrs. Paul Mellon's daughter, Liza Lloyd, at the Mellons' 3,200-acre Virginia estate, with First Lady Jacqueline Kennedy a guest, soon gave Dorothy a chance to use the tricks she'd learned covering crime. Two days before the debut ball, she drove to Oak Spring, the Mellon estate near Upperville, boldly went up to the guard at the gate, and announced she was to see Mrs. Mellon.

Since Dorothy looks far more like somebody's aristocratic aunt than a snooper, the guard politely gave her directions for finding the main house. Roaming around the grounds and house, she talked to dozens of people putting up tents and decorations, and was on her way out before actually coming face-to-face with the shocked Mrs. Mellon. It didn't matter, for by then Dorothy had all the background material she needed.

The day of the party, the *Post* sent Dorothy and Maxine Cheshire to Upperville to cover the debut, which was not open to the press. The two reporters checked into the local inn, and while the Mellons' guests were scattered all over the hunt country, attending pre-ball dinners (Mrs. Kennedy went to the one given by Mrs. Kingman Douglas, the former Adele Astaire), Maxine and Dorothy went out to Oak Spring, where the dance was to be.

"Maxine drove," says Dorothy, "and we went all around the place. We found a little narrow lane, pitch dark and muddy, but Maxine assured me all was well, that she had a gun locked in the glove compartment and a carving knife on the back seat. Once we got out and crawled through the bushes, in the mud, trying to get to the party. That's the story of my life, crawling through bushes. I scrambled through them, over rain-soaked ground, when I covered the Lindbergh case . . . that time I got right up under the window which was open, and heard everything Lindbergh was saying, but at the Mellons we were frightened away by someone with a flashlight.

"Back at the main gate we watched people arriving. We saw Mrs. Kennedy at about 12:30 A.M., and then we went back to the inn. Maxine went to bed, but I stayed up and sat on the porch, waiting."

Hours later, two college boys who had been hired by the decorating firm to work on party preparations, and who had been "allowed in as sort of semi-guests," came up and asked Dorothy where they could get a bus into Washington, so they could catch their train back to Philadelphia.

"They knew all the details of the party, but said they didn't have time to tell me. I said, 'Don't worry, I'll take you to Washington.' I went upstairs and got my things (Maxine was fast asleep) and arrived at the *Washington Post* at 8:00 A.M. with my story.

"One of the best stories I ever had," continues Dorothy, "was when the Johnsons gave their first party, for members of Congress, in December, 1963, just a month after the assassination . . . after the party President Johnson asked Fran Lewine, Isabelle Shelton, Hazel Markel (of *Palm Beach Life*), and me to stay. He talked to us for about a half hour, giving us this fantastic thing about foreign affairs. Then he asked if we had seen his office and waved to his photographer, Okamoto, to take our pictures. On the way to his office, he took us to see the swimming pool. No representative of the press had ever seen it since Joe Kennedy had commissioned that tremendous mural of the Virgin Islands on the wall for President Kennedy. We stopped in the Cabinet room, had our pictures taken again, and when we got them signed, mine said, 'To Dorothy McCardle, who keeps me *Posted* every day.' In his office he autographed pictures of the whole family and gave us each one. Then, he said, 'I think I'll call Jackie.' He told us we could say he called her, but not to report the conversation, because 'I don't think she would like it.'

"President Johnson said, 'Hello, Jackie, how are you,' then 'When are you coming to see me?' She apparently laughed it off, and he said, 'If you don't come to see me, I am coming out there and picket your house.' The rest of it was about the children, and then, 'Oh, he is?' He whispered to us, 'John is playing with the fire truck I sent him for Christmas.'" Dorothy reports that the whole scene felt unreal.

After he hung up, the president shuffled through papers on his desk, some marked "confidential," saying, "You're just as good reporters as the men, I'm going to give you a story." Then he gave them the new budget figures, which, of course, was front-page news. Continuing her story, Dorothy says, "President Johnson asked the reporters if they had seen his hideaway, the first anyone knew he had a little private office created at the side of his regular office. The walls were lined with pictures of Eisenhower, Roosevelt, Kennedy, and Sam Houston, among others, together with autographed letters from important people of the day to his grandfather. The women were floating on air."

On inaugural night of 1965, Dorothy had another intimate glimpse of the president. She was assigned to the press pool car in the motorcade which took the presidential party to the various inaugural balls. After the last stop, she was running up the ramp of the hotel, trying desperately to catch up with the press car before it pulled out, when the Johnsons, seeing her distraught state, offered her a ride back to the White House. On the way, LBJ gave her a plum that made the whole nightmarish evening worthwhile: he told her that while dressing that morning, he had rewritten his entire inaugural address.

Reporters on the diplomatic beat, to be successful, must have razor-sharp memories, since without a working acquaintance of the cast of characters on the scene they could not possibly make sense, let alone news, out of a party. A recent story by Ruth Dean in the *Washington Star* about a reception given by Uruguayan Ambassador Hector Luisi and his wife illustrates the need for a clear picture of who's who. Ruth mentioned within a brief 15 paragraphs her conversations with more than a dozen ambassadors and officials, including John McClintock, who provided the first printed information that his twin brother Robert was expected to be appointed the next ambassador to Venezuela.

On the same evening, Joy Billington, also of the *Star*, was knee-deep in tulips at the Netherlands Embassy's annual reception to show off Holland's most famous flower. She, too, chatted with dozens of VIPs, including White House Curator Clem Conger who told her that Jacqueline Onassis' new portrait was being hidden at the National Gallery until it was hung in the White House, because the ceremony had been delayed by Jackie's statement that she "would never enter the White House again."

In memorizing faces, reporters even become familiar with those of the party crashers, a special Washington breed. It's easy to drop into embassy receptions and national day celebrations uninvited, because the crowds are so large that no one, certainly not the ambassador-host, knows all his guests. Judy Axler once wrote in the *New York Daily News* about a government secretary and her boy friend who built a small nest egg to buy their first home by getting their dinners free every night at embassy parties.

Many of the most memorable parties given on Embassy Row are those ambassadors give for each other. "The best party I ever went to was at the Algerian Embassy. I wrote about it and was never asked back," says Ann Wood of the *New York Daily News.* Ann, who was born into the newspaper business (her father, J. Howard Wood, is chairman of the *Chicago Tribune* Company) was the only reporter at the farewell party former Ambassador Cherif Guellal gave for the popular Hervé Alphands. Ann, then working for the *Star,* thinks she was invited because she was single and young, a great advantage when covering the Washington social scene. Cherif, a bachelor beau of the seductive former Miss America, Yolanda Fox, gave the party at the embassy residence, The Elms, which the Algerians bought from Lyndon Johnson when the LBJs moved into the White House. All the ambassadors from the countries IN at the time, along with a sprinkling of residential society, were there. What made the party extraordinary was the amateur hour that followed dinner. The Russian Ambassador Anatole Dobrynin danced a *pas de deux* with the Marquesa de Merry del Val, in which she took the male role since her narrow dinner skirt limited her movements, and during which the couple did pirouettes, leaps, and turns until his dinner jacket caught on the jeweled bodice of the Marquesa's dress. Ann reported, "They were trapped until he removed it." Ambassador Alphand, a superb mimic, performed his standard repertoire, imitations of Sir Winston Churchill and of a hen laying an egg: "He became a hen, head atilt, eyes blinking, slowly lifting a foot outward to take a step. His cackles were perfect, ending in a triumphant crow as the hen produced an egg." Mme. Dobrynin played the piano while she and her husband sang duets such as "Moscow Nights" and "How Much Is that Doggy in the Window?"

Anne's story was an instant sensation and furnished material for gossip columnists for weeks.

Another time Ann beat her competition on a story was when she got the first interview with Trenny Robb after the precocious teen-ager had been a bridesmaid at the wedding of her brother, Chuck, and Lynda Bird Johnson. The bridesmaids were house guests at the White House, a move said to be for their convenience and pleasure but which the press interpreted as managing the news, since no one could ask any of them the simplest questions without going through Liz Carpenter. Ann tracked down the senior Robbs and talked them into letting her follow Trenny to her home in Milwaukee.

From Ann's interview came Trenny's story about being caught by a pajama-clad President Johnson, late at night in a White House hallway, as he strolled through the mansion turning out the lights: "Who's that?" "It's Trenny." "It would be you." Trenny said she was worried about her father's expense for the rehearsal dinner, since "He'll spend money and be in debt the rest of his life to do the right thing." She told Ann the White House was set up so "everything that's said can be listened to later."

"I got a bonus for that story," says Ann, who stopped covering embassies for two reasons: she found she couldn't remember what day it was (with so many parties, night after night, that doesn't become difficult), and she had worn out her welcome on the diplomatic beat.

"Diplomats are here on assignment, and it's a business. They want you to write a good story so they can send a clipping home. I'm critical, although I'm not mean, and primarily I think I should amuse my readers instead of pleasing the people I cover."

Ann worked for two years at the *Post* before going to the *Star* which she left for her present job at the *News*. Along the way, she learned that hostesses rate reporters according to the papers they represent. She believes her social standing as a reporter was highest when she worked for the *Star.*

Another familiar face on the embassy beat is Donnie Radcliffe of the *Star,* who was catapulted, so to speak, into learning how to cover affairs of state. "It was the very first party I covered," Donnie says, and even recalling it brings back the awe. "I was sitting at Dean Rusk's table, right across from him. I'd never seen Secretary Rusk before, except in pictures."

The then-secretary of state was entertaining ambassadors to the Organization of American States in the elaborate John Quincy Adams, Thomas Jefferson, and Benjamin Franklin State Dining rooms, on the top floor of the State Department. "I went in a short dress," says Donnie. "Everybody else was in long— the last long dress I bought was in my senior year in college, and that had been sixteen years before. I didn't know anyone, nor did I know the procedure. When a reporter was at one of these things, sitting between two ambassadors, was what they told you off the record? Or, if not, did you sit there and scribble your notes?"

Fortunately, one of the ambassadors was so charming, and such a good conversationalist, that Donnie forgot she was a new Washington reporter and it was her first time as a State Department guest.

"Somehow, the conversation got around to Castro and the Bolivian Ambassador to the OAS, Diez de Medina, asked Secretary Rusk about the rumor that the Castro-Communist infiltration questions might be taken to the United Nations. Secretary Rusk said that he felt it was an OAS, not a U.N. problem. My reporting Rusk's answer caused such a flap that the ambassador was called by the wires to learn more about the U.S. position. Apparently he handled it very well, because he later said it all came out satisfactorily."

Thus, Donnie learned her first night out that covering Washington Society was nothing like being women's editor of the *Salinas Californian.* Here she could make news going to a party; she also could know that it would be read by men as well as women, even if it did appear in the women's section of the paper.

Society writers are often asked how they can accept an invitation and then criticize the hostess or her party; Nancy Ross of the *Post*, a member of the tell-it-like-it-is school of reporting, says:

"Undoubtedly the reason I have a reputation for being bitchy is that I think society should be covered like politics, finance, music, anything else . . . You should apply the same standards to society that you apply to all types of critical and analytical reporting. In this respect, Charlotte Curtis has taken the lead, by far, and I respect her enormously for what she has done."

An article Charlotte wrote from Cap Martin, France, in August 1969, is a case in point. Charlotte wrote about a group of the Beautiful People partying at an outdoor restaurant, when someone threw an unshelled almond ("there are those who suspected the Marquis, Spain's gregarious heart surgeon and Generalissimo Francisco Franco's son-in-law") and started a "fun and games thing" which included guests lobbing champagne glasses into the fire and Count Giovanni Volpi climbing into a tree high above the tables taking his plate of vanilla ice cream and raspberries along, then dropping blobs of the dessert on his friends, who included Mrs. Giancarlo Uzielli, her sister Charlotte Ford Niarchos, and their father Henry Ford II. Mr. Ford squirted water from a bottle at the Marquis, an unidentified girl rode a burro in among the tables, and the owner of the restaurant fired a cap pistol while throwing another chair onto the fire, all, as Charlotte pointed out, a typical little evening on the Riviera with the Beautiful People.

This is the sort of thing Washington's never had even under the Kennedys, which is probably one reason Jackie stayed here as little as possible when she was First Lady. The closest the capital ever came was probably the swimming-pool dunkings at the Bobby Kennedys, or the night there was a belly dancer at the Moroccan Embassy. Though the parties here fascinate everybody with a nose for intrigue, they drive some of the Beautiful People like Marion Javits, the theater-and-fashion-minded wife of New York Senator Jack Javits, right up the walls of a typical Georgetown drawing room. Marion feels, and has repeatedly stated in TV and magazine interviews, that Washington is a sort of super "hick town" where all the preoccupations are essentially provincial.

It is in an effort to correct this that slim, unflappable Nancy Ross, a Proper Bostonian with elegantly understated clothes ("I don't subscribe to fads") who went to Swiss, French, and New England private schools, was assigned by the *Washington Post* to what many would consider its most glamorous beat, covering not only city society, but the rich and super-rich at play everywhere.

From the first, Nancy hasn't hesitated to be outspoken about any event she covers, trying to relate the doings of the rich to the average reader by criticism, by showing that the *grande dame* in the tiara can have her make-up smeared, her slip or other foible showing, that "we are all human and the rich can do silly things, too. You run into people who argue that 'You knocked such-and-such a party and it was for *charity*. How could you do such a beastly thing?' They feel it's like striking a nun or something, and in their eyes you are a terrible demon."

There were many repercussions from a piece of Nancy's about the way local and national charities pressure embassies into tremendous contributions of time, money, and gifts. She pointed out that charities abroad did not ask American embassies to give all these dances, dinners, tours, and contributions of wine and perfume. Many a benefit committee woman called to say she had "maligned their motives and their causes." But a number of ambassadors told Nancy "Thank God someone has told the story, for we are sick to death of being used this way."

Nancy says there are many stories like this. She wanted to write about segregation in the diplomatic corps, telling how the Africans stick with the Africans, how they are almost never invited to the European, Asian, and Latin American embassies. Her editors didn't want her to write it.

Another story she proposed was on the kind of reception people like Mrs. Strom Thurmond and Mrs. William O. Douglas, both very young wives of old men, get from the older Congressional and Supreme Court wives. "You can see it in their pattern of entertainment that the young women are completely cold shouldered, but nobody dares to write this."

Having too many tell-it-like-it-is reporters on one newspaper has its disadvantages, though: "We had to have a whole new campaign at the *Post*. To put it quite frankly, our party sources essentially dried up. So after we took a good hard look at what the social situation was, it was decided to try to get back in the good graces of people we supposedly have maligned in the past so we could open the doors which were being closed to us."

She strongly believes there are certain ethics to follow, even in her kind of reporting. For example, she thinks it unfair to eavesdrop, to misrepresent, or get her information under false pretenses. "You have to weigh what is being said and ask yourself, 'Would quoting this hurt the person?' " she says.

"Then there are the social climbers, many who make a career of it and use the press to their advantage. If they use the press, then it is fair for the press to use them by reporting some of the silly things they say."

On the other hand, when a Cabinet member, a married man, while dancing with Nancy discussed his current girl friend, plus revealing other intimate details from his past, Nancy chalked it up as normal for a man to boast while talking with a pretty girl. She didn't write about his remarks, saying, "Just because he happened to be a Cabinet member didn't mean he wasn't a man."

"More women work in Washington after dark than anywhere in the world since the brothels were closed in Paris."

It isn't hard in Washington to become part of society, or even to become one of the close-to-the-throne power people: not if the aspirant is smart, knows how to entertain, has stamina, wit, thick skin, a fat bank account, and determination. Taste is an asset, but some have made it without much of that, as anyone who's gone to many Washington parties can testify. The first step toward being a Capital socialite is to get "involved." The second is to make sure of good coverage in the local society columns. For the press is so powerful it actually can make one a socialite.

Gwen Cafritz became a famous Washington hostess because a local paper deliberately set out to make her one. The *New York Daily News'* Washington-based reporter Paul Healy tells in his book, *Cissy,* how the colorful and powerful Cissy Patterson, owner of the old *Washington Herald* (later she added the *Washington Times* to make the *Times-Herald,* which was subsequently bought by the *Post*), suddenly decided one morning in 1938 that the town needed a new hostess. She explained to

Luvie Pearson, wife of Drew, that she had picked Gwen Cafritz, wife of Washington builder Morris Cafritz, because she thought the exotic Hungarian-born Gwen had the "ambition, the vitality, the *savoir faire* and the wealth" to make it as a hostess, plus having a large house on fashionable Foxhall Road. Cissy immediately started dropping Gwen's name in the *Herald*'s society and gossip columns. Top people accepted Gwen's invitations and, says Paul, "Gwen Cafritz was launched, and for the next several decades made Cissy look good as a drawing-room talent scout."

Another example of how the press creates the very scene it then reports was the "Democratic inaugural ball" given by a fervent Adlai Stevenson worker and admirer in her Georgetown house on the night of the second Eisenhower inaugural in January of 1957. Only Democrats were invited, even the waiters and musicians had to have full party credentials, and no friend, however close, was allowed to cross the threshold if known to have defected to Eisenhower even temporarily.

Adlai refused the invitation, on the grounds that his presence at such a gathering would be in "poor taste," but candles were lighted next to his charming letter, and Senators Kennedy, Humphrey, and Symington came in their white ties from the various real inaugural balls and almost literally "danced all night."

The party received some passing attention in the press, because it was a funny idea, and because it was a marvelous silly party in the days before Vietnam, the War on Poverty, and the assassinations made fun synonymous with frivolity. One well-known national correspondent (male) was discovered naked in one of the children's bathtubs the following morning at 8 A.M. Nobody ever found out how he got there, for he jumped into his clothes and rushed out the door in terror when the children shouted, "Mummy! Daddy! Help! There's a dead man in the tub!"

The story of the party hit *Time* and *Newsweek*, which meant it went into the library folder marked "Kennedy, Senator John F., Social Life," of virtually every paper in the country. When Kennedy was elected president four years later, and reporters started pulling out the files, there it was: positive proof that the hostess was an intimate friend of the Kennedys. The fact that she knew them only as pleasant acquaintances, never as close friends, didn't daunt the press, which day after day listed the embarrassed giver of the party as one of Jackie's most intimate confidantes.

It got so embarrassing that it was painful to run into Jackie's real friends, like Toni Bradlee, wife of Ben Bradlee, now executive editor of the *Washington Post*, or Martha Bartlett, wife of Charles Bartlett, now a syndicated columnist, for fear they'd think these stories had been planted out of a self-advancement motive. And it wasn't much fun staying home by the fire while those dazzling dancing parties were going on at the White House, answering calls from reporters wanting to know first who was going, and then who had been there. Once a myth is created by the press, it becomes a part of folklore, and dies hard. The "Democratic ball" hostess found that the invitations to fancy parties multiplied like guinea pigs during the early days of the Kennedy administration.

Media power works another way, too; it can put the one having it in a position to become a hostess whose parties will "draw" Cabinet members, important senators, ambassadors, administration officials, nationally known columnists, and who knows, maybe the president. (In society-writer language, a party which will "draw" is more important than one at which guests will be merely "seen.") Nothing short of an illness requiring hospitalization would keep anyone away from a party given by Katherine Graham, probably the most powerful woman in Washington if not in America. Columnists Marianne Means and Betty Beale and TV commentator Nancy Dickerson also give parties which draw the nation's great, *including* presidents.

The Power Society here really isn't many years old. Mrs. E. Taylor Chewning, an authentic "cave dweller" (the nickname given to those whose families have been prominent here for generations), whose ancestors include Richard Wallach, the next-to-last mayor of Washington before it came under the jursidiction of Congress in 1881, Senator Charles L. Mitchell of Connecticut, and President Lincoln's Postmaster General, Montgomery Blair, thinks the picture began changing during FDR's administration.

"I was only a child then, but I remember how divided my

family was about these new people with only money moving in, and how upset some of them were when Aunt Rose Merriam, who had fallen upon hard times and became the first social secretary, began helping girls to be debutantes whose families nobody had ever heard of before.

"But the final blow to the old order was the Kennedys coming in . . . there were two people with the right background who had all the style and elegance you could dream of in the White House, and Jackie had grown up here and gone to the Dancing Class, which was *the* party which stamped you as Society, and they formed their own society, the brain people, New York café society, entertainers, the press, which made Old Washington feel provincial and out of it."

When the Dancing Class, which was started in 1910, held its Swan Song in 1967, with Meyer Davis practically in tears because he'd played at every party since World War One, the last of the elegance went out of residential society, Mary feels.[*] "Alice Roosevelt Longworth is about the last link between the old world and new."

According to Mary, since the center of the new society is power, the press, people like Kay Graham and columnists like Joseph Alsop and Rowland Evans have taken over the roles that famous hostesses used to play. "It's at their houses you'll find the secretary of state or the secretary of defense for dinner, because everybody's too busy now, and Washington's too important, for them to spend time with people who aren't connected with their work. Of course it helps that the taste and the food are exquisite . . . when Joe Alsop has a party he might fly the dinner over from Paris, for example."

What used to come with family and breeding now can be had by involvement, and politics is a good place for a would-be socialite to start. Take the case of Barbara Howar. Barbara, until recently a panelist on Metromedia's TV show, "Panorama," is a pretty blonde from North Carolina with a Southern accent and

---

[*] This is something of a hyperbole. Mary Chewning, together with Dorcas Hardin, "Ceci" Carusi, and "Oatesie" Charles, all with impeccable social credentials, give two subscription dances a year called "The Fivers." No reporters or photographers are invited, as is also the case with the dances given by the Potomac Marching Society.

sharp wit. She was a natural for the Johnson administration, which featured blonde bombshells like Mary Margaret Valenti, who had been LBJ's secretary before marrying motion picture czar Jack Valenti, and Ann Hand, whose husband, Lloyd, was chief of protocol.

Barbara went to Washington's fashionable Holton Arms and married the son of a Lebanese immigrant who made a fortune in the construction trade (Ed Howar's father built the Washington Mosque). In 1964 Barbara became one of the young matrons in the badly fitting maroon dresses who acted as hostesses for the VIPs at the Atlantic City Democratic Convention, which introduced her to such key Democratic women as Lindy Boggs, wife of Hale Boggs, the House majority whip and congressman from New Orleans. Lindy invited her to go on the "Lady Bird Special" campaign train.

"At a meeting before the trip, someone asked 'Can anyone here comb hair'?" says Barbara. "I had combed everyone's hair at boarding school, so I said I could, and I combed Lady Bird and Lynda's hair on the Whistle Stop."

Mrs. Johnson called her to the White House one day and asked if she would help get some clothes together for the girls for the inaugural. By now, the election was won and Barbara had been named coordinator for the inaugural balls. After that, she saw one Johnson or another four or five times a week. They would either call her, or if she found something she thought they would like, she would call them.

When she was busy selecting clothes for Luci Johnson's wedding, over a year later, a reporter asked if she had had professional experience in fashion. Barbara answered, characteristically: "No. Just a great deal of experience in spending money."

Soon Barbara was dining *en famille* at the White House, and was a guest, along with her husband, Ed, at the swinging dinner-dance the LBJs gave for Princess Margaret and Lord Snowdon (on the dance floor, she later said, "Lynda was draped around George Hamilton like a fox fur"). She read movie magazines with Luci in the privacy of White House limousines, watched movies in the White House theater, chaperoned Luci and Pat Nugent on a New York trip, and helped Pat buy Luci's engagement ring from Harry Winston at a discount.

Her picture appeared in local and out-of-town papers, in designer evening gowns and in mini-dresses with 14-K gold chain straps; her remarks were duly reported ("there aren't enough swingers in Washington to fill a phone booth") so often by one Society reporter it's rumored the editor banned the name of Barbara Howar from her section for weeks; and even *The New York Times* covered a "Zowie" party Barbara and Ed gave at a local discotheque, running the story under a four-column picture of the modly attired hostess.

More publicity came when Barbara and Ed booked the Washington Hotel roof for a pre-wedding party for Luci and Pat. Noted decorator Dick Ridge planned the decorations, the band from Sybil Burton Christopher's New York discotheque "Arthur" was engaged, invitations to match the sharp yellow and poison green decorations were ordered from *haute société papeterie* Mrs. John L. Strong, and the guest list was approved by Mrs. Johnson after several names suggested by Barbara were deleted.

The day the invitations, already addressed and stamped, were to go into the mail, Barbara received a call from the White House. The party was cancelled; so was Barbara's friendship with the Johnsons.

She blames jealousy on the part of two members of Mrs. Johnson's staff, Press Secretary Liz Carpenter and Social Secretary Bess Abell, for her downfall. Discussing *l'affaire* Barbara three years later, a member of the Johnson White House staff said, "The party was cancelled because it was becoming a party to promote Barbara, not a party for Luci. A national magazine was covering it, a network was covering it, and the guest list was generously sprinkled with Barbara's friends."

Barbara said three years later: "I think they were strange folks to turn their kids over to someone for two years and then drop them . . . [but then] that was a very jealous group of people over there, and I had a strong influence over the girls and I think people just got tired of it . . . also, I was against beautification and against the war during the time I was at the White House, and I said beautification was kinda like buying a wig when your teeth are rotting. I thought it was a ridiculous waste of time and money, and of the energy of a woman who could put it into so many other things. For me to see her planting

$15,000 of tulip bulbs from Mary Lasker when there was no inside plumbing in many areas around here was just more than I could bear, and I was most outspoken about it, because it has never been my bag not to be. I don't think Mrs. Johnson appreciated it.

"I did get a couple of nice subtle hints that I should knock it off. Then I told the *Chicago Daily News* that if all these do-gooders in New York want to spend their money down here, let them send it down and we will pay the police a little more and if they want recognition I will personally wear a bronze plaque on my back saying, 'Today I was not raped or mugged, through the kind generosity of Mary Lasker.' Well, I thought Mrs. Johnson was going to faint over that."

Barbara admits that her experience with the Johnsons was a painful turning point in her life: "I was dropped right and left around the city, by people I had thought were friends. They were scared, it was as simple as that."

Now divorced from Ed Howar, Barbara lives with her two children in the old Georgetown townhouse which was home to Teddy and Joan Kennedy before they built their $750,000 house in McLean, Virginia.

Instead of being a rich young society matron, Barbara became a controversial television personality, appearing two hours a day, five days a week, on the Metromedia program, when she wasn't fainting in the Rive Gauche restaurant "from lack of energy and lack of funds," as her remark was duly recorded in Maxine Cheshire's column.

Her social life wasn't completely shattered ("I don't go anymore to the vapid, black-tie dinner parties where they talk about somebody who brought a Jew into the Chevy Chase Club"), since many of Washington's IN people felt being dropped by LBJ was not a major disaster.

Her name did disappear from The Social List of Washington, commonly called the Green Book, a suede-covered volume which reposes on most fashionable tables, and is invaluable as a protocol guide and as a reference book for checking the names and numbers of diplomats, congressmen, and the like—neither the enterprising hostess nor the society reporter could be without one. It is published by Carolyn Hagner Shaw, who has a mystery board which decides on who makes it or doesn't in Washington (some disgruntled OUTs claim the board has one member, "Callie" Shaw), and the slightest hint of scandal bars your name from her book. Former Supreme Court Justice and Mrs. Abe Fortas were the most newsworthy names dropped in 1970.

Barbara isn't bitter about Washington newspaper women, who following her fall from Johnson grace didn't always treat her with what she calls "utmost kindness and sincerity." As she puts it, "I owe the fact that some TV station wanted to show my face all over the country to my having had an image created by the women's press, purely and simply that. Without them I'd be nowhere . . . I have no ax to grind, although some of them bore the Bejesus out of me."

Newspaperwomen still find Barbara always good for a quote and one, Gwen Dobson of the *Star,* even found Barbara willing to discuss her "searing runaway romance that rocked the White House." Gwen wrote in her column, "Luncheon With . . ." that it was during her romance that her son was stricken with spinal meningitis. "He was only 14 months old, and the illness left him with a serious hearing defect. With her strict Catholic upbringing, Barbara still frets that her son's illness was retribution for her fling."

Barbara's TV career consisted of doing a news commentary and being the one woman on a three-member panel which on a live broadcast, *Panorama,* five times weekly quizzes people whose names are in the news. ("I was the screaming liberal of the three of us. I got the Lowensteins, the Shirley Chisholms, and the George McGoverns.") Her questions were knowledgeable, sometimes witty, often caustic, and occasionally what some people called downright nasty. When Hollywood columnist Sheilah Graham was on, she found Barbara and her questioning so "obnoxious" she threatened to walk off the show. "I've never been so insulted in all my life," said Sheilah.

"Between my mini-skirts and multi-mouth, I didn't think I'd last a month when I started in April 1968, but the show's rating went up. Women are interested in what other women are saying, particularly if you are a reconstructed jet-setter or a reclaimed Beautiful People. I had so much frivolousness to live down, I've had to work twice as hard as a regular newswoman."

Perle Mesta is another who made it socially through political involvement. But her choices over the years of politicians to support has caused her social status to go up and down like a Yo-Yo. Mrs. Mesta, loaded with Oklahoma and Texas oil money from her father, William Skirvin, and steel money from her late husband, George Mesta, was foresighted enough to entertain the then-Senator Harry Truman when few members of Washington's social world cared a hoot about the piano-playing former haberdasher from Missouri. She supported him for the vice-presidential nomination in the 1944 Democratic Convention, and campaigned for him as a presidential candidate in 1948. When Truman walloped Thomas Dewey, Perle *Call Me Madam* Mesta became minister to Luxembourg (after she had told Truman she'd like the job, and after Washington newspaper woman Hope Miller had suggested to her that it would be a good idea).

During the Eisenhower administration, Democratic Perle's social star didn't dim, although her old pal Ike (who had loved to cook in her Luxembourg kitchen and entertain her dinner guests by singing "Drink to Me Only with Thine Eyes," when he headed NATO) didn't do right by Perle. He fired her from her Hostess with the Mostes' job in Luxembourg less than a month before the coronation of Queen Elizabeth II, in London. Mrs. Mesta said later that Ike did it under pressure from the Women's Division of the Republican National Committee because it didn't want a Democrat representing the U.S. at the coronation.

The unsinkable Perle went to England on her own, rented luxurious Londonderry House and gave a smashing dinner for 125, followed by a supper dance for an additional 575 which made almost as much news as the festivities for the new queen.

Returning to Washington, Mrs. Mesta continued giving her newsmaking parties, such as a luncheon for First Lady Mamie Eisenhower, a dinner for Dr. and Mrs. Wernher von Braun, and a Thanksgiving Day party honoring several foreign ambassadors.

When LBJ made a bid for the Democratic presidential nomination in 1960, Perle was right there in Los Angeles at the Democratic National Convention, giving a huge party for him. She was taken aback when Lyndon took the second spot on the ticket, and not too many days later called a friend to say she was coming out for Richard Nixon. She refused to change her mind, although warned she might be making a fatal mistake, saying that "President Eisenhower, himself, told me last night that Nixon can't lose." Nixon lost and Mesta was OUT. But not for long. She was continually hospitable to Vice President and Mrs. Johnson, as well as members of their staffs like Liz Carpenter, while Kennedy people were virtually snubbing the Texans. When LBJ became president, Mrs. Mesta was IN and at the Atlantic City nominating convention of 1964 she gave a series of such splashy private parties that even the snobbiest Kennedy friends were angling for invitations.

During the 1968 campaign, Perle supported Hubert Humphrey, so after the election people started saying "Two-party Perle is OUT again." They were selling her short. Mrs. Spiro Agnew went to a Mesta party soon after the inaugural, Cabinet members and other administration VIPs followed, so Perle, while perhaps not still the Mostes', is certainly still a Hostess.

The bash she recently gave for Clare Boothe Luce was such a swinging affair that Clare did the hula, Perle danced the Charleston, Peruvian Ambassador Fernando Berckemeyer and Carol Finch, wife of the secretary of HEW, swished through a *paso doble*, Claribel Berckemeyer sang "I Could Have Danced All Night," and Senator Strom Thurmond toasted Perle in rhyme. When she gave a supper-dance for Ethel Merman, following a screening of *Call Me Madam*, a member of the Nixon Cabinet entered the dance contest. George Romney, Secretary of Housing and Urban Affairs, and Mrs. Romney didn't win. Turned out they could do a wicked waltz, but only a sedate rock.

Even in this political town, diving into politics isn't everyone's bag. Some devote their time to the symphony and the opera. ("A great deal of social climbing is done to music," says Hope Miller.) Others, some of whom can't tell a Miro from a Murillo, take up art—becoming a Friend of the Corcoran is helpful—and being on the board of the Friends of the Kennedy

Center for the Performing Arts is like being a member of the Racquet Club in New York.

Two of Washington's most trim and fashionable matrons, "Ceci" and "Lily" (if you don't know they are Mrs. Eugene Carusi and Mrs. Polk Guest, you're starting out way behind the eight ball), work almost full time for the Center, and the International Best Dressed List. "Deeda" is the wife of William McCormack Blair, former law partner of Adlai Stevenson, ambassador to the Philippines, then Denmark under JFK and LBJ, and now chairman of the Center. The Ralph Beckers are a couple constantly in the news whose rise to social security can be attributed at least in part to his position as General Counsel of the Kennedy Center.

You can, of course, achieve the same end by building a Cultural Center of your own, as did the David Lloyd Kreegers when they erected a marble palace on Foxhall Road a few years ago to house what former National Gallery Director John Walker called "one of the truly distinctive collections of impressionist and post-impressionist art," complete with Renoirs and Monets.

Just as a political worker must pick a winner, the aspiring socialite must choose a *chic* charity. Anything Kay Halle is working on will do, for this dynamic blonde knows all the key political and what few literary figures there are in town, and gives romantic parties on her Georgetown terrace which always include such visiting celebrities as Arthur Schlesinger, Jr., and Kenneth Galbraith.

Or one would do well, now, to develop an absorbing interest in children's hearing and speech problems, if she wants to meet Mesdames Hugh D. Auchincloss, David Bruce, Joseph or Steward Alsop, Christian Herter, Paul Nitze, Frank Wisner, Robert Charles (the former Oatsie Leiter of Newport and Washington, whose first husband's family owned a marble palace on DuPont Circle), or the former Mrs. Neylan McBain, the San Francisco heiress who recently married author Marquis Childs.

Occasionally the Children's Hearing and Speech Center gives a benefit, such as the $25-per-person "old fashioned barbecue" it has held for three years in a row at Polly and Jack Logan's Firenze House overlooking Rock Creek Park. Polly Logan was the widow of Colonel Robert Guggenheim until she married bachelor-about-town Jack Logan, and her house is so magnificent that Allen Drury used it as the model for the home of one of the heroines in his best-selling *Advise and Consent*. EVERYBODY attends the barbecue, including Alice Roosevelt Longworth, who munches spareribs between spars with the press. One of the first people President Nixon invited to the White House for dinner was Alice Longworth. It was served in her old White House bedroom, which Jackie Kennedy had turned into an upstairs family dining room. Later, some Washingtonians said that having Alice Longworth over for a little family dinner was the smartest thing Nixon had done, socially, since his inaugural.

The charity ball as a fund-raising operation has been going downhill for the past few years, though to borrow Mark Twain's phrase, reports of its death would be premature. Also on the wane, though still surviving, is the political cocktail party. Only the fact that it was at Mrs. Eugene Meyer's house, and that it was for Adlai Stevenson III and his delightful wife, Nancy, to help their campaign for the U.S. Senate from Illinois, kept a spring party in 1970 at $100 per person from turning into a sparsely attended disaster. Only nine thousand dollars was raised, enough for a five-minute television program, but hardly a drop in the bucket for a candidate for the Senate from the third most populous state in America.

No matter which cause is chosen, it's important to have a house, or under the Republicans an apartment at the Watergate, fancy enough to hold committee meetings in. This establishes that one has money and knows how to serve tea as well as "they" do. So much the better if the abode will handle a crowd large enough for the "after the concert," "after the opening," or "before the ball" supper habitually given for a benefit's $100-and-up ticket holders. In fact a shortcut to success would be to buy a large house with several acres and offer to lend it for the benefit, an especially good gambit now that the large ball at a hotel has fallen into disfavor. At some point, "they" will have to invite the hostess back, because they want her house lent again next year. And of course the benefit will be covered by the society reporters.

After holding the charity's committee meeting at her house, the aspiring socialite provides a divine little lunch or tea with light food and light conversation. Hopefully she has met a few embassy wives (there usually are several on every benefit committee), who provide the seasoning in the stew, since everyone is curious about them and since it's easier to get "asked back" by diplomats. Preferably one starts with an ambassador's wife as honor guest, but that's not necessary. As Gwen Cafritz once said, "I started out having little attachés, and worked my way up to the Supreme Court."

Courting the embassies can get a little sticky at times. One Jewish couple was solidly entrenched with the Arab countries when the Israeli-Arab war started in 1967. After what must have been much soul-searching about loyalty to heritage versus fear of losing newly gained social standing, the couple decided to continue going to Arabian Embassy parties, although these parties were boycotted by other Washington Jews. Seeing them at another embassy a few days after the fighting had ceased, a Washington lawyer, Jewish himself, walked over to remark acidly, "Well, I see your side lost."

"Making the scene" is work, work, work, even for those who thoroughly enjoy it. Marie Ridder, writer, well-known hostess, and wife of publisher Walter Ridder, remembers Senator Eugene McCarthy telling her that after going through his invitations he had come to the conclusion that "more women work in Washington after dark than anywhere in the world since the brothels were closed in Paris."

Marie, an astute observer of the merry-go-round, adds that "Some of these women are members of the press or married to one. Others are wives of lobbyists, lawyers, diplomats. They run the gamut of those married to men whose business it is to be well informed to those who simply want an active and glamorous social life, for a Washington party is almost never completely dull."

It goes without saying that one invites the press to one's parties.* Perle Mesta's first "do" after returning from her diplomatic

---

* Stephen Birmingham, in his best-seller *Right People,* quotes one Washington wife as saying, "Socially, the press corps here is more powerful than the diplomatic corps. At every party I give, I make damn sure that the press people are having a good time."

post in Luxembourg was a black-tie dinner honoring news-women. The food and music were first class, and VIPs were generously sprinkled about. For after-dinner entertainment, Perle had important stars then appearing on Broadway. Nothing is too good for the women who keep your name in the paper.

Perle Mesta says she has never had a party flop ("I wouldn't let it!"), but she admits some have produced embarrassing moments. One occurred at a luncheon Perle gave for Mamie Eisenhower, then First Lady. "There are two women here with the same last name; I made a mistake and invited the wrong one," says Perle. "I didn't realize it until she walked in the door. I didn't say a thing, naturally, but I know she's wondering to this day why I asked her to a party."

Society reporters are constantly looking for tidbits which spice up their stories, and smart politicians know this. At the first Congressional reception—a black-tie affair—given by President and Mrs. Nixon, the new president held up the receiving line many times to say a few words to a senator or a representative. Each time, a newspaper woman would ask what the president had discussed. Most congressmen would frown and brush off the question. Not Senator Jack Javits of New York. He replied, "Sex!" Then, observing another reporter jotting down what the women were wearing, he added, "I'm wearing basic black." Naturally he was quoted, and his constituents knew he'd been a guest at the White House.

Senator Eugene McCarthy, at the same reception, toured the rarely seen second floor of the White House, peeked into the Queen's bedroom, and told the press, "If I'd known it was this lovely, I would have worked harder." He was quoted, too.

At the same party, Joan Kennedy, wife of Senator Edward Kennedy and a good-looking blonde who certainly knows how to get the attention of the press, arrived in a six-inches-above-the-knee dress. Nothing fashion-wise shocked Washington quite as much in 1969 until Mrs. M. Robert Rogers went to the always-proper Symphony Ball wearing a metal bra. The sylph-like Mrs. Rogers, wife of the National Symphony's managing director, wore a hip-hugging black skirt topped with a wide metal belt and a brief bra of clanking metal platelettes. The outfit prompted Georgetowner Mrs. George Webster to cry, "Her husband is a PAID employee and she had the nerve to upstage all the volunteers!" But Mrs. Dale Miller, a close LBJ friend better known to her many friends as "Scooter," said she thought Mr. Rogers must be planning on resigning, which is just what he did a few months later.

Some regular party-goers are so full of news for reporters they have been labeled "professional informers." Gwen Cafritz, when defending her position as one of Washington's foremost hostesses, always said or did something a reporter could mention. One evening a *Washington Post* reporter, seeing Gwen surrounded by a small group of party guests, asked what she was up to. "She's demonstrating a new exercise for girth control," replied another reporter. Misunderstanding the explanation, the *Post* reporter wrote that Gwen was demonstrating a new exercise for birth control.

Knowing that the quickest way to keep a society reporter from even mentioning one's name again is to complain to her editor, Gwen didn't say a word, but the next time she saw the reporter at a party, she walked up and said, "Tomorrow I am leaving for Paris for the Grand Prix, and that is spelled, G-R-A-N-D P-R-I-X." The *Post* reporter duly reported her announcement, complete with spelling.

Gwen, a widow, is possessed of a talent for quotable remarks. At a party in honor of the then-Italian Ambassador and his wife, neither of them young, Gwen closed the dinner with the disclosure that she had invited the Italians "because I love old ruins." Her statement that she gave parties "in order to save Western Civilization" was ridiculed from here to Timbuctoo, but Gwen knew what she was doing: getting famous from here to Timbuctoo. Asked at a reception after the opening of Ford's Theater about the beaded Grecian-type evening dress she was wearing, she told Nancy Ross of the *Washington Post*, "Darling, it can eat and drink, but it can't dance or it sheds."

The press, like a flock of hungry turkeys, gobbles up this sort of thing, gleefully reporting each witticism. Barbara Howar was, for months, the most quotable woman on the Washington scene with such lines as: "I'm the poor man's Nichole Alphand," "Everyone has his own personal scene, mine is to be young and have fun," and when describing a new Washington boutique, "It's a sort of unsanforized Henri Bendel."

Her good friend Margot Hahn, wife of the District's City Council chairman, is often good for a quote, too. When her husband was running against an Italian restaurant owner, and Margot was asked what she was doing to help him, she quipped: "I've given up pizza."

Margot and Barbara, without saying a word to each other, had the same idea for their Christmas cards a few years ago. Barbara, left with several hundred addressed and stamped invitations to the dance she had planned for Luci Johnson and Pat Nugent until it was cancelled by the White House, announced that she was going to send them as Christmas cards, if the White House didn't "cancel Christmas." Margot, who had been co-chairman that year of the Symphony Ball with Mrs. Edward Kennedy, had already had 650 replicas of the ball invitation stamped with red letters proclaiming, "Merry Christmas, Margot and Gil Hahn." Afraid of looking like "copycats," neither mailed the cards. Margot sent all 650 of her invitations to Barbara.

A blue-eyed brunette who has a way with clothes, Margot established herself as a swinging Washington hostess when she gave a fund-raising tea at her home. The caterer didn't show up with the tea service and her coffee set leaked, but undaunted, Margot served martinis and took the women on a tour of the house. She later said, "Everyone got high and we had a wonderful time."

Comparatively new as a Washington hostess is Mrs. Sidney Zlotnick, whose husband's family made a fortune in the fur business. For years, a huge, somewhat grotesque stuffed polar bear standing at the entrance to the Zlotnick fur store at F and Fourteenth Streets was a landmark of downtown Washington. The Zlotnicks now own a house on fashionable Massachusetts Avenue, where they give dinner parties which "draw" Supreme Court justices, ambassadors, Cabinet members and congressmen. Since Sidney Zlotnick was president of the Friends of the Corcoran and also a trustee of the Washington Theater Club, many of their guests are also patrons of the arts.

Something that happened at a Zlotnick dinner soon after President Nixon took office shows just how dramatically Washington can symbolize its changing priorities. Dorothy McCardle of the *Post* covered the party, a farewell for Tunisian Ambassador and Mrs. Rachid Driss, and told how "Former Secretary Dean Rusk found himself in the out-of-office position of being seated at the foot of the table. His host had worried greatly about this. Twice, Sidney Zlotnick phoned the protocol office at the State Department to determine whether a man who used to be at the head of every table in Washington as secretary of state now really belonged at the bottom. He was assured that all the other guests now out-ranked the Rusks. Among these were the ambassadors of India, Pakistan, Ceylon, and Norway and their wives. Even Senator Charles Percy of Illinois was seated above the former secretary of state."

Like Gwen Cafritz, Evelyn Zlotnick gets off highly quotable remarks for an eager press. At a tea given by Mrs. George Maurice Morris in her eighteenth-century house, "The Lindens," which she moved painstakingly down from Massachusetts and is now on every historical society's list of carefully restored old houses, Maxine Cheshire reported in the *Post* that Mrs. Zlotnick inquired about the cookies. "These are eighteenth-century cookies," replied Mrs. Morris, one of the *grandes dames* of Old Washington society. "They are!" Mrs. Zlotnick exclaimed. "Boy, would I like to go downstairs and see that freezer!"

One evening when she was in a tight, empire-style evening dress (she has a superb fashion figure and wears French designer clothes), she walked up to a reporter and said, "I can't breathe. I had to be squeezed into this dress. You may think these are my breasts, but they're not. They are my knees." That, the paper didn't print.

Except for the occasional debut ball, the local papers seldom write about the fascinating and brilliant Negro society that exists here. Not only do the beautifully staged parties in the large rambly houses on Washington's "Gold Coast" and "Platinum Coast," as the area housing some 700 affluent Negroes is called, go unreported in the *Post*, *Star*, and *News*, but they also are unnoticed by the Negro press as well.

The "white" press apparently ignores Negro society for the same reason it ignores the cave dwellers it used to write about in such gushy, glowing terms: they aren't running the country and the press is Power minded.

The Negro press doesn't agree as to why they seldom report the interesting parties given by such couples as Dr. E. C. Mazique and his beautifully dressed wife, Marguerite, who was at one time married to Harry Belafonte; Dr. and Mrs. Alvin Robinson who live in fashionable McLean, Virginia, and are among an ever-growing group of Negroes moving to the suburbs; or the handsome Dr. William Funderburk and his wife, Marilyn, who wears marvelous designer clothes and who went to Manhattanville College with Joan Bennett Kennedy, or the Belford Lawsons, whose seated dinners for 30 or 40 are among the best in town.

"We cover Negro society only when someone of national interest is involved," says Fannie Granton, a reporter in the Washington Bureau of the Johnson Publishing Company, which puts out *Jet* and *Ebony*. "We write about the political appointees, and of course we cover the African embassies when there is a head of state visiting."

Fannie, who went to Howard University, graduated from Shaw, and has a Master of Science from the Atlanta University School of Social Work, covers social events at the White House and travels with the First Lady whenever there is a Negro angle. She considers herself lucky that though she was born in Newport News, Virginia, she came to Washington at age 11 and thus knows her way around. Her most exciting White House story was the Nixon dinner for Duke Ellington ("he's such a remarkable fellow"), and the biggest event she's missed lately was the Nixon-Eisenhower wedding ("We couldn't find a Negro angle in that at all . . . there were just the maid and the valet").

Mabs Kemp, a society columnist for the *Afro-American*, though a full-time employee at the Department of Housing and Urban Development, says the chief difference between Negro and white society is that the former is largely professional, composed of doctors, lawyers, educators, government workers, and, of course, Mayor and Mrs. Walter Washington. "Just as with the whites," she says, "job status here has a lot to do with social status."

Other than write-ups now and then in the *Star* by Anne Christ-mas or Cissy Finley of doings in the hunt country around Mid-dleburg, Virginia, or Potomac, Maryland, white residential soci-ety is also largely ignored in Washington. The typical news item in most papers around the country, beginning, "Mr. and Mrs. John Doe were surrounded by all their children yesterday for the celebration of their silver wedding anniversary," no longer exists here. Perhaps its demise was hastened during World War II, when Eva Hinton, now one of Georgetown's *grandes dames* but then writing for the *Washington Post*, had it in one of her columns that Mrs. So-and-So "came to the cocktail party in her uniform, after a long lay at headquarters with her boss at the Red Cross." Eva thinks to this day that the composing room had a ball with that typographical "error."

Ironically, many of the most accomplished hostesses in town are the ones who receive the least publicity: mostly, they're the wives of important newspaper men. In the first place, govern-ment officials need to be on good terms with the top columnists, so for them a star-studded guest list is not the problem it is for the ordinary mortal; and in the second place, since the enter-taining is for business as well as pleasure, they can deduct enough from their income taxes to be able to do it frequently on a small scale, which is, many think, the only scale that's fun in a city which specializes in good conversation.

One almost never reads the names of Kay Evans, Polly Kraft, Tish Alsop, Sherry Geyelin, Luvie Pearson or Marie Ridder on the society pages, and they like to keep it that way. They would no more invite a reporter, not even a Betty Beale, to a party just so she would write about it than they would invite the butler to sit down for a drink; if newswomen are invited, it's because they are friends, and they are often asked not to mention the event in print. The first two hostesses live in Georgetown and are the wives of columnist Rowland Evans and Joseph Kraft, both widely syndicated. Tish Alsop and husband Stewart live in Cleveland Park. Sherry's husband, Philip, is the *Post*'s editorial page editor and they have a house just off fashionable Foxhall Road. Marie Ridder lives in McLean and is herself a working newswoman, though her husband is one of the owners of Ridder publications, a vast chain of papers stretching from New York (*Journal of Commerce*) to San Diego, California, and including the St. Paul, Minnesota, *Pioneer-Press.*

Marie and Walter spent their honeymoon with Hubert H. Humphrey, although Marie says, "The saddest part of that statement is that Humphrey was unaware of it." Walter was at the Democratic Convention of 1948 covering the "Young Turk" Mayor of Minneapolis for his Minnesota paper while Marie was there, assigned by the *Philadelphia Bulletin* to the civil-rights platform. Marie's mother, when told that her daughter would honeymoon at the convention, murmured that it was an odd way to spend a honeymoon. It turned out she was right. Walter worked for morning papers while Marie worked for an evening one, and they rarely saw each other except in that least cozy of rendezvous, the press box.

Marie has a big, sunny house on the banks of the Potomac, just up the stream from Nancy Dickerson's Merrywood. In it she raises four children, innumerable enormous dogs including St. Bernards that visitors are always tripping over, a lavish rock garden around the swimming pool, and money for her favorite causes, such as the election of liberal Democratic politicians like Congressman John Brademas of Indiana. For the last few years, she has been deep into the War on Poverty at the Office of Economic Opportunity, but she also helped Theodore White with his *Making of the President 1968*, traveled with Eugene McCarthy during the campaign for her husband's papers, and covered the 1968 Democratic Convention in Chicago.

Walter's company recently bought the Gary, Indiana, *Post-Tribune*, the most important paper in that troubled steel-mill city, and he has spent most of the past two years in Gary. Thus, the Ridders haven't done much entertaining lately, but nobody who has ever been to one of their glittering "small dances" for 100 and more congressmen, senators, administration bigwigs, and close friends which of necessity means many press people, can ever forget them. Even at their small dinners, carefully supervised by Marie, who loves cooking almost as much as horseback riding and gardening, Hubert Humphrey was apt to drop in, breathless, and keep the company enthralled for hours with tales of who was doing what to whom.

Recently George Worthington Baker, described by Marie as "that last word in Washington bachelors—the dinner hostess' dream, unmarried, friend of politicians, connoisseur of fine food and furniture," chided her for not making the effort to keep on being a top Washington hostess. He reminded her that "If you don't entertain your news sources, you might just as well be living in Istanbul. The toe always has to be in the water or you are left high and dry, and Madame de Stael serves a purpose. Bringing intelligent people together pleasantly is not a waste of time in this city."

Marie was reminded of Stewart Alsop's advice to his English bride when she first arrived in Washington: "You may refuse cocktails, but never dinner, without asking me." He was right, Marie says, because the Washington dinner is used to exchange ideas in an unpressured atmosphere. Her examples:

· After a dinner given some years ago by Henry Brandon of the *London Sunday Times* for the new British Ambassador Sir Harold Caccia, a plan for withdrawing all British troops from Germany was discussed. The ambassador wanted to try out an idea involving an important change in his country's planning on this small, carefully chosen group. If the idea had met with a hostile reception, the diplomat could have claimed that the whole conversation had just been a kind of sophisticated parlor game. If it seemed to them a workable plan, he would have already consulted those who mattered most in Washington in a manner that in no way forced them to an official statement.

· More recently, at a small dinner, Presidential Assistant Bryce Harlow and Health, Education and Welfare Secretary Robert Finch agreed on the timing and method of transferring an agency of the Poverty program from the Office of Economic Opportunity to HEW. The comment Finch made was, "So glad to have had this talk with you. I've been planning to call you all week." The secretary explained to the other guests that since the issue was not explosive, and one that could be resolved relatively easily, it had been left to drift while more pressing matters were dealt with. "It's always nice," he added, "to combine business and pleasure."

· At one particularly gay soiree, Theodore H. White's wife asked him over the din of music, "Darling, are you having a good time?" The distinguished author's gruff reply was, "I am working." A rundown later of the conversations he had had during the evening indicate he was not exaggerating. White chatted with two Cabinet members, three presidential aides, one general and several ambassadors. His evening was spent the way most Washington evenings are—gathering or cautiously disseminating the information that is the warp and the woof of Washington life.

Luncheons are important, too. On the quiet Sunday that heralded the building of the Berlin Wall, Senator Jack Javits of New York, Presidential Assistants McGeorge Bundy and Walt Rostow and several journalists were lunching together. The New York Senator disagreed with the presidential aides on the importance of the Berlin action. Those differences so lightly expressed over Bloody Marys remained a major White House-versus-the-Senate issue for the ensuing seven years.

The little dinner or lunch as a functioning part of the business of government reached its apex during the Kennedy administration, Marie feels. From the private dining room of the White House through Georgetown and out into the more modest suburbs where young government employees live, she says Jackie's "ideal number, eight to ten" was the way of life. It was a time when brilliant talk pervaded the atmosphere.

"For a few of us," she adds, "it was at just such a gathering that the worst moment of that brief bright time occurred. Presidential Assistant Walt Rostow was having lunch with several reporters at the 1925 F Street Club. Rostow was about to answer the question, 'Why, Walt, do you think there is so much hate in this country now?' when Timothy, manager and father figure of the Club, came into the small dining room, and hesitated between several tables. In one corner Senator William Fulbright was lunching with two of our senior ambassadors. Timothy chose the table with a member of the president's own staff. 'Mr. Rostow,' he said, 'the President has been shot.' From Senator Fulbright's table came the agonized cry, 'I begged him not to go to Texas!' "

Marie notes that Washington dinners are not always amicable:

· At one Joseph Alsop dinner Italian Ambassador Egidio Ortona went out into the garden. When questioned about his sudden horticultural interest, he answered, "Joe and his brother Stewart want to kill each other, blow up the United States, do away with Europe. This is no place for an Italian."

· On another occasion a famous newsman described a government white paper as "the stupidest document I have ever read." The U.S. government does not give by-lines to its authors, so the dinner party was rather shaken when the guest of honor excused himself from the table with the remark, "I wrote the paper in question."

· One recent dinner was upset when a guest, surrounded by Republicans still flushed with victory, announced he was leaving because, he was "up to his ass in Republicans."

· Jules Stein's daughter, Jeanne, and her husband, William Van den Heuvel, one of Attorney General Robert Kennedy's assistants, gave a cozy dinner for eight one night. Among their guests were columnist Drew Pearson and Kennedy Presidential Assistant Mike Forrestal whose father, James, our first secretary of defense, had ended his distinguished and controversial career by committing suicide. When Mike Forrestal found Pearson at the Van den Heuvel's dinner, he excused himself immediately, saying, "I do not find it necessary to dine with my father's assassin." Pearson had written scathingly of Jim Forrestal on the morning of the secretary's death.

Marie once wrote for *The New York Times* (Sunday) *Magazine* section that: "Washington is the kindest and cruelest of cities. Kindest because since the population is a transient one, strangers are quickly accepted. It's cruelest, however, because what counts is your job. It's got to be either interesting or influential, preferably both."

Arthur Schlesinger, Jr., she says, defines it as "jungle warfare with your clothes on." Marie prefers to think of it as a parlor game: "There are many other games to be played in life, and quite frankly, with the world in the state it's in at the moment, Walter and I haven't been particularly in the mood to play this one. But it's nice to know it will be there to be played as long as there's a Washington."

Washington women have come a long way in the news world since *Editor and Publisher*, the venerable trade magazine, noted with astonishment in 1912 that "it is getting to be a regular thing for the press gallery to boast of a lady correspondent." Trying not to raise its eyebrows too archly, it added that "time was when these precincts were almost inviolate, and the rustle of silk would have sent half the scribes scurrying for cover. But with the advance of the suffrage movement, woman's invasion of the press gallery seems to be permanent."

Suffrage helped, and so did women like Doris Fleeson whose brilliant political columns made her so influential that once a Truman cabinet appointee asked her how he could win her approval. "It's quite simple," Doris answered. "If you answer my calls, you're a statesman. If you don't, you're a bum." Adela Rogers St. John, the spectacular Hearst reporter who covered Washington politics during Franklin D. Roosevelt's New Deal was another twentieth-century pioneer. It's unlikely that an editor today would give a girl in his city room the kind of bawling-out she received at the age of 18 from her first boss. "You'd better take up streetwalking," he told her, "since obviously you aren't going to make it as a reporter."

Mrs. St. John was the only woman among eight outstanding political reporters awarded the Presidential Medal of Freedom by President Nixon in late April 1970. The president said that she was a longtime friend, and that after the 1962 elections when he lost the race for California governor he told her he had decided to leave political life. Mrs. St. John informed Nixon that Jack Dempsey had once confided to her that what makes a champion is the ability to get up off the floor when you have been knocked down and think you never want to get up again. What the president didn't tell his guests was that he had first known Adela Rogers St. John in Whittier, California. He delivered groceries from his father's store to the even-then famous reporter-lecturer-novelist.

Bureau chiefs such as Mel Elfin who heads *Newsweek*'s Washington office are another cause for the advance women have made in journalism. When asked to compare women reporters on his staff with men reporters, he answers: "That's like asking me to compare tall reporters with short reporters." A self-styled "White Panther," Mel resigned from the prestigious National Press Club because it would not permit women to be members. No women reporters were hired by the *Newsweek* Washington bureau in the ten years before Mel took over; he now has five women reporters on a staff of twenty, a much higher percentage of women than one finds in most news operations.* As for women's so-called temperament, Mel says, "Women reporters are no more temperamental than male reporters who throw tantrums in a different way."

Lloyd Schwartz, Washington Bureau Chief of Fairchild Publications which includes *Women's Wear Daily* among its posses-

* Forty-six women from the editorial staff of *Newsweek*'s New York office filed a complaint with the Equal Employment Opportunity Commission, in March 1970, charging discrimination in the magazine's hiring and advancement policies. The women said there were more than 50 men writing at *Newsweek*, but only one woman. Osborn Elliott, editor in chief, said: "The fact that most researchers at *Newsweek* are women and that virtually all writers are men stems from a news-magazine tradition going back 50 years . . ."

sions, says: "I have a conviction that women can do as well as men. About half of the people in this office are women and we have them on the same basis, competing with men. I have one woman, Heather David, covering the Pentagon full time and she is terrific. She writes for technical publications on the most complex subjects as well as reporting for general circulation, and she can hold her own with the best of them. She's aggressive, digging, and she gets out and sees people, she doesn't wait for a handout."

However, the City Room Suffrage Battle is far from over. Evidence of discrimination is everywhere. Many male editors still resist hiring women for other than women's news or "soft" news. An award-winning woman reporter, who wishes to remain unidentified, says she is the only reporter of stature at her paper who has never been inside her editor's office, though male writers are called in regularly for conferences. "I don't think he feels comfortable with women," she says. Mary Wiegers of the *Washington Post* adds: "Often a male editor won't take a woman's reporting seriously, no matter how good she is." As discussed earlier, some Washington officials frequently hold "backgrounders" with women visibly, if not deliberately, excluded. Even President Johnson, who often told women reporters that he thought they were much better than the men, held all-male backgrounders. And one candidate for election to president of the National Press Club based his whole campaign on one issue: he was against letting women into the Club.

A recent head-count at the *Washington Post* revealed only 33 women among 272 reporters, columnists, and editors. Of 14 editors and 22 reporters on the national desk, only 2 were women. None of the 33 were with the *Post*'s overseas bureau, neither were any on the foreign desk, the news desk or the city desk. As Bonnie Angelo of *Time* magazine says, "when you get into a position of authority, of going up the corporate scale, women fall off the ladder." The percentage at the *Washington Daily News* was better than at the *Post*, but not much—10 women out of 54 editorial staff members. The *Washington Star* listed 63 women out of an editorial staff of 256, but included in these figures were secretaries, news aides, dictationists, copy girls, and those who work in the library.

While well aware of their disadvantages, some newswomen shrug them off. Nona Brown, Washington editor of *The New York Times* (Sunday) *Magazine* is one. She says, "If you're going to be worked against, you might as well let it work for you." She recalls that when a reporter and *The Times* wanted something about Vice President Alben Barkley, they sent her, because a woman could get more out of him. "The only times it really annoys me," says the blonde, serene Nona, "is when I'm dealing with someone's secretary. She asks me what I want to talk to the man about, assuming I couldn't possibly be important enough to talk to him directly." Nona, who went to the Columbia University School of Journalism after she graduated from Vassar, had her first experience along these lines when *The Times* inadvertently sent her to cover a stag dinner at the all-male and very conservative St. Nicholas Society in New York:

"There were 300 men and not a woman in sight . . . a pleasant, correct old gentleman came over and told me I was in the wrong place, and when I said in all innocence that I was supposed to be there, he took me over to meet the president. In the end I was allowed to sit at the press table, but when I went to work on Monday the editor told me there had been an irate call from the wife of a St. Nicholas member, asking whether he knew that 'some blonde' had crashed the dinner by passing herself as a reporter for *The Times*."

Not everyone has a job like Nona's, in the driver's seat, so to speak, where one can be philosophical about discrimination. Dozens of eager writers come to her each week, not she to them. It's out in the hard world that the subtle male barrier becomes less subtle. Myra MacPherson of the *Washington Post*, while trying to cover a Mets baseball game, was barred from the press box where, as she said, the men were "spoon-fed . . . programs, number of paid attendance, how many young fans were there, background on baseball players." One official complained to her, "We're trying to do something nice for you. I just don't understand you." His "niceness" had consisted of issuing Myra a press pass "with every possible area reporters could go crossed out" except the stands.

When Fran Lewine was covering President Nixon in California, she wasn't allowed in the press box at a San Diego football game he attended. She had to go outside to telephone the AP office in Los Angeles, which in turn phoned their man in the press box to tell him to go outside to talk to Fran. This would be funny if it weren't for the fact that even the most liberal-minded bosses might stop assigning women reporters to cover events where they could run into discrimination.

In fairness, it must be noted that the nature of the work, requiring as it does total, undivided attention, makes a newspaper career especially unsuited to all but the hardiest women attempting to raise children. It is the one business, possibly excluding medicine, in which nothing important can ever be put off until tomorrow, and a public-relations job with more predictable hours, especially in Washington where there are so many trade-association headquarters, is a compromise many women make who started off as potential Nellie Blys.°

Those who do stick with reporting have much in common: they are dedicated to the principle that the public has a right to know (Helen Thomas says she sometimes feels like "the watchman at the Tower of Freedom"); they are motivated by an unflagging curiosity; and they are too busy to worry about whether or not they are "fulfilled." They are keeping the watch on the Potomac, and because they have to work harder than men to keep afloat, their wits are often sharper. They also are the social historians of their time, a function once performed only by those rare women who wrote copious memoirs or letters, like Abigail Adams to her husband John. Historians writing a hundred years from now—if indeed Western civilization lasts that long—will need to know what life was like in the sixties and seventies, and there will be no better place to look than in newswomen's stories. Pat Nixon, Lady Bird Johnson, and Jackie Kennedy, for example —could any three women better symbolize Life in America? One from a background of poverty, one imbued with the graces of the Old South, one the quintessence of the Eastern Establish-

---

° Nellie Bly, a New York newswoman, created a sensation in January 1890 when she completed an around the world trip in 72 days, 6 hours, 11 minutes, having traveled via ship, burro, train, jinrickshaw, sampan, and barouche. All this Nellie colorfully reported in Joseph Pultizer's *New York World*.

ment debutante—each one responding in her own way to the implacable demands of the job.

If nothing else, Washington newswomen would make H. L. Mencken of the *Baltimore Sun*, possibly the greatest newsman of his time, proud. An ardent crusader for women's rights, he pronounced in 1919:

"That it should still be necessary, at this late date in history of the human race, to argue that women are gifted with an acute and valuable form of intelligence is surely an eloquent proof of the defective observation, incurable superstitiousness, and general dunderheadedness of man."

Abboud, Ibrahim 90
ABC (American Broadcasting System) 74, 156, 161
Abell, Bess 94, 121, 213
Abell, George 94
Abell, Tyler 94, 121
Abrams, Creighton W. 41
Adams, Abigail 236
Adams, John Quincy 168, 204, 236
Adenauer, Konrad 155
Afro-American 20, 225
Agence France Presse 47
Agnew, Spiro 19, 30, 33, 56, 70, 80, 89, 103, 151, 188, 198
Agnew, Mrs. Spiro 70, 89, 145, 159, 217
Ahoua, Ambassador and Mrs. Timothee 174
Albert, Carl 42
Alexander, Shana 17
Al-Ghoussein, Ambassador and Mme. Talat 193
Alphand, Herve 186, 187, 190, 202
Alphand, Mme. Herve 186, 187, 190, 202, 222
Alsop, Joseph 119, 211, 230
Alsop, Mrs. Joseph 119, 218
Alsop, Stewart 226, 228, 230
Alsop, Mrs. Stewart 218, 226
American Newspaper Women's Club 21, 137
American Women in Radio and Television 137
Angelo, Bonnie 46, 86, 169-71, 234
Arden, Elizabeth 18
Arkansas Gazette 158
Associated Press 20, 48, 52, 54, 67, 68, 74
Atlanta Constitution 165
Auchincloss, Mrs. Hugh 87, 218
Axler, Judith 76, 85, 99-101, 202

Bacon, Mrs. Robert Low 165
Bailey, Pearl 89
Baker, George Worthington 228
Baker, Robert G. 126, 139, 140
Baker, Russell 148
Baldrige, Letitia (Mrs. Robert Hol-
lensteiner) 43, 52, 70-72, 87, 94, 183
Ball, George Wildman 25
Baltimore Sun 54, 55, 93, 94, 237
Barkley, Alben 235
Bartlett, Mr. and Mrs. Charles 210
Beale, Betty 18, 19, 39, 76, 95, 108-15, 118, 167, 169, 210, 226
Becker, Mr. and Mrs. Ralph 218
Beene, Geoffrey 145
Belafonte, Harry 225
Bender, Heinz 178
Bengelloun, Ali 190, 191
Bengelloun, Mrs. Ali 190
Berckemeyer, Ambassador and Mrs. Fernando 217
Billington, Joy 174, 201
Birmingham, Stephen 220
Black, Shirley Temple 40
Blair, Ann 156
Blair, Mr. and Mrs. William McCormack 218
Blunt, Ellen Key 71
Bly, Nellie 236
Boggs, Congressman and Mrs. Hale 212
Bolling, Richard 133
Bonaparte, Jerome 177
Boston Globe 36, 149
Boston Herald 33
Brademas, John 133, 227
Bradlee, Ben 163-65, 210
Bradlee, Mrs. Ben 210
Brandon, Henry 36, 228
Brandt, Willy 89
Brinkley, David 138, 151
Brooks, Congressman and Mrs. Jack 28
Brown, Nona 235
Bruce, Mrs. David 94, 218
Bucher, Lloyd M. 148
Bui Diem 174
Bundy, McGeorge 229
Burros, Marian 177, 178
Burton, Richard 195
Byrd, Mr. and Mrs. Harry 154

Caccia, Sir Harold 228
Cafritz, Morris 209

Cafritz, Mrs. Morris 115, 208, 209, 220, 222, 224
Cameron, Mrs. Peter 41, 42
Capote, Truman 163
Cardin, Pierre 190
Carpenter, Elizabeth 21, 50, 57, 58, 69, 72, 73, 93, 94, 101, 102, 104, 105, 107, 112, 117, 118, 121, 144, 157, 169-71, 178, 195, 203, 213, 217
Carpenter, Leslie 117
Carpenter, Rene 103, 104
Carpenter News Service 135
Carper, Elsie 166
Carswell, G. Harold 31, 95, 158
Carusi, Mrs. Eugene 211, 218
Casey, Phil 165
Castro, Fidel 204
CBS (Columbia Broadcasting System) 147, 156
Cavin, Patty 18
Cerf, Bennett 148
Chafee, John 148
Chamberlin, Anne 181, 182, 185
Channing, Carol 90, 93
Charles, Mrs. Robert 211, 218
Charlotte, Grand Duchess 90
Chattanooga Times 135
Chavez, Dennis 197
Chennault, Anna 177, 195, 196
Chennault, Clair Lee 195
Cheshire, Herbert 118, 119
Cheshire, Maxine 19, 114-19, 167, 191-92, 197, 199, 200, 214, 224
Chewning, Mrs. E. Taylor 210, 211
Chicago Daily News 214
Chicago Tribune 78, 139, 202
Childs, Marquis 218
Chisholm, Shirley 215
Chotiner, Murray 39
Christian Science Monitor 27
Christmas, Anne 49, 226
Christopher, Sybil Burton 195, 213
Christy, Marian 149
Churchill, Winston 202
Clements, Earl 94
Cleveland Plain Dealer 126
Clifford, Clark 138
Coleman, Barbara 158, 159
Coleman Enterprises Inc. 158
Collins, Michael 41
Conger, Clement 92, 201
Congressional Record 125, 126, 134
Conroy, Richard 180
Conroy, Sarah Booth 158, 170, 181
Coolidge, Calvin 101

Cooper, John Sherman 95, 146, 147
Cooper, Mrs. John Sherman 95, 146, 155, 177
Coplon, Judith 35
Cormier, Frank 48
Cornell, Douglas 48
Cosmopolitan 181
Courrèges 145
Craig, May 38, 127, 160
Crawford, Clare 18, 59, 61, 62, 91, 94-97, 101-104, 175
Crawford, Joan 100, 101
Crawford, Victor 103
Crimmons, Margaret 166
Cronkite, Walter 151
Crutcher, Anne 177
Curley, James Michael 34
Curtis, Charlotte 87, 205

Dacey, Norman 159
D'Ambroise, Jacques 90
D'Angers, Yvonne 195
David, Heather, 234
Davis, Meyer 211
Davis, Mrs. Spencer 113
Dean, Ruth 201
De Gaulle, Charles 116, 184, 187
Dempsey, Jack 233
Des Moines Register Tribune 139
Detroit Free Press 173
Detroit Times 173
Dewar, Helen 20
Dewey, Thomas 216
Dial, Mr. and Mrs. Morse 115
Dickerson, C. Wyatt, Jr. 117, 149, 153
Dickerson, Nancy 21, 45, 50, 117, 121, 145-56, 210, 227
Dietrich, Marlene 195
Diplomat magazine 109
Dirksen, Everett 94, 121
Dirksen, Mrs. Everett 94
Dixon, Ymelda 39, 167, 195-97
Dobbin, Muriel 54-56, 93
Dobrynin, Anatole 202
Dobrynin, Mrs. Anatole 203
Dobson, Gwen 163, 164, 167, 168, 197, 215
Dolan, Mary Anne 168
Douglas, Mrs. Kingman 199
Douglas, William O. 100
Douglas, Mrs. William O. 100, 101, 206
Drayton, Katherine 15

Driss, Ambassador and Mrs. Ra-
    chid 224
Drury, Allen 36, 219
Dunham, Charles 95

Ebony magazine 225
Editor and Publisher 48, 232
Edstrom, Eve 144
Edwards, Sherman 91
Ehrlichman, John 64
Eisenhower, David 62, 65, 122, 169,
    171
Eisenhower, Mrs. David 18, 19, 62,
    65, 66, 79, 80, 82, 95, 122, 169,
    171
Eisenhower, Dwight David 38, 50,
    67, 69, 87, 89, 92, 127, 136-38,
    192, 201, 209, 217
Eisenhower, Mrs. Dwight David 51,
    68, 89, 175, 216, 221
Eisenhower, John 116
Elder, Shirley 25, 128, 130-34
Eleni 176, 177
Elfin, Mel 233
Elizabeth II 54, 87, 216
Elizabeth, Queen Mother 87
Ellender, Allen J. 78
Ellington, Duke 90, 91, 225
Elliott, Osborn 233
Ellsworth, Robert 40
Epstein, Sid 176
Erhard, Dr. Ludwig 90
Esquire 181
Evans, Mrs. Robert F. 178
Evans, Rowland 149, 211, 226
Evans, Mrs. Rowland 226

Fairchild Publications 120, 233
Feldman, Trude B. 85
Fillmore, Millard 127
Finch, Robert 39, 115, 145, 228
Finch, Mrs. Robert 217
Finkelstein, Dr. Louis 61
Finley, Cissy 226
Flanagan, Peter 39
Flatley, Mary Margaret 168
Fleeson, Doris 35, 38, 232
Ford, Gerald R. 42, 131, 134, 147
Ford, Henry, II 205
Foreman, Percy 174
Forrestal, James 230
Forrestal, Michael 183, 230
Fortas, Mr. and Mrs. Abe 100, 215
Fox, Yolanda 202
Franklin, Ben 204

Frederika, Queen 87
Friendly, Alfred 164
Fritchey, Clayton 25, 26
Fulbright, J. William 148, 150, 158,
    229
Fulbright, Mrs. J. William 158
Funderburk, Dr. and Mrs. William
    225
Furlow, Barbara 20
Furman, Bess 67, 171
Furness, Betty 87

Galbraith, John K. 143, 218
Gallagher, Mary 43, 179, 180
Gandhi, Indira 99
Gardner, Arthur W. 191
Gardner, Mrs. Arthur W. 116, 191,
    192
Gary Post Tribune 227
Gernreich, Rudi 93
Geyelin, Mr. and Mrs. Philip 226
Gifford, Mr. and Mrs. Dun 148, 149
Gilbert, Ben 103, 164
Gilpatric, Roswell 167, 183
Gingras, Angele 87
Glaser, Vera 39-43, 72
Glenn, John 170
Goldberg, Arthur 42, 188
Goldwater, Barry 28, 38, 89
Goldwater, Barry, Jr. 104
Gordon, Stephanie and Rachel Marie
    98
Gore, Louise 56
Gorton, Prime Minister and Mrs.
    John 95
Graeber, George 109, 114-15
Graham, Katherine 23, 116, 122, 162-
    67, 210-11
Graham, Philip 163, 166, 187
Graham, Sheilah 215
Granton, Fannie 225
Green, Edith 133
Greenfield, Meg 107
Groebli, Betty 156
Guellah, Cherif 202
Guest, Mrs. Polk 218
Guggenheim, Robert 219

Hahn, Gilbert 223
Hahn, Mrs. Gilbert 116, 223
Hall Syndicate 108
Halle, Kay 218
Haller, Henry 92, 178
Halsell, Grace 8, 160
Hamilton, George 212

Hand, Lloyd 188, 211
Hand, Mrs. Lloyd 188, 212
Hardin, Dorcas, 211
Harkness, Rebekah 90
Harlech, Lord and Lady 190
Harlow, Bryce 228
Harper's Bazaar 146
Harriman, Averell 35
Harris, Fred 24
Hartke, Vance 174
Hassan II 113, 191, 193
Hauptmann, Bruno 198
Hauser, Rita 122
Haynsworth, Clement 95, 157
Hays, Wayne 41
Healy, Paul 208, 209
Healy, Robert 36
Hearst Headline Service 21, 26, 27, 135
Helm, Edith 68
Helms, Mrs. Richard 180, 181
Hemingway, Ernest 194, 195
Herald Tribune (Paris edition) 163
Hershey, Lenore 74
Herter, Mrs. Christian 218
Hess, Steve 29
Hinton, Eva 226
Hiss, Alger 35
Hitchcock, Alfred 86
Holyoake, Keith 96
Hoover, Mrs. Herbert 171
Hoover, J. Edgar 117, 141, 151, 173
House, Toni 168
House & Garden 184, 192
Houston, Sam 201
Howar, Barbara 26, 211-15, 222-23
Howar, Ed 212, 213, 214
Howard, Jack 99
Hoyt, Mary 17
Hruska, Roman 31
Humphrey, Hubert H. 24, 32, 40, 63, 85, 88, 102, 121, 129, 146, 192, 193, 196, 209, 217, 227
Humphrey, Mrs. Hubert H. 63, 98, 121
Hunter, Marjorie 128-30
Huntley, Chet 151
Hurd, Peter 91, 116, 139
Hussein I 85
Hyde, Lloyd 176
Hyde, Nina 175-77

Iran, Shah and Empress of 90
Irwin, Don 40

Israeli News Agency 100
Izvestia 47

Jackson, Henry (Scoop) 146
Jacobs, Andy 133
Jaidi, Abdeslam 191
Javits, Jack 206, 221, 229
Javits, Mrs. Jack 205, 206
Jefferson, Thomas 46, 92, 204
Jenkins, Walter 31, 139, 140
Jet magazine 225
Jewish Press 85
Jewish Telegraphic Agency 100
Johnson, Luci Baines *see* Mrs. Patrick Nugent
Johnson, Lynda Bird *see* Mrs. Charles Robb
Johnson, Lyndon B. 15, 24, 25, 28, 29, 32, 36, 37, 46, 49, 50, 55-58, 60, 62, 63, 72, 78, 79, 85, 88-94, 96-98, 100, 102, 104, 105, 107, 116, 117, 120, 121, 126, 127, 129, 134, 136, 138, 139, 140, 142, 145-47, 150, 152-54, 157, 160, 161, 175, 188, 193, 194, 198, 200-203, 212-14, 216-18, 222
Johnson, Mrs. Lyndon B. 9, 17, 21, 28, 29, 54, 56, 58, 62, 63, 67, 72, 75, 77, 78, 83, 87, 88, 92, 93, 94, 98-100, 104, 105, 117, 121, 135, 147, 154, 157, 159, 175, 176, 189, 194, 200, 212-14, 217, 236
Johnson Publishing Company 225
Journal of Commerce 227
Juliana, Queen 87

Katzenbach, Nicholas 28
Kaufman, George S. 15
Keating, Kenneth 42, 146
Kemp, Mabs 225
Kendrick, Tom 167
Kennedy, Caroline 48, 71, 108, 170, 175, 198
Kennedy, Edward 119, 148, 214, 221
Kennedy, Mrs. Edward 146, 159, 214, 221, 223, 225
Kennedy, Jacqueline *see* Mrs. Aristotle Onassis
Kennedy, John F. 15, 16, 24-27, 29, 32, 37, 38, 43, 44, 49, 50, 54, 57, 62, 72, 87-90, 92, 93, 97, 107, 113, 121, 127, 134, 136, 137, 140,

Kennedy, John F. (*continued*)
142, 144-46, 151, 153, 155, 169, 170, 174, 181, 182, 186, 188, 190, 192, 200, 201, 205, 209-11, 217, 218
Kennedy, John F., Jr. 50, 200
Kennedy, Joseph 46, 200
Kennedy, Mrs. Joseph 166
Kennedy, Robert 37, 38, 72, 103, 104, 113, 121, 175, 205, 230
Kennedy, Mrs. Robert 103, 104, 113, 121, 175, 205, 230
Kennedy, Rory 119
Khan, Ayub 71, 77
Khrushchev, Nikita 54, 136
Kiesinger, Kurt 95
Kilgore, Margaret 135
King Features News Syndicate 22, 26
King, James 98
King, Martin Luther 38, 141, 159, 174
King, Mrs. Martin Luther 159
Kirk, Samuel 177
Kissinger, Henry 29, 147, 148
Kitt, Eartha 93
Klein, Herb 39, 160
Kleindienst, Richard G. 39
Klotz, Herbert 115
Knight Newspapers 39, 72
Knowles, John 20
Knoxville News Sentinel 116
Kober, Barbara 135, 136
Kraft, Mr. and Mrs. Joseph 226
Kreeger, David Lloyd 218
Krock, Arthur 129
Ky, Nguyen Cao 195, 196
Ky, Mme. Nguyen Cao 196

Ladies' Home Journal 17, 74, 180
La Fayette, Marquis de 177
La Hay, Wauhillau 17, 21, 67, 75, 88, 94, 95, 98, 99
Lahey, Edwin A. 34
Laird, Melvin 42, 133, 147
Laird, Mrs. Melvin 147, 177, 178
Lalla Nezhas, Princess 113, 191
Lamotte, Bernard 46
Langley, Jane Pickens 155
Lanvin 177
Laraki, Ahmed 191
La Rue, Fred 39
Lasker, Mrs. Albert 117, 214
Lawson, Mr. and Mrs. Belford 225
Lebel, M. and Mme. Claude 16

Lee, Elinor 177
Leighton, Frances Spatz 179
Lerner, Micheline 191
LeSueur, Dorothy 176
Levine, Lois 178
Levy, Christopher 170
Levy, Harold 170
Levy, Stan 78
Lewine, Frances 20, 48-54, 61, 93, 200, 236
Lewis, Caroline 156
Life magazine 17, 77, 117, 118, 140, 181
Lincoln, Abraham 127, 153, 210
Lincoln, Evelyn 26
Lincoln Journal 24
Lindberg, Charles 72, 198, 199
Lindley, Ernest K. 134
Lindsay, John 30, 103
Lippmann, Walter 29
Lloyd, Liza 199
Logan, John 218, 219
Logan, Mrs. John 115, 218
London Sunday Times 36, 228
Longworth, Alice Roosevelt 107, 211, 219
Los Angeles Mirror 168
Los Angeles Times 40, 163
Louis XIV 116
Lowell, Robert 84
Lowenstein, Allard K. 215
Luce, Clare Boothe 94, 217
Lucet, Charles 187
Luisi, Hector 201

McBee, Susanna 17
McCaffree, Mary Jane 68, 69
McCall's 17, 74, 181, 184
McCardle, Carl 198
McCardle, Dorothy 17, 61, 166, 198-201, 224
McCarthy, Eugene 30-32, 35, 36, 38, 121, 150, 156, 197, 220, 221, 227
McCarthy, Mrs. Eugene 121, 197
McCarthy, Joseph 34, 35, 38, 87
McCarthy, Richard D. 133
McClendon, Sarah 38, 137-42
McClintock, John 201
McClintock, Robert 201
McCone, John 44
McCormack, John W. 131
McCormick, Anne O'Hare 38
McGovern, George 177, 215
McGraw-Hill 118

McGrory, Mary 20, 22, 27, 30, 32-39, 45
McHugh, Godfrey 57
McLaughlin, Marya 156, 158
McLendon, John Benjamin 12
McNamara, Robert 17, 37, 42, 72
McNamara, Mrs. Robert 17
Macomber, William B. 148
MacPherson, Myra 171-73, 235
Mafia 20, 61
Mahon, Mr. and Mrs. George H. 28
Mann, Ted 167
Mansfield, Mike 134, 150, 175
Marcy, Carl 148
Margaret, Princess 212
Markel, Hazel 200
Marshall, Mr. and Mrs. Sylvan 174
Martin, Judith 73, 96, 101, 102, 104, 105, 167, 171, 190, 192-95
Martin, Nicholas 192
Martin, Robert 194
Mazique, Dr. and Mrs. E. C. 225
Means, Marianne 21-29, 38, 39, 210
Medina, Diez de 204
Meir, Golda 120, 122
Mellon, Mrs. Paul 92, 199
Melzer, Helene 90, 163-65, 168, 174
Melzer, Leo 168
Mencken, H. L. 237
Merman, Ethel 159, 217
Merry del Val, The Marquis 114
Merry del Val, The Marchioness 114, 155, 179, 202
Mesta, George 216
Mesta, Perle 8, 74, 115, 119, 155, 159, 165, 216, 217, 220, 221
Metromedia 214
Metropolitan Sunday Newspapers 179
Meyer, Mrs. Eugene 163, 219
Miller, Dale 28
Miller, Mrs. Dale 28, 222
Miller, Hope Ridings 109, 216, 217
Milligan, Norma 128, 134
Millspaugh, Samuel Kirk 177
Mitchell, Charles L. 210
Mitchell, Clarence 31
Mitchell, John N. 24, 39, 156, 157
Mitchell, Mrs. John N. (Martha) 39, 115, 156, 157, 174
Mollenhoff, Clark 140
Monberg, Helene 142, 143
Monroe, Marilyn 23
Moore, Ellen 51
Morgan, Raymond 75
Morocco, King of see Hassan II

Morris, Mrs. George Maurice 224
Morton, Rogers B. 23
Morton, Thruston 42
Mosbacher, Emil, Jr. 179, 198
Mosbacher, Mrs. Emil, Jr. 89, 179
Moss, John 133
Moyers, Bill 50, 85
Moynihan, Pat 129
Muskie, Senator and Mrs. Edmund 95

NAACP 31
Naughton, James M. 46
NBC (National Broadcasting Company) 18, 21, 50, 117, 145, 146, 150
Newsday 50, 85, 169, 170
Newsweek 32, 59, 115-17, 128, 134, 163, 209, 233
New York Daily News 67, 76, 85, 99, 100, 202, 203, 208
New York Herald Tribune 184
New York Times 16, 18, 19, 36, 46, 67, 69, 77, 78, 86, 87, 100, 128-30, 135, 138, 148, 173, 180, 183, 213, 230, 235
New York Tribune 127, 184
New York World 236
New Yorker, The 49, 183
Niarchos, Charlotte Ford 205
Nightingale, Florence 77
Nitze, Mrs. Paul 218
Nixon, Julie see Mrs. David Eisenhower
Nixon, Richard M. 15, 17-19, 23, 24, 26, 27, 29, 38-42, 46, 47, 49, 50, 52, 54-56, 59, 61, 62, 64, 65, 67, 70, 72, 74, 80, 87, 89-92, 94-97, 101-104, 107, 108, 116, 120-22, 129, 137, 138, 140, 142, 144-47, 153-55, 157, 159, 160, 169, 173, 175, 176, 195, 217, 219, 221, 224, 225, 233, 236
Nixon, Mrs. Richard M. 9, 15, 16, 18, 19, 42, 48, 51, 52, 57, 59, 62-65, 67, 74, 75, 78-84, 86, 87, 89-92, 95, 97, 109, 112, 116, 120, 121, 146, 154, 159, 160, 172, 176, 221, 236
Nixon, Tricia 18, 19, 55, 65, 79, 104, 113
Nomikos, Marco 51
North American Newspaper Alliance 40, 68, 139, 199
Northern Virginia Sun 25, 30

Novak, Robert 149
Noyes, Newbold 34, 35, 197
Nugent, Patrick J. 50, 62, 100, 105, 134, 212, 213, 223
Nugent, Mrs. Patrick J. 18, 50, 62, 73, 100, 102, 105, 121, 134, 178, 212, 213, 223

Oberon, Merle 191
Ohliger, Gloria 173
Onassis, Aristotle 104, 180
Onassis, Mrs. Aristotle 16-18, 26, 43, 47, 48, 50-52, 54, 55, 62, 70, 71, 76, 77, 79, 87, 88, 92, 94, 112, 113, 135, 145, 146, 153, 154, 167, 175, 179, 180, 182, 183, 190, 198-201, 205, 210, 211, 219, 229, 236
Ortona, Egidio 230
Osman, Ahmed 191
Ottenberg, Miriam 20

Packenham, Mary 78
Palm Beach Life 200
Patterson, Cissy 208, 209
Peale, Norman Vincent 101, 169-70
Pearce, Lorraine 198
Pearson, Drew 209, 230
Pearson, Mrs. Drew 94, 146, 209, 226
Pell, Senator and Mrs. Claiborne 146
Percy, Charles 116, 157, 179, 224
Percy, Mrs. Charles 179
Peterson, Russell 23
Philadelphia Bulletin 198, 227
Philadelphia Inquirer 198
Philip, Prince 19
Phillips, B. J. 165
Phillips, Cabell 8
Pickle, Congressman and Mrs. James Jarrell 28
Pompidou, Georges 198
Portland Oregonian 81
Post, Mrs. Merriweather 76, 164, 166
Poulain, Simone 58
Powell, Adam Clayton 136, 172, 173
Powell, Mrs. Adam Clayton 136
Powell, Adam Clayton, III 108, 172
Powell, Jean 157
Pravda 41, 47, 102
Prologue magazine 175
Pucci, Emilio 176
Pulitzer, Joseph 236

Quinn, Sally 196

Radcliffe, Donnie 204
Radio Corporation of America 18
Radziwill, Lee 51
Raleigh News and Observer 128
Randal, Judith 20
Rathbone, Basil 90
Rawley, James 27
Ray, James Earl 174
Rayburn, Sam 57, 105, 151
Reagan, Ronald 103
Rebozo, Charles Gregory 23, 108
Redbook 184
Reedy, George 60
Rees, Thomas M. 187
Reporter magazine 107
Reuss, Henry 133
Reuters 47
Rheault, Robert B. 40
Rheault, Mrs. Robert B. 40, 41
Rhodes, James 24
Ridder, Walter 220, 227
Ridge, Richard 213
Risher, Eugene 48
Robb, Charles 115, 170, 171, 203
Robb, Mrs. Charles 18, 93, 100, 108, 115, 121, 170, 171, 178, 203, 212
Robb, Trenny 203
Robbins, Jerome 90
Robertson, Nan 16, 69, 77, 78, 86
Robinson, Dr. and Mrs. Alvin 225
Robinson, Julie Marr 66
Rockefeller, Mr. and Mrs. John D., IV (Jay) 100
Rockefeller, Nelson 17, 31, 95, 102, 103, 121, 151
Rogers, Robert 222
Rogers, Mrs. Robert 221
Rogers, William 29
Rogers, Willie May 86, 87
Romney, Mr. and Mrs. George 217
Roosevelt, Eleanor 59, 67, 68, 73
Roosevelt, Franklin D. 46, 47, 67, 137, 175, 184, 201, 232
Roosevelt, Theodore 46
Rosenstiel, Lewis 117
Ross, Harold 49
Ross, Ishbel 8
Ross, Nancy 61, 205-207, 222
Rostow, Walt 154, 229
Rostropovich, Mstislav 190
Rowan, Carl 170
Royall, Anne 168
Rusk, Dean 88, 154, 204, 224

Rusk, Mrs. Dean 88, 224
Ryan, Will 57

Sagalyn, Arnold 25
St. John, Adela Rogers 232, 233
St. Laurent, Yves 176
St. Paul Pioneer-Press 227
Salinas Californian 204
Saltonstall, Mrs. William 108
Sanders, Marlene 74
Saturday Evening Post 181
Sauer, Marie 164, 165, 197
Schlesinger, Arthur, Jr. 113, 183, 218, 230
Schnyder, Mrs. Felix 197
Schwartz, Lloyd 119, 233
Scott, Hazel 108, 172
Scott, Hugh 31, 134
Scripps-Howard 17, 21, 67, 78, 88, 94, 98, 99
Secrest, Merle 167
Seppala, Rickhard 188
Sevilla-Sacasa, Guillermo 69
Shaffer, Sam 134
Shanahan, Eileen 19, 135
Shaw, Carolyn Hagner 215
Sheehan, Neil 183
Sheehan, Sue 183
Shelton, Elizabeth 141, 175
Shelton, Isabelle 68, 70, 71, 75, 81, 141, 158, 200
Sheppard, Eugenia 155
Shillito, Barry J. 138
Shriver, Mrs. Sargent 152
Siegel, Morris 173
Simpson, Adele 175
Skirvin, William 216
Slocum, Beryl 108, 172
Slocum, Mr. and Mrs. John J. 108, 172
Smathers, George 24, 108
Smith, Helen 66
Smith, Marie 18, 56-58, 60, 65, 66, 96, 148, 174, 175
Smith, Merriman 49, 63
Snowdon, Lord 212
Sorensen, Theodore 25, 26
Sothern, Ann 191
Sperling, Godfrey 27
Standish, Miles 108, 172
Stanton, Kelly 161
Stanton, William 156
Stanton, Mrs. William 156, 161
Starr, Malcolm 177
Stars and Stripes 78

Steber, Eleanor 167
Steers, Mrs. Newton 108, 135
Stein, Jeanne 230
Stein, Jules 230
Stennis, John 36
Stephenson, Malvina 39-43, 72
Stern, Philip M. 25
Stevenson, Adlai 38, 108, 111, 187, 209, 218
Stevenson, Mr. and Mrs. Adlai, III 219
Stewart, George 124
Stone, Clement 56
Stone, Walker 99
Storer Broadcasting 159, 160
Strelnikov, Boris 41
Strong, Mrs. John L. 213
Stroud, Frank 121
Stroud, Kandy Shuman 75, 101, 119-22
Stuart, Charles 64, 65
Stuart, Constance Cornell 59, 64-67, 86
Sulzberger, Arthur Ochs 148
Suzy (Aileen Mekle) 189
Swisshelm, Jane Grey 127
Symington, James W. 99
Symington, Stuart 209

Tallchief, Maria 90
Tass 46, 47
Tejera-Paris, Enrique 188
Tejera-Paris, Mme. Enrique 189
Thayer, Mary Van Rensselaer 8
Thomas, Helen 19, 20, 42, 49, 50, 53, 54, 60, 70, 93, 160, 161, 236
Thompson, Dorothy 38
Thurmond, Strom 217
Thurmond, Mrs. Strom 196, 206
Time magazine 46, 86, 140, 157, 169, 181, 209, 234
Thomasina, Sister 57
Travell, Janet 77
Triangle Stations 156
Trudeau, Pierre Elliott 72, 178
Truman, Harry 107, 216
Truman, Mrs. Harry 68
Tuckerman, Nancy 183
Tufty, Esther Van Wagoner 136
Turner, Lester 100
Turnure, Pamela 70-72

UPI (United Press International) 19, 20, 48, 63, 74, 118, 119, 128, 135, 160

U.S. News and World Report 20
Uzielli, Mrs. Giancarlo 205

Valenti, Jack 28, 212
Valentino, Rudolph 192
Van den Heuvel, Mr. and Mrs. William 230
Van der Heuvel, Gerry 48, 59, 60, 63, 64, 66, 83, 87
Van Wagoner, Murray D. 137
Variety 145
Verdon, René 92
Viorst, Anthony 184
Viorst, Judith 184
Viorst, Milton 184
Vishneyskaya, Galina 190
Vogue 146, 181
Volpi, Giovanni 205
Von Braun, Dr. and Mrs. Wernher 216
Von Hoffman, Nicholas 165

Walker, John 218
Wall Street Journal 67, 90, 163, 174
Wallace, George 41, 104, 105
Wallace, Lurleen 104
Wallach, Richard 210
Walton, William 183
Waltzman, Sanford 126
Washington, Mayor and Mrs. Walter 225
Washington Daily News 18, 59, 61, 91, 94-96, 103, 158, 162, 173, 175, 177
Washington Post 17-20, 22, 23, 25, 49, 51, 56, 60, 61, 65, 71-73, 90, 96, 101, 103, 107, 109, 114-17, 119, 122, 138, 139, 141, 144, 148, 156, 162-67, 171, 173-77, 187, 190-94, 196-200, 203, 205-208, 210, 222, 224, 226, 234, 235
Washington Star 18, 20-22, 25, 30, 34-36, 49, 68, 76, 81, 95, 108, 110, 128, 130, 135, 141, 157, 158, 162, 164, 167, 173, 174, 176, 177, 195, 197, 201, 203, 204, 215, 224, 226, 234
Washington Times Herald 51, 168, 208

Washingtonian Magazine 101, 114, 163, 184
Watkins, Arthur 38
Wayman, Stan 77
Webster, Mrs. George 221
Wee Jun Jon, Chief 86
Wells, Fay Gilles 159
Wells, Linton 160
Werner, Mary Lou 20
"Western Resources Wrap-Up" 143
Wharton, Liz 128
Wheeler, Earle G. 174
Whitaker, John 29
White, Theodore H. 32, 195, 227, 228
White, Mrs. Theodore H. 228
Wiegers, Mary 72, 166, 167, 234
Wiggins, Lillian 20, 21
Wilhelmina, Queen 87
Wilkins, Roy 90
Williams, Roger 108, 172
Williamson, Nichol 196
Wilson, Harold 95
Wilson, Mrs. Woodrow 68
Winchester, Lucy 61, 94
Windle, Mary J. 127
Windsor, Duke and Duchess of 95, 97, 166
Winston, Harry 212
Winston Salem Journal 128
Wisner, Mrs. Frank 218
Wohler, Milly 81
Women's Wear Daily 18, 73, 75, 119-21, 176, 234
Wood, Ann 202, 203
Wood, J. Howard 202
WRC–TV 61, 103
Wright, Zephyr 57, 58
WTOP–TV 156
Wyeth, Andrew 91, 116

Yates, Sidney R. 131
Young, Milton 196

Ziegler, Ron 46, 89, 160
Zlotnick, Mr. and Mrs. Sidney 157, 223, 224